BY THE SAME AUTHOR:

Smith's Moscow

This is a Borzoi Book,
published in New York by Alfred A. Knopf

SMITH'S MONTREAL

Alfred A. Knopf, New York, 1976

SMITH'S
MONTRÉAL

by Desmond Smith

THIS IS A BORZOI BOOK

PUBLISHED BY ALFRED A. KNOPF, INC.

Published in the United States by Alfred A. Knopf, Inc.,
New York, and simultaneously in Canada by
Random House of Canada Limited, Toronto.
Distributed by Random House, Inc., New York.

LIBRARY OF CONGRESS CATALOGING IN PUBLICATION DATA
Smith, Desmond (Date) Smith's Montreal.
Includes index.
1. Montreal—Description—Guidebooks. I. Title.
F1054.5.M83S54   1976   917.14′281′044   75-34258
ISBN 0-394-73170

Printed and Bound in Canada

First Edition

For Nicholas

Contents

Acknowledgments   ix

Introduction   5

History   10

Planning Your Trip   16

Arrival   42

Language   64

Getting About Montreal   70

A Drive and Four Walks   90

Children's Montreal   123

Shopping and Services   135

Eating and Drinking   189

Montreal After Dark   230

Entertainment   241

Quebec City   255

Sports   279

Appendix:

   BASIC MENU FRENCH   295

   EMERGENCY   300

Index follows page   300

A special supplement on the 1976
Olympic Games in Montreal is included
with all copies of the first edition.

Acknowledgments

It would have been impossible to write this book without the counsel and help of a platoon or so of Montrealers. I wish to thank, in particular, Eric Koch, André Dufresne, David Waters, David Knapp, Don Brown, Yvon Vadnais, Maurice Baudry, Gordon Atkinson, Bob McDevitt, Doreen Kays, Fred Langan, John Kalena, Pat Cook, Stephanie Brunell, Paul Wright, Les Niremberg, and Claire Lebeau, my friends and colleagues at the Canadian Broadcasting Corporation who cheerfully provided answers to some of the most difficult questions about *la vie Montréalaise*.

I am especially indebted to Ian McDonald and Gillian Cosgrov of the *Montreal Gazette*, and to Bill and Barbara Borders of *The New York Times*.

I would also like to express my appreciation to Pierre Petel, for sharing with me his expertise in the field of wine and food; to Professor Jill Baker, David Bazay, and Richard Inwood, for checking my Quebec City chapter; and to Professor Laurier Lapierre, for his comments on Quebec history.

I must thank my friend and agent, David Obst, and my editor, Judith Bailey Jones of Knopf, for their helpful comments. Mel Rosenthal and Barbara Rulison also earn my gratitude for their help with the manuscript.

Finally, my appreciation for all her help to Marjaleena Jappinen of Etela Suomern Sanomat.

SMITH'S MONTREAL

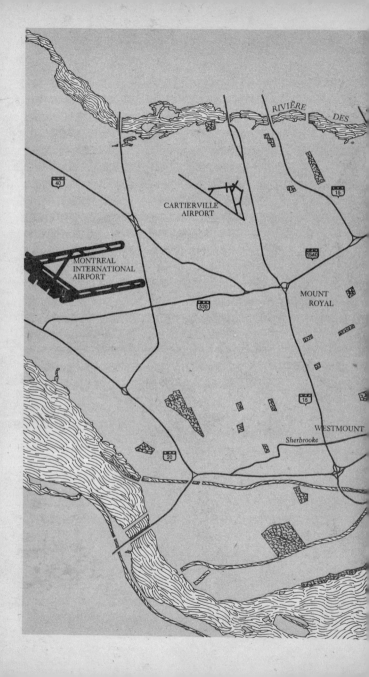

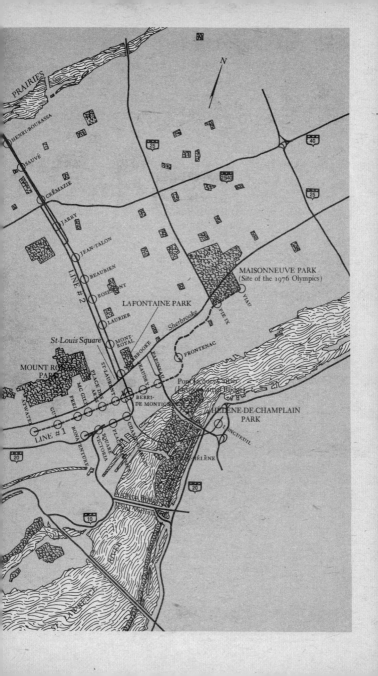

MONTREAL
6 km

QUEBEC 130
ST-LOUIS-DU-HA! HA!
CAP-AUX-OS
LATUQUE
ST-ÉMÉLIE-D-L'ÉNERGIE
MANCHE-D'ÉPÉE
RIVIERE-AUX-RATS

Introduction

Pride, intense vitality, a zestful and enterprising spirit are the hallmarks of Canada's greatest city, Montreal. Part European ghetto, part English country town, it is above all, of course, French—French in the cobbled streets of the Old City; the sedate façade of City Hall; the cafes along Rue St-Denis with their hanging clouds of Gauloise smoke; the old men playing *pétanque* near Lafontaine Park; the popular *chansonniers* whose songs are peppered with *joual*, the working-class argot of Quebec. A visitor from New York or Vancouver finds himself abroad at home. As he drives into the city along the Décarie Expressway, the signs and billboards look at once familar and strange—

There are more French-speaking people today in Montreal than in any other city in the world outside of Paris! More than half of its 3,000,000 population speak French—and that's why it is the official language; for some 700,000, English is the native tongue, and about 250,000 speak other languages. Yet, despite its size and diversity, this is a friendly town, with neither the hauteur of Paris nor the push-and-shove of a city like New York.

A visitor doesn't have to speak French to get along in Montreal: almost everyone you are likely to meet speaks or at least understands English. Of course, if you do have a few words of French (something this book aims to supply you with, among many other things), then so much the better; but no one will give you the cold shoulder if you don't.

Few visitors, no matter how many photographs of Montreal they may have seen, are prepared for the architectural beauty of the city. A morning's easy stroll from Place Jacques-Cartier to Place Ville-Marie will take you through the seventeenth, eighteenth, nineteenth, and twentieth centuries—all within a couple dozen city blocks. Here is the warehouse of John Jacob Astor, one of the greatest fur traders of his day; there, the place where Benjamin Franklin set up his printing press during the American Revolution. Tramping about, you will discover Notre-Dame Church, one of North America's finest examples of Gothic revival architecture, and next door to it, the original Seminary of the Sulpician Fathers, Montreal's most treasured link with the past. Part of it dates back to 1660.

It is from the air that you see clearly that Montreal is an island-city, engirdled by the prodigious St. Lawrence River, a stretch of water as wide as six superhighways put together. The city rises in a series of terraces from the water's edge. The Lower Terrace includes Le Vieux Montréal (Old Montreal), Notre-Dame Church, the financial district, and the courthouses. It is separated from Sherbrooke Street—the Upper Terrace —by a short but steep grade. And towering above Sherbrooke, the city's central and most famous landmark, the mountain which has given the town its name: "Mount Royal."

Just thirty years ago, almost all the buildings in the heart of Montreal were between four and eight stories, with only the silvery church steeples standing higher. Indeed, for more than 200 years the sound of church bells and the sight of church spires offered the principal sense impressions of North America's largest Catholic city. Mark Twain, for one, wryly observed that "This is the first time I was ever in a city where you couldn't throw a brick without breaking a church window."

Today Montreal is in the middle of a tremendous

building boom. From the observation deck atop the Bank of Commerce Building (see page 70) you can take in at a glance what is happening. The whole city seems to be shifting eastward, and the East End—flat, urban, choked with traffic and people—is being linked to the West by a series of bold architectural strokes. Place Dupuis, Place Desjardins, the $75-million (Radio Canada) broadcasting center (see page 80), and, of course, the 1976 Olympic site are revitalizing a section of the city that, until recently, had all the charm of an automobile junkyard. The well-to-do prefer the town of Mount Royal (an area whose Member of Parliament is Prime Minister Pierre Elliott Trudeau), Outremont, and Westmount, which are among the most gilded residential neighborhoods to be found anywhere. And to the north and south lie the great, sprawling bedroom suburbs: St-Laurent, Laval, St-Leonard, St-Lambert, Longueuil, and Brossard.

Yet, in spite of change, Montreal remains one of the most elegant cities in the world. The town's favorite color—silver-gray—comes from nearby limestone quarries. But from any small height it looks entirely green. Montrealers love trees. Almost every tree that stands on city property—close to 300,000 maples, birches, pines, and Chinese elms—is tagged with a serial number so that any damage can be quickly attended to. Each summer Montreal's Botanical Gardens, second largest in the world behind London's Kew Gardens, supplies the city with 15,000 saplings which are planted in boxes along the main boulevards. The Sanitation Commissioner is as fussy as any Paris concierge when it comes to street cleanliness. And in what other North American city can you find baskets of fresh geraniums and trailing vines hanging from every lamppost?

There are many other aspects of the city's daily life

that will enhance the pleasure of your visit. You can walk the streets by day or night in safety. Taxi drivers are courteous in the extreme. The hotels and restaurants are among the world's finest. Privacy is respected, and you will rarely be bothered by panhandlers, pimps, or prostitutes.

In contrast to such "melting pot" cities as New York and Toronto, where upwards of 60 percent of the population have been born and raised somewhere else, Montrealers tend to have their roots deep in Quebec. Many visitors—although there is no reliable sociological evidence on this point—have been impressed with the townspeople's willingness to go out of their way to make an out-of-towner feel welcome. To Montrealers, there is something fascinating about strangers, whether they come from the United States, from the Canadian West, from distant India, or from Europe. Not long ago, a woman wrote the "Action Line" column of the Miami *Herald*: She wanted help in locating a Montreal cabbie who had taken two hours off from work just to show her and her husband the city sights. Didn't charge them for it, either.

Montreal is like that. *Bienvenue!*

History

THE BEGINNINGS

The Indians inhabited Montreal Island long before the white man came. Not far from where McGill University now stands there was once a stockaded Iroquois village called Hochelaga. The first white man to arrive—in 1535—was the explorer Jacques Cartier. It was he who named the island *Montréal*, after its maple-covered mountain.

A century later, in 1642, inspired by the great religious revival in France, a group of philanthropists formed the Association of Montreal and sent Paul de Chomedey, Sieur de Maisonneuve, along with fifty others to establish a Christian outpost and to convert and instruct the Iroquois "in the practice of Christian life." In time, the entire island was taken over by the Gentlemen of St. Sulpice, a religious order which has

maintained its wealth, power, and influence to the present day. Religious idealism rather than commerce was the bedrock out of which Montreal grew.

GROWTH

By the year 1701, Ville-Marie, the first settlement, had a population of nearly 2,000, and Montreal was attracting some of the most remarkable and colorful characters ever to grace history's pages. Among them: the Chevalier de la Salle, founder of Chicago; Antoine de la Mothe Cadillac, who settled Detroit; Greysolon du Luth, who portaged and canoed as far as Lake Superior and gave his name to what is now the largest city on its shores; and the dashing Le Moyne brothers, two of whom established New Orleans and Louisiana. The town grew and prospered, as the saying goes, and by the middle of the century it had a population of some 40,000. Then, a pivotal turn of events: war between rival European powers spread from the Old World to the New. Montreal was besieged by British forces under General Amherst in 1760, and capitulated virtually without a struggle. In 1763 Great Britain took formal possession of all of what had been French Canada.

A dozen years later, during the American Revolution, the army of the Continental Congress occupied Montreal for several months. The indefatigable Benjamin Franklin arrived, and set up a printing press on which he turned out hundreds of leaflets in French and English, trying to persuade Canadians to join the American colonists against the British. But Franklin left in a hurry after the Americans were defeated at Quebec (see page 265).

Montreal became a great fur-trading center in the eighteenth century, and tremendous fortunes were made by the lucky few. Among them was a sharp-witted New Yorker named John Jacob Astor who was to finance much of his real-estate deals in New York City out of his Montreal profits (you can still see his fur warehouse on St-Jean-Baptiste Street in Old Montreal—Walk Two, page 103).

THE IRISH

In the 1820's and 1830's, tremendous waves of Irish immigrants arrived. It's probably fair to say that much of nineteenth-century Montreal was built with the sweat of their backs. They dredged the Lachine Canal, built the Victoria Bridge (as a monument at the city approach to the bridge attests), built the railroads to New York, Toronto, Quebec, Ottawa, and finally across

the continent. Intermarriage between the Irish and
their French fellow Catholics was not uncommon, with
the result that today's Montreal phone book is full of
Kellys, O'Reillys, and Shaughnessys whose first language
is French. Now almost as many French-Canadians—
some of them descendants of these early immigrants—
march in the annual St. Patrick's Day parade as do
ethnic Irish.

VICTORIAN MONTREAL

The nineteenth century marked the rise of commercial
Montreal; and a population which had remained a fairly
constant 40,000 for almost a century and a half, had
increased over fivefold to 220,000, by 1891. Throughout
the early part of the century, the English-speaking
population was in the majority, but industrialization
shifted the balance in favor of the French-speaking
inhabitants, who by 1901 constituted 61 percent of the
total.

The Gothic churches that still abound in Plateau
Mount Royal, the lower East End, Hochelaga, and
St-Henri are a reminder of the time when the Roman
Catholic Church reached into every aspect of French-
Canadian life. Jews, some driven out of Russia by
pogroms, others from Eastern Europe (many of the
latter came by way of the United States), settled along
St-Laurent (St. Lawrence) Boulevard; the area east of
St-Laurent was exclusively French-Canadian, the section
west of it primarily English-speaking—a separation
that continues to this day.

The rich, chiefly English and Scottish merchants,
lived on the slopes of Mount Royal: in Westmount
or Outremont, or in great mansions in the "golden
mile" above McGregor Street. What the Main Line

was (and is) to Philadelphia, the Mountain was (and is) to Montreal. Here lived the most complacently entrenched oligarchy in Canada. Stephen Leacock, a friend of Mark Twain and Canada's greatest humorist, once observed that "the rich in Montreal enjoyed a prestige in that era that not even the rich deserved."

Here was the origin of the "two solitudes," a city divided between French and English, between poor and rich. Strolling around Montreal today, you can see the lasting mark that these influential McGills, McTavishes, van Hornes, and Redpaths made on the city. Among them, Mount Royal Park, designed by Frederick Law Olmsted (architect of New York's Central Park), Mount Royal's stately cemetery, the Windsor and Viger railway stations, the Bank of Montreal on Place d'Armes, the Mount Stephen Club (where even the soap in the washroom is British), and McGill University.

NEW MONTREAL

The Roaring Twenties brought notoriety to Montreal. If Toronto was called "Toronto the Good," Montreal —only 40 miles from the Vermont border—had a far different reputation. The Prohibition years in the United States turned Montreal into a bootlegger's paradise, and the city became the unofficial U.S. port of entry for illegal booze.

Between the wars Montreal was a raucous, wide-open city, a sinkpot of municipal corruption with a smeary reputation as the vice capital of Canada—so much so that part of the city was off limits to the Canadian army during World War II. As late as 1947, the city center looked about as inviting as a decayed tooth, and St. Catherine Street was a gaudy, honky-tonk neon

strip filled with clip-joints, gambling clubs, and dime-a-dance parlors. Then came Jean Drapeau, a vice-busting prosecutor who became mayor in 1954, at the age of 38. Apart from one defeat at the polls in 1957, he has been in office ever since. Not since the late Fiorello La Guardia of New York has any North American city seen a municipal leader like Jean Drapeau. Stern, autocratic, given to working seven days a week, he is single-mindedly devoted to one goal: making Montreal the first city in the world. The renovation and rebuilding of the city center, the $38-million Place des Arts, Expo '67, the building of the subway system, the '76 Olympic Games are all part of Drapeau's hopes and dreams, realized or about to be realized, for Montreal.

Planning Your Trip

The city says *Bienvenue* to more than 5,000,000 visitors a year, the vast majority of whom pour in between May and September. At the most recent count, however, there were in central Montreal, all told, less than 16,000 hotel rooms for them. The present building boom will add at least a dozen new hotels to the city skyline, but even the additional 5,000 or 6,000 rooms thus provided will barely keep pace with the demand.

Your first step, then, is self-evident: reserve your accommodations *before* leaving home. You can make the necessary arrangements through your travel agent; through Air Canada, CP Air, American Airlines, Eastern Airlines or Allegheny, if you are flying; or through the nearest Canadian Government Travel Bureau (most major U.S. and European cities have branches). You might also wish to get in touch with the nearest office of the Quebec (Province) Travel Bureau. There, in addition to descriptive literature, you can obtain *Hotels of Quebec*, a free guide to most of the province's hotels and motels which evaluates them individually and gives current room rates. Write, phone, or visit any of the following offices:

IN U.S. AND CANADA

The Tourist Information Division
    Parliament Buildings, Quebec, Canada G1A, 1R4
    2 Place Ville-Marie, Montreal
    17 West 50th St., New York City
    Park Square Bldg., Room 409, 31 St. James Ave., Boston
    72 West Adams St., Chicago
    510 West Sixth St., Los Angeles

IN EUROPE
Agent-General for Quebec
   66 rue Pergolese, Paris
   12, Upper Grosvenor Street, London
   16, via Manzoni, Milan
   30, Königsallee, Düsseldorf

VISAS AND PASSPORTS

Getting into Canada is simple. Permanent residents of the United States, whether citizens or not, need no passport. For citizens it's advisable to have some proof of identity such as a driver's license or voter registration card, while citizens of other countries who live in the U.S. must take along their alien registration cards.

A valid passport (no visa) is all that is required for nationals from the following areas and countries who intend to stay three months or less: countries of the Western Hemisphere; member states of the British Commonwealth; Austria, Belgium, Denmark, Finland, France, Great Britain, Greece, Italy, Japan, Luxembourg, Monaco, the Netherlands, Norway, Portugal, Spain, Sweden, Switzerland, Turkey, West Germany.

MEDICAL REGULATIONS

Vaccination certificates are not required of travelers who are permanent residents of the United States. All others must hold a current International Smallpox Vaccination Certificate.

WEATHER AND CLOTHING

Montreal, with more than 110 inches of snowfall annually, is one of the snowiest cities on earth. The city and its residents spend more than $20-million a year just removing the stuff, and it is hard to estimate when a blizzard is likely to strike. There has been an 18-inch snowfall in February (when the snow is heaviest), and a 10½-inch fall in May. During the three winter months —December, January, February—the mean temperature is around 15° above zero. Things start to warm up by late February or March, and by April, rain is more probable than snow. But there is definitely no guarantee. If you visit anytime between November and April, be sure to bring along heavy clothing and overshoes.

Spring, which local wits solemnly declare takes place on a single afternoon in early May, can be slushy. Summers are warm and generally sunny, although July is the rainiest month of the year according to meteorological records. In June, July, and August, daytime temperatures range from the cool 60's to the hot and humid 80's and 90's. October can be glorious, a time of the year when the maple leaves turn brilliant red and when the air is clear, with a hint of frost in it.

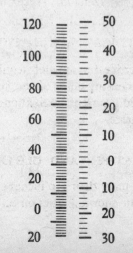

FAHRENHEIT   **CELSIUS**

For weather information in Montreal, dial 636-3302. Keep in mind, however, that (as part of Canada's transition to full adoption of the metric system) temperature readings are now given in degrees Celsius, not Fahrenheit. See conversion table on preceding page.

MONEY AND CREDIT

Canadian money is in dollars and cents, just as in the U.S. The coins differ only in design from U.S. coins; they are identical in name, denomination, and size: 1¢ (penny), 5¢ (nickel), 10¢ (dime), 25¢ (quarter), 50¢ (half dollar). Paper money comes in denominations of $1, $2, $5, $10, $20, $50, and $100. U.S. coins and currency are acceptable everywhere; most Canadians, however, prefer that you use their currency—this, after all, is just plain good manners.

For currency transactions, it's best to go to a bank, where the exchange rate will be somewhat better than that offered by restaurants and shops. However, bringing in or using currency in large denominations is not recommended—Montreal has a considerable reputation as a counterfeiting center, and $50 bills, whether U.S. or Canadian, are treated with suspicion.

The most widely used credit cards are Chargex, American Express, and Master Charge, followed by Carte Blanche and Diners Club. U.S. visitors who possess BankAmericard and British visitors with Barclaycard should note that these are valid wherever Chargex is accepted. (Occasionally you may have difficulty; in that case, have the dealer or manager call Chargex.)

Traveler's checks can be cashed at banks, hotels, and travel agencies. The banks close at 3 p.m. on weekdays, but a number of trust companies (e.g., Royal Trust) provide various banking services until 5 p.m., and at least a few offer services on Saturday.

It is useful to know that many shops and hotels (and even a few restaurants) will accept personal checks, providing you have sufficient identification with you.

CUSTOMS

You'll generally find Canadian customs officials to be fairly easygoing. There is, however, a $15 limit on items brought in other than for personal use—a duty is imposed on anything above that amount. Visitors are allowed to bring in up to 50 cigars or 200 cigarettes or 2 pounds of tobacco, and 50 fluid ounces of alcoholic beverages per adult; and if you do smoke and/or drink, it's a good idea to take your full allowance with you. A pack of American cigarettes will cost about 75 cents in Montreal. Canadian cigarettes are made of unblended tobacco, which many Americans may find too mild; in any case, they're not much cheaper. A pack of regular-sized "Craven A" or "Macdonald's Export A," for example, is 75 cents. Most cigarettes in vending machines cost 85 cents a pack. Cigarettes are cheapest in supermarkets, where they usually sell for $5.80 a carton. A bottle of whiskey or vodka is similarly expensive—between $7 and $11—by U.S. standards.

ELECTRIC CURRENT

Same as in the U.S.: 110 volts, 60-cycle A.C.; all 220-volt appliances require a transformer. Most outlets use a plug with two flat prongs.

FIREARMS

If you expect to go gunning for elk or moose, you can obtain a temporary permit (form E-29B) at the border. Sporting firearms, standard or automatic loading, are admitted for hunting purposes. Two hundred rounds of ammunition may also be brought into Canada duty-free. You must obtain a Quebec Province hunting permit once you arrive. Pistols and revolvers, as well as air-pistols, are prohibited, except when the person bringing them in is participating in authorized competitions.

ACCOMMODATIONS

Montreal has about a hundred hotels and motels, and about the same number of guest homes and tourist lodges. You can pay as much as $76 for deluxe single accommodations at the Queen Elizabeth, or as little as $3.50 a night at the Nanking Tourist Rooms on Lagauchetière. While the Queen Elizabeth is the most expensive, it is the Ritz-Carlton on Sherbrooke Street that offers the city's most truly elegant lodgings.

Businessmen opt most often for the centrally located Queen Elizabeth, Château Champlain, Bonaventure (the major convention hotel in the city), or Sheraton–Mount Royal. Families tend to prefer one of the several Holiday Inns (which, as of late 1976, will include the world's largest, on Dorchester Boulevard), while writers, painters, poets, and others on a limited budget are likely to choose the Iroquois or Nelson in Old Montreal.

St-Denis and St-Hubert streets are where you'll find dozens of inexpensive tourist rooms and the plainer and simpler sort of hotels.

What follows are the major hotels and motels listed by area. Between October and April many of these places offer reduced rates, worth checking on if you plan to visit during the off-season. Parking facilities are free at all motels, of course, but at hotels there is usually a charge for overnight parking. Most of the establishments listed are fully air-conditioned. Partial air-conditioning is indicated by an asterisk (*). Dogs and cats are accepted at most places; exceptions in this regard are indicated by the symbol (#).

Credit card abbreviations are as follows:

Air Canada-CN–AC-CN	Chargex–Chx
American Express–AE	Diners Club–DC
BancardCheck–BaCh	Master Charge–MC
BankAmericard–BaAm	Canadian Pacific–CP
Carte Blanche–CB	British Petroleum–B.P.

RITZ-CARLTON

Keep in mind also that Quebec law requires an official rate card to be on display in every room. Guests cannot be obliged to pay more than the charge listed. Should advance payment be requested, you may demand to inspect your accommodations first.

Midtown Area

This includes the main shopping district north of Windsor Station: Place Ville-Marie, Place Bonaventure, and the leading department stores. The hotels listed below are all within walking distance of many of Montreal's art galleries, fine restaurants, and most elegant boutiques.

RITZ-CARLTON · 1226–28 *Sherbrooke St. West*

842-4212. 249 rms. Baby-sitter avail., $1.50 per hr.
No swimming pool. Parking $4.50.
Accepts AC-CN, AE, Chx, DC, MC, Texaco, CP.
Singles $32.00–$60.00, Doubles $40.00–$68.00

This is a hotel in the grand manner. It has recently been completely renovated without the least impairment of its old-fashioned splendor. Rooms are large and spacious and the service is impeccable. The Maritime Bar is Montreal's smartest rendezvous. Le Café de Paris, with its superb chef, Pierre Demers, ranks as one of the city's great dining rooms. Easily the poshest hostelry in town.

LE CHÂTEAU CHAMPLAIN · *Place du Canada*

878-1688. 612 rms. (#) Baby-sitter avail., $2.00 per hr.
No swimming pool. Parking $2.00.
Accepts AE, CB, DC, MC, Chx, Esso, Imperial, CP.
Singles $33.00–$45.00, Doubles $41.00–$53.00

Built in the late 1960's and owned by Canadian Pacific, this hotel offers every conceivable luxury. The rooms enjoy views of either the river (on the south side) or the city (north side). Service is excellent. The rooftop restaurants and bars offer the pleasantest dining and dancing in town.

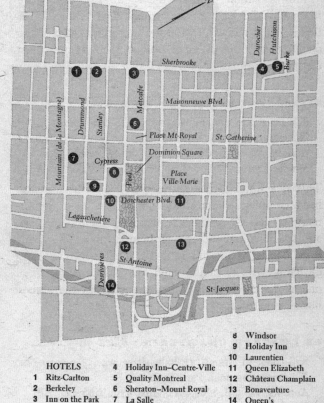

HOTELS
1	Ritz-Carlton	
2	Berkeley	
3	Inn on the Park	
4	Holiday Inn–Centre-Ville	
5	Quality Montreal	
6	Sheraton–Mount Royal	
7	La Salle	
8	Windsor	
9	Holiday Inn	
10	Laurentien	
11	Queen Elizabeth	
12	Château Champlain	
13	Bonaventure	
14	Queen's	

BONAVENTURE · *Place Bonaventure*

878-2332. 395 rms. Baby-sitter avail., $1.50 per hr.
Outdoor heated pool. Parking $2.35.
Accepts AE, BaAm, CB, DC, MC, Western Int. Hotels.
Singles $34.00–$51.00, Doubles $40.00–$59.00

Heavily patronized by businessmen and convention-goers. Year-round heated outdoor pool, sauna, and health club. Convivial rather than elegant. An outstanding dining room, Le Castillon, with its fireside bar and view of the Bonaventure gardens, attracts the expense-account set.

INN ON THE PARK · *Peel and Sherbrooke*
To be opened in late 1976.

HOLIDAY INN · *Dorchester Blvd.*
To be opened in late 1976.

HOLIDAY INN · *420 Sherbrooke St. West*

842-6111. 493 rms. Baby-sitter avail., $2.50 per hr.
Indoor pool. Free parking.
Accepts AE, Chx, DC, MC, Gulf.
Singles $24.50–$26.50, Doubles $31.50–33.50

On busy section of Sherbrooke, close to McGill University and midtown business area. Lots of construction in the neighborhood.

SHERATON–MOUNT ROYAL · *1455 Peel St.*

488-0665. 1015 rms. Baby-sitter avail., $1.50 per hr.
No swimming pool. Free parking.
Accepts AE, BaAm, CB, Sheraton, Am. Torch Club,
  Barclay.
Singles $23.00–$48.00, Doubles $29.00–$48.00

As close as could be to the geographical heart of the city. This hotel, so popular in the 1940's, seems out of place in the 1970's—the cavernous lobby more attuned to the gathering of sightseeing tours than to quiet conversation.

QUEEN ELIZABETH · 900 *Dorchester Blvd. West*

861-3511. 1167 rms. (#) Baby-sitter avail., $2.00 per hr. No swimming pool. Parking $2.00.

Accepts AC-CN, AE, BaCh, Chx, DC, MC, BC, Hilton, Esso, Eurocard, TWA Getaway, Am. Torch Club, Pan Am Take-off, Scotia Bank.

Singles $34.00–$76.00, Doubles $34.00–$76.00

Overlooking Place Ville-Marie, this hotel is big, comfortable, and friendly. It has outstanding entertainment, and an exceptionally fine (and expensive) restaurant, The Beaver Club. And there are altogether another 20 restaurants in and around the hotel that are served by its famed kitchen.

CONSTELLATION (FORMERLY SONESTA) · 3407 *Peel St.*

845-1234. 162 rms. (#) Baby-sitter avail., $1.50 per hr. No swimming pool. Parking $3.50.

Accepts AC-CN, AE, CB, Chx, DC, MC.

Singles $20.00–$30.00, Doubles $28.00–$40.00

Conveniently located in the heart of shopping and business district. Lots of construction taking place in the area. Has rooftop dining and dancing.

BERKELEY · 1188 *Sherbrooke St. West*

849-7351. 75 rms. Baby-sitter avail., $2.00 per hr. No swimming pool. Parking $2.00.

Accepts AC-CN, AE, CB, Chx, DC.

Singles $22.00–$29.00, Doubles $24.00–$35.00

Small, comfortable, and friendly, with charming terrace restaurant. Convenient for galleries and shopping.

WINDSOR · 1170 *Peel St.*

866-9611. 289 rms. (*)
No swimming pool. No parking.
Accepts AC-CN, AE, CB, Chx, DC, MC.
Singles $24.00–$38.00, Doubles $30.00–$40.00

King George VI once slept here. Since then this
dowager of Montreal hotels has grown a lot older. A
quiet, respectable place to stay in the heart of the city.

CHATEAU RENAISSANCE ● *700 Peel Street*

866-2531. 317 rms. (*) Baby-sitter avail., $1.25 per hr.
No swimming pool. No parking.
Accepts AC-CN, AE, BaAm, CB, Chx, DC.
Singles $8.00–$30.00, Doubles $14.00–$36.00

Formerly the city's leading railroad hotel. Today, somewhat left behind by the Jet Age. Rooms are clean and
comfortable. Extensively renovated in 1976.

QUALITY INN HOTEL · 410 *Sherbrooke St. West*

844-8851. 183 rms. Baby-sitter avail., $1.75 per hr.
Indoor pool. Free parking.
Accepts AE, BaAm, CB, Chx, DC, MC, American Oil,
  Esso, Phillips 66, National Car Rental.
Singles $23.00–$25.00, Doubles $32.00–$33.00

Close to the McGill campus and all shopping. Sherbrooke is noisy by day but quiet by night.

LA SALLE · 1240 *Drummond St.*

866-6492. 176 rms. No swimming pool. Parking $2.00.
Accepts AE, BaAm, CB, Chx, DC, MC.
Singles $18.00–$60.00, Doubles $24.00–$60.00

Clean and decent.

City Center East

What is happening here is the development of a French-speaking city core that, in time, will rival the

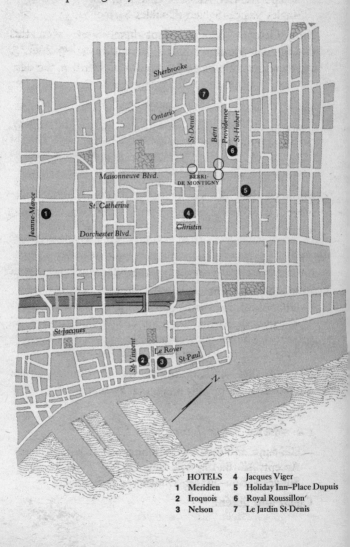

HOTELS		
1	Meridien	**4** Jacques Viger
2	Iroquois	**5** Holiday Inn–Place Dupuis
3	Nelson	**6** Royal Roussillon
		7 Le Jardin St-Denis

midtown area and West End, which are English in character. It includes: Place Desjardins; the area on either side of St-Denis, between St-Jacques to the south and Sherbrooke to the north; the artists' and writers' *quartier* around St-Louis Square; Old Montreal; and the beginning of the city's industrial belt. Maison du Radio-Canada, the world's most modern broadcasting studios, is located here, as is the '76 Olympic site. The hotels and tourist lodges range in price from super-expensive to dirt cheap. *Le Métro*—the subway—connects you to midtown in a matter of minutes.

HOLIDAY INN · *Place Dupuis, 1415 St-Hubert St.*
  842-4881. 360 rms. (#)
  Indoor swimming pool. Free parking.
  Accepts AE, BaCh, BaAm, CB, Chx, DC, MC.
  Singles $26.50, Doubles $33.50

The second biggest HI in the city, opened in 1974; it is part of a huge shopping center. Fare in the dining rooms is quite a cut above the usual HI standard. Convenient to East End—Olympic site, CBC, and 5 minutes from Old Montreal.

MERIDIEN · *Place Desjardins*
  Due to open in September 1976.

ROYAL ROUSSILLON · *1610 St-Hubert St.*
  849-3214. 52 rms.(#) (*) Free parking.
  Accepts AE, BaCh, BaAm, Chx, DC, MC.
  Singles $10.50–$19.50, Doubles $10.50–$19.50

A small, neat, and clean hotel around the corner from the Central Bus Terminal. Its ace-in-the-hotel is an outstanding kitchen which serves the restaurant Au Tromblon d'Argent located downstairs.

LE JARDIN SAINT-DENIS · 1611 *St-Denis St.*

288-2023. 7 rms.
Accepts AE, Chx, DC, MC.
Singles $8.00–$12.00, Doubles $10.00–$15.00

A converted townhouse in the heart of the St-Denis area, beautifully decorated with antiques. There are sinks in all rooms, and this small hotel is as clean as your own home.

ARGOAT TOURIST LODGE ·
524 *Sherbrooke St. East*

842-2046. 29 rms. TV.
Singles $13.00–$20.00, Doubles $16.00–$25.00

JACQUES VIGER · 1254 *St-Denis St.*

861-6331. 66 rms. (*) Parking $1.00.
Accepts AE, CB, DC.
Singles $25.00, Doubles $25.00

A cheerful place in a somewhat run-down (but safe) neighborhood. Lively at night, with three restaurants that attract a largely French-Canadian clientele.

AUBERGE RICHELIEU · 505 *Sherbrooke St. East*

842-8581. 330 rms. (#) Baby-sitter avail., $1.50 per hr.
Accepts AE, Chx, DC, MC.
Singles $27–$35, Doubles $35

NELSON · 425 *Place Jacques-Cartier*

861-5731. 64 rms. (*)
Singles $7.00–$12.00, Doubles $7.00–$12.00

Place Jacques-Cartier is Montreal's version of Piccadilly Circus. A focal point from April to November for the young, the vocal, and the footloose, the crowds wash in and around the Nelson in one great human tide.

Some years ago the hotel had a reputation as the gathering place for Quebec nationalists. The talk in the bar below still runs to politics and rock music. Not a place to stay if you prefer peace and quiet, but one of the liveliest hostelries in Montreal. The rooms are nothing special, but are clean and neat.

IROQUOIS · 446 *Place Jacques-Cartier*

861-5416. 109 rms. (#) (*)
Baby-sitter avail., $2.50 per hr. Parking $2.50.
Accepts AE, CB, DC.
Singles $6.50–$13.00, Doubles $9.00–$16.00

Across the street from the Nelson. Rooms are clean and decent and the hotel has a popular terrace-cafe that overlooks the action in Place Jacques-Cartier.

JACQUES-CARTIER MOTEL ·
14070 Sherbrooke St. East

642-4533. 60 units. Baby-sitter avail., $1.00 per hr.
Outdoor pool.
Accepts CB, Chx, MC.
Singles $18.00–$24.00, Doubles $28.00–$40.00

Clean and decent.

LE LUCERNE MOTEL · 4950 *Sherbrooke St. East*

255-2806. 136 units. Baby-sitter avail., $2.00 per hr.
Outdoor pool.
Accepts AE, CB, Chx, DC, MC.
Singles $19.50, Doubles $23.50–29.50

LE MARQUIS MOTEL · 6720 *Sherbrooke St. East*

256-1621. 77 units. (*) Baby-sitter avail., $2.00 per hr.
No swimming pool.
Accepts AE, Chx, DC, MC.
Singles $16.50–$34.00, Doubles $16.50–$34.00

RAMADA INN-EAST · 5500 *Sherbrooke St. East*

256-9011. 249 units. (#) Baby-sitter avail., $1.25 per hr.
Outdoor pool.
Accepts AC-CN, BaAm, CB, Chx, DC, MC, Esso,
Exxon.
Singles $21.50–$50.00, Doubles $26.50–$50.00

The largest and most modern motor inn in the East
End. About 2–3 minutes' drive from Olympic Park,
10 minutes from downtown.

LE VERSAILLES MOTEL ·
7200 *Sherbrooke St. East*

256-1613. 124 units. Baby-sitter avail., $1.50 per hr.
Outdoor pool. Accepts AE, BaAm, CB, Chx, DC.
Singles $16.50–$35.00, Doubles $21.50–$42.00

Easy access to Olympic site. Ten minutes from downtown.

In addition to those listed above, there are many
smaller motels located on Sherbrooke Street East.

City Center West

This includes the area on either side of Guy Street, between Dorchester Boulevard to the south and Sherbrooke Street to the north. Here you will find Radio and TV headquarters for the Olympics (ORTO), as well as the city's major indoor sports arena, the Forum; Alexis Nihon Plaza, a giant shopping center; and Westmount Square, Montreal's most expensive shopping center.

This part of Dorchester is primarily a getaway route for Montrealers heading for the West Island. The side

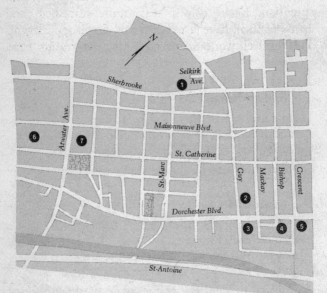

1 Château Versailles
2 Seaway Motor Inn
3 Ramada Inn
4 De Province
5 Colonnade
6 Westmount Square
7 Forum

streets contain many fine restaurants, as does St. Catherine Street near Guy. You can reach downtown in three minutes by bus, subway, or taxi (or by a five-minute walk).

CHÂTEAU VERSAILLES ·
1659 Sherbrooke St. West

933-3611. 79 rms. (#) (*) Baby-sitter avail., $1.00 per hr. No swimming pool. Free parking.
Accepts AE, Chx, MC.
Singles $12.00–$26.00, Doubles $15.00–$30.00

One of the most charming, if not *the* most charming small hotel in Montreal. The owner has transformed four old mansions into an oasis of personal service and attention. Each room is beautifully furnished, and many of them have chandeliers and fireplaces. Elegant, tasteful; well worth trying hard for a reservation here.

HOTEL DE PROVINCE ·
1484 Dorchester Blvd. West

861-7201. 82 rms. No pool. No parking.
Accepts AE, CB, DC.
Singles $12.00–$18.00, Doubles $19.50–$24.00

An apartment hotel on a noisy street.

RAMADA-MOTOR INN · *1005 Guy St.*

866-4611. 205 rms. Baby-sitter avail.,$1.50 per hr. Outdoor pool. Free parking.
Accepts AC-CN, AE, CB, DC, MC, Esso.
Singles $18.00–$30.00, Doubles $28.50–$39.00

Patronized by denizens of the world of show business and sports. Excellent restaurant. Across the street from the former headquarters for Radio Canada (now ORTO hq.).

SEAWAY MOTOR INN · 1155 *Guy St.*

932-1411. 222 rms. (#) Baby-sitter avail., $2.00 per hr.
Outdoor and indoor pools.
Accepts AE, CB, Chx, DC, MC, B.P., Esso.
Singles $18.50–$25.00, Doubles $24.50–$35.00

Clean, comfortable, convenient.

COLONNADE · 1366 *Dorchester Blvd. West*

861-1234. 62 rms. No swimming pool. Free parking.
Accepts AE, BaAm, CB, Chx, DC, MC.
Singles $20.00, Doubles $26.00

Apartment hotel in busy neighborhood.

BISHOP GUEST HOUSE · 1242 *Bishop St.*

866-0011. 10 rms. TV. Parking. Telephone.
Singles $12.00–$16.00, Doubles $14.50–$18.50

Airport Row

There is hardly an airport in the world that offers a
pleasant drive from the terminal to the city. Montreal's
Dorval Airport is unfortunately no exception to this
rule: the route is a dreary, semi-industrial sprawl of
bowling alleys, freight warehouses, golf-driving ranges,
and assembly plants. The only good thing to be said
for it is that the ride doesn't last long—the terminal
is only 12 miles from the city center, which makes it
especially convenient if you have a car.

MONTREAL AEROPORT HILTON ·
12505 Côte-de-Liesse Rd.

631-2411. 492 rms. Baby-sitter avail., $1.50 per hr.
Outdoor Pool. Free parking. 24-hour room service.
Accepts AC-CN, AE, BaAm, CB, Chx, DC, MC,
   Hilton, Esso, Eurocard.
Singles $35.00–$40.00, Doubles $42.00–$48.00

A lively bar, a pleasant restaurant. Usual high Hilton standards in everything else. Hotel is within the airport grounds.

SKYLINE · *6600 Côte-de-Liesse Rd.*

342-2262. 220 rms. (*) Indoor pool. Free parking.
Accepts AC-CN, AE, Chx, Din-Skyline Hotels,
   Supertest, Shell.
Singles $28.00, Doubles $34.00

Located on the service road from the airport to the city. First-class accommodations.

LE SEVILLE · *4545 Côte-Vertu Rd.*

332-2720. 94 rms.
Singles $18.00–$26.00, Doubles $22.00–$26.00

A recent addition in the Spanish style. Restaurant: El Conquistador.

HOLIDAY INN CHÂTEAUBRIAND ·
   6500 Côte-de-Liesse Rd.

739-3391. 193 rms. Baby-sitter avail., $1.50 per hr.
Outdoor pool. Free parking.
Accepts AE, BaAm, Chx, DC, MC, Gulf.
Singles $22.50–$26.00, Doubles $28.00–$31.50

Neat, well run, familiar.

HOLIDAY INN SEIGNEURIE ·
   7300 Côte-de-Liesse Rd.

731-7751. 197 rms. Baby-sitter avail., $1.50 per hr.
Outdoor pool. Parking free.
Accepts AE, Chx, DC, MC, Gulf.
Singles $22.50–$35.00, Doubles $28.00–$30.50

Neat, well run, familiar.

FLEUR DE LYS MOTEL · 7900 *Côte-de-Liesse Rd.*

733-8223. 42 rms. Baby-sitter avail., $2.50 per hr.
Outdoor pool. Free parking.
Singles $19.00–$20.00, Doubles $28.50–$30.50

Décarie Strip

An unlovely stretch of steak joints, shops, and slub-
urbia. Sole asset: a drive of less than ten minutes to
the city center.

RUBY FOO'S · 7815 *Décarie Blvd.*

731-7701. 118 units. Baby-sitter avail., $1.50 per hr.
Outdoor pool.
Accepts AE, BaAm, CB, MC.
Singles $30.50–$39.00, Doubles $35.50–$39.00

The outstanding motel on the strip, and a winner of
numerous design awards.

SEAWAY CAPRI · 6445 *Décarie Blvd.*

739-2771. 100 rms. Baby-sitter avail., $2.00 per hr.
Outdoor pool. Free parking.
Accepts AE, CB, Chx, DC, MC, B.P., CP.
Singles $20.00–$26.50, Doubles $21.50–$28.50

Inexpensive lodgings

If you don't mind sharing a bathroom, there are dozens
of tourist rooms and guest lodges within a few minutes
of the city center. Accommodations range in price from
a low of $3.50 a night for single accommodations to
around $20 for doubles. And there are plenty of
rooming houses that offer spartan but clean accommodations for as little as $15 a week. Sherbrooke
Street, St. Catherine Street, and especially St-Hubert
and St-Denis are the places to look.

VILLE-MARIE GUEST HOUSE ·
1430–32 Bishop St.

849-0117. 30 rms. Parking. TV.
Singles $6.00, Doubles $12.00

ST-LOUIS TOURIST ROOM · *317 St-Louis Square*

845-1078. 7 rms. Parking. TV.
Singles $5.00–$10.00, Doubles $10.00–$15.00

AMERICAN SUNSHINE LODGE ·
1042 St-Denis St.

849-0265. 19 rms. Parking. TV.
Singles $6.00–$9.00, Doubles $10.00–$12.00

AUBERGE CHEZ BÉBERT INN ·
4109–11 St-Denis St.

849-0265. 21 rms. Parking. TV.
Singles $9.00–$19.00, Doubles $12.00–$21.00

CHESTER LODGE · *1177 Dorchester Blvd. West*

861-7186. 14 rms. Parking. TV.
Singles $6.00–$12.00, Doubles $9.00–$12.00

NANKING TOURIST ROOMS ·
56 Lagauchetière West

866-4815. 7 rms. Parking.
Singles $3.50–$4.00, No doubles.

YMCA · *1441 Drummond St.*

Singles $8.00–$10.00 ($13.50 with private bath),
Doubles $16.00–$27.00

The "Y" is centrally located, only a block from St.
Catherine Street, and two blocks from the action on
Crescent and Mountain streets. Both men and women
allowed.

Y W C A · *1355 Dorchester Blvd.*
866-9941.
Singles $23.00 per week, Doubles $19.00 per week
Women only. No curfew.

Hostels and Student Accommodations

There are always plenty of available accommodations in dormitories and private rooms during the summer months.

French-speaking students should contact:

Université de Montréal
  Edouard Montpetit St., Corner of
  Louis-Colin 343-6111
Université du Québec à Montréal
  255 St. Catherine St. West 876-5448

  English-speaking students:

McGill University
  805 Sherbrooke St. West 392-4311
Sir George Williams Campus, Concordia University
  1455 Blvd. de Maisonneuve West . . . 879-2852
or
Loyola Campus, Concordia University
  7141 Sherbrooke St. West 482-0320

Some fraternities near the McGill campus rent rooms. A visit to such well-known student haunts as the Mansfield Tavern (see page 195), the Yellow Door Cafe (see page 239), or the Rainbow Bar & Grill (see page 197) should yield further information. Two housing registries are: **Info-Loge**, 3480 McTavish Street, 392-8927; and, for the French-speaking, **La Banque de Logement**, Université du Québec, 876-5868.

The **Canadian Youth Hostel Association** operates

a year-round hostel in the heart of Montreal. Technically for members only, but nonmembers can obtain a "guest pass" at the Regional Office. Despite its name, the CYHA is open to everyone, regardless of age. The Regional Office is located at: 1324A Sherbrooke Street West, 842-9048; and the Hostel itself at: 3541 Aylmer Street, 843-3317. Card-holders $2 per night, nonmembers $3. There are 80 beds in rooms of four to eight. Separate quarters for males and females. Running water in each room. The Hostel is open at 5 p.m. and closes at midnight.

Free Lodgings

Men who are stranded in Montreal with no place to stay should try the **Salvation Army Men's Residence,** 1620 St-Antoine, near Guy Street. Both men and women are welcome at the **Jesus People Hostel,** 1836 Dorchester West.

Camping

Whether you arrive in an Airstream land-cruiser or with a tent in your backpack, you will find all of 168 camping and trailer (caravan) grounds in and around Montreal. One of the handiest guides to what is available is *Camping Quebec,* available free from: Quebec Department of Tourism, Fish and Game, Place de la Capitale, 150 East Boulevard Saint-Cyrille, Quebec, Que. G1R 2B4.

Arrival

INTRODUCING YOURSELF TO
MONTREAL

Early morning or late at night, your first stroll might
be along Sherbrooke Street, walking west from Peel
Street, until you reach Mountain Street. Down Mountain, with its fine boutiques housed in some of Montreal's cheeriest nineteenth-century townhouses, and
you reach Maisonneuve. On the corner you will spot
Chez Bourgetel, one of the city's many sidewalk cafes.
A scent of beer, red wine, and the smoke of Gauloises
floats in the air. No matter if you are a family of
four, or a single person looking for a chance conversation, or merely want to read your newspaper, having
coffee or an aperitif at Chez Bourgetel offers you a
fine tableside introduction to Montreal life.

If "The Bourge" is too crowded, you can usually
get a table next door at **Casa Pedro**. There is a back
room (up a flight of stairs) with a bar that is popular
with young people. Two blocks east of Mountain is
the **Rainbow Bar & Grill**, 1430 Stanley (see page 197).
Students, and the young generally, gather here to talk,
flirt, and play electronic games such as "Pong."

Between May and September, **Place Jacques-Cartier**,
in Old Montreal, rivals the Mountain Street area in
popularity. Every hotel and restaurant in this steep,
cobblestoned square has its own terrace-cafe. Here
you can talk, eat, and drink from early morning to
early the next morning. Just off Place Jacques-Cartier
and down the narrow lane known as Rue St-Amable,
you will discover the barnlike **Boîte à Chanson**, where
you can sit and enjoy the folk-singing for the price
of a beer or a *carafon* of wine. Should you tire of that,
then walk around the corner and along colorful St-Paul

Street—the oldest street in Montreal—with its ice-cream parlors, discotheques, and many restaurants.

The French student quarter is around St-Denis Street above Sherbrooke. One quite popular spot is the **Jardin St-Denis**, but there are lots of places to choose from as you stroll along the street. For a family, one of the very nicest ways to get a feel for the city is to take a horse-drawn ride in a *calèche*. You can tour Old Montreal or clip-clop through Mount Royal Park, with its big old trees and gentle slopes. From the **Lookout** you can see the city below you, and on a clear day you can even sight Vermont.

To capture fully the ambiance of Montreal, you must get out into the streets. Montreal is the most northerly of North American cities where so much of daily life is spent outdoors, and going about on foot is the best way to savor it properly. The French have a verb for it: *flâner*, meaning to lounge, to saunter, to stroll, to loaf. It's a word that has nothing to do with any sense of active purpose and it offers an important key to a true appreciation of this very special city.

In summertime, one pleasant idea, among many, is to buy a bag of oven-fresh croissants in Simpson's Department Store (Metcalf Street entrance) and enjoy them while you sit in the plaza of Place Ville-Marie. In wintertime Montrealers no longer have to don snowshoes to go *en flânant*, because now they have created (and are still creating) a unique two-level city, one above ground, one below. All important points—large apartment buildings, stores, offices, the Forum, Place Ville-Marie—are being connected by underground concourses to the Métro. Civic boosters declare solemnly that a decade from now, you will never need to wear an overcoat in Montreal.

Now let's get acquainted with the city.

ORIENTATION

It's hard to get lost in Montreal. Five great thoroughfares—Sherbrooke, Maisonneuve, St. Catherine, Dorchester, and Notre-Dame—traverse the city center from
east to west. There are half a dozen major north–
south arteries; from west to east, these are Atwater,
Guy, Peel, University, St-Laurent (St. Lawrence), and
St-Denis, and they all connect Sherbrooke (northern-
most of the five above) to Notre-Dame (the southern-
most). Street numbers start from the river for streets
going north, while St-Laurent divides the east and west
numbers for streets running in this direction. Parallel
north–south streets bear the same numbers between
intersections: Dorchester to St. Catherine is the 1200
block, for example, and Maisonneuve to Sherbrooke,
the 2000 block.

Spend a few minutes studying the map on the following pages, and the main outlines of downtown Montreal
will become clear to you.

CITY TRANSIT

Montreal's urban transit system, a combination of
bus and Métro routes, is fast, cheap, and efficient. As
a visitor, you'll find that the Métro alone will take
you to most of the places you wish to go. For the price
of a single Métro or bus fare, you can switch from
one system to the other: on the bus, you ask for a
transfer when you board; on the Métro, you take one
from an automatic dispenser after going through the
turnstile. Adult cash fare (exact fare only) on the bus
is 50 cents; on the Métro, 50 cents or thirteen tickets for
$5.00. Children between the ages of five and thirteen
pay a cash fare of 10 cents, but you can get six children's

1	Concordia University	8	Université du Québec
2	U.S. Consulate	9	Notre-Dame-de-Bonsecours
3	McGill University	10	Maison de Radio-Canada
4	Mary Queen of the World Cathedral	11	Cross of Christ
5	Château Champlain	12	Mount Royal Lookout
6	Bonaventure	13	St. Joseph's Oratory
7	Place Dupuis	14	Aquarium

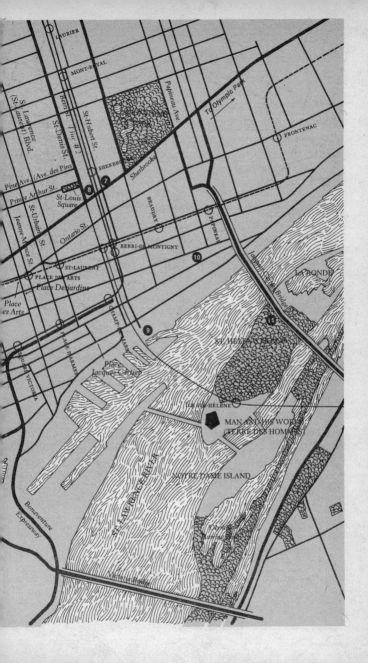

tickets for 50 cents for use between the hours of 7 a.m. and 7 p.m. All Métro tickets are good indefinitely, and can be used anytime. There is no charge for children under five.

The Métro operates between 5:30 a.m. and 1:30 a.m. Autobuses on St. Catherine and St-Denis streets are in operation 24 hours a day. For more information on routes and schedules phone 849-4761.

The Métro

The Métro is the pride and joy of every Montrealer. No visitor should leave without visiting it. This $500-million subway, opened in October 1966, is far more than a people mover; it is also an incredible underground art gallery. The city hired Quebec's most talented architects, artists, and designers to create a network of stations that are both functional and beautiful. No two are alike. Its paintings, sculpture, stained-glass windows, murals, tapestries, frescoes, ceramics, and mosaics make Montreal's Métro the seventh wonder of North America.

At **Place des Arts**, for example, Frédéric Bach created a 45-foot stained-glass mural that relates the

"Story of Music in Montreal"; it can be seen from one end to the other of the 800-foot-long mezzanine; at **Crémazie**, artist Georges Lauda used the symbols of the solar system and the signs of the zodiac in a multicolored ceramic mural that towers over the subway platform; at **McGill**, a richly woven tapestry in deep red, black, blue, violet, and gold depicts the life of James McGill, founder of the university that bears his name.

Spotlessly clean, the Métro is used by an estimated quarter-of-a-billion passengers each year. The trains run on rubber-tired wheels at speeds up to 50 mph, and—like those of the Paris Métro on which the Montreal system is modeled—they are amazingly quiet. The 8-mile journey on Line No. 2 takes about 20 minutes, the equivalent of about an hour's taxi ride in the rush hour. The system is still expanding; but at present there are three lines: one leg is the east-west Maisonneuve line, which runs from Westmount Square to Olympic Park in the east; the north-south line runs parallel to St-Denis Street, from Place Bonaventure to the south, all the way across Montreal Island to Henri Bourassa in the north. The third line begins at the triple-level Berri-de-Montigny station, goes under the river, emerges at St. Helen's Island (site of Man and His World), and continues to Longueuil on the south shore. The map preceding the Introduction explains how the system works.

Buses

Some 1,850 buses operating on 122 regular and 8 express routes cover the rest of the city, and a dozen other municipalities on the island as well. You will need the exact fare, but if you don't possess it, the driver will take your name and address and, in time, the amount of your overpayment will be refunded. Remember that transfers are free, so if you are planning on taking a bus after a Métro ride, make sure you get a transfer from the machine before you leave the station.

Taxis

Taxis are plentiful in Montreal, and drivers courteous in the extreme. Metered rates are 60 cents for the first seventh of a mile, then 10 cents for each additional seventh of a mile. An average ride in the downtown area costs around $1.50 (but fares are due to go up in Spring '76). There is an extra charge of 25 cents for each piece of baggage, but no charge for extra passengers. The usual tip is 10 to 15 percent of the fare.

The three biggest fleets are La Salle: 861-2552, Diamond: 273-6331, and Veterans: 273-6351. By all means use the phone, most Montrealers do.

Airport Service

International flights arrive at the world's largest airport, Mirabel International, which opened in 1975, and is 34 miles from the city, 29 from Dorval. By bus the trip takes from 45 to 65 minutes. Buses leave from the Queen Elizabeth Hotel (central station) on the hour from 5 a.m. to noon, and on the half-hour from noon to 11:30 p.m. For both airports, the fare is $5 each way to and from Montreal. The taxi fare to Mirabel from downtown is about $25, a rate that will go up if taxi fares are increased.

The cheapest way to get to or from Dorval Airport is offered by the Murray Hill Bus Service. Buses leave every 20 minutes throughout the day and evening. Once downtown, the airport bus picks up and discharges passengers at the Queen Elizabeth, Sheraton-Mount Royal, Windsor, Château Champlain, and Bonaventure. Fare is $2.75, $1.25 for children under twelve, and free for children under two.

A taxicab to or from Dorval will cost you around $10, depending upon where you are heading—slightly less if your ultimate destination is Westmount, somewhat more if it is the Olympic site.

You can also order a limousine to take you to the airport. It'll come to your door, will arrive early, and costs about the same as a taxi. Call Murray Hill Limousine Service the day before: 937-5311.

Trains and Buses (out-of-town)

Commuter and long-distance trains operate from Windsor Station (Canadian Pacific: 861-6811), 215 St-Jacques Street West, and from Central Station (Canadian National: 877-6550), next door to the Queen Elizabeth Hotel, Dorchester Boulevard. Amtrak operates through service to New York, Washington, Miami, Los Angeles, San Francisco, and Seattle from Central Station. For reservations and information, phone 877-6550. Out-of-town buses leave from the Central Terminal, corner of Berri Street and Maisonneuve Boulevard (842-2281). Bus service to all points in Quebec and the rest of Canada and the U.S. *Greyhound Bus Lines* runs a VIP bus service between Montreal and New York. Bilingual hostess, lunch served, soft drinks, tea and coffee (no liquor), wall-to-wall carpet, stereo music, newspapers and magazines. Express service. Round-trip $46.70. In Montreal call 843-3888.

AUTOS AND DRIVING

Montreal is not Paris, but its reputation comes a close second when one speaks of the quality of city driving. The Montrealer drives with the Frenchman's dash and *élan*, but with none of his skill. You have to look out for the other fellow, since he will rarely be looking out for you. It is a common sight to find your neighbor in the left lane cutting across to the right lane without so much as a blink of his tail indicators. Moreover, turns are allowed from the center islands that run down many of the major east-west streets. Not surprisingly, this is the single greatest cause of accidents in this accident-prone city. Monday mornings are always gloomy occasions for local residents, for this is when the newspapers list the weekend accidents, a morbid accounting that often runs to half a page of fine print. In a word, take care.

The following traffic signs are in use in Montreal (one general point to note is that all signs in green circles indicate "can do"; all signs in red circles, "can't do").

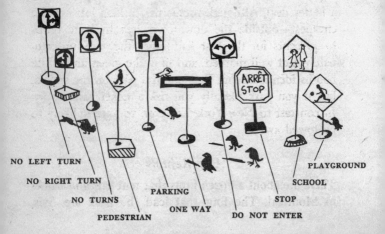

NO LEFT TURN

NO RIGHT TURN

NO TURNS

PEDESTRIAN

PARKING

ONE WAY

DO NOT ENTER

STOP

SCHOOL

PLAYGROUND

RULES OF THE ROAD

1. Maximum speed on city streets is 30 miles per hour, which must be reduced to 20 miles per hour at intersections.
2. No right or left turns permitted at red lights.
3. You must stop after an accident, even a minor one, and furnish any person involved or the police with information concerning identity, driver's license, car registration, and insurance. If the accident is serious, police should be notified immediately with mention of injuries. Hospitals and ambulances are called by police, not by the driver.

Parking

If you have your own car, be aware that rates in local parking lots vary a good deal. In the city center, prices range from 60 cents for the first and second *half-hours*, then 60 cents for each hour thereafter, or $4 per day, in municipal parking lots to 85 cents for the first half-hour in private parking lots. So it pays to look at the tariff before blithely turning over your keys. By cruising the neighborhood you will almost certainly find a better deal. Although municipal parking lots are the cheapest—outside the downtown area the rate drops to 40 cents for the first half-hour—they are, unfortunately, not well marked, and only the green and white booths identify them. You can also park on the streets, but if you park illegally you risk a ticket, usually $5. In contrast to New York, however, you are unlikely to be towed away.

Car Rentals

There are about a dozen firms that rent cars and trucks in Montreal. The four that lead the pack are Avis,

Budget, Hertz, and Tilden, the last-named being a wholly Canadian-owned enterprise. Hertz and Avis are somewhat more expensive than Budget and Tilden; and if you plan to do a lot of driving, the latter two offer the considerable advantage of no car-mileage charges. In effect, these companies are betting that you are the average car renter, and that you will therefore not drive more than 75 miles before turning in the keys. If you're figuring on exceeding this limit by any significant amount, Tilden or Budget is the place to go.

If you can book ahead, do so. Tourism is booming these days, and the car-rental situation in Montreal is, in a word, tight. If you can't book ahead, the airport is where you have the most choice among rentals. Your best bet is to gather the literature from each rental agency (they're all lined up next to each other) in the airport arrival hall, and sit down and compare them.

MONTREAL RESERVATION CENTERS

AVIS	(toll-free) 1-800 261-2600
HERTZ	(toll-free) 1-800 261-1311
	in Montreal 636-9530
TILDEN	Airport 631-6343
	Stanley St. 878-2771
BUDGET	Airport 636-0052
	Guy St. 937-9121

COMMUNICATIONS

The main post office, 1025 St-Jacques Street West, is open daily (except Sundays) from 8 a.m. to 11 p.m., Saturday 8 a.m. to 12 noon. Information, 24-hour service: 283-2564. First-class surface mail (ordinary letter) costs 8 cents per ounce (or fraction thereof) and airmail is 10 cents per ounce for the U.S. and Canada, 15 cents for the rest of the world. Air letter forms can be sent anywhere in the world for 15 cents. The Canadian Postal Service would appreciate it if American visitors would remember that no matter how alike our two countries are, the postcards and letters you mail home  must have *Canadian* stamps affixed. You can use U.S. money to buy them, but you can't use U.S. stamps.

The charge for a local call is 20 cents for most public telephones, although there are still a few 10-cent public telephones here and there. If you call from your hotel room, there is usually an additional service charge. For calls abroad, dial long distance and ask for the overseas operator. The charge for a three-minute daytime call to most countries is $12, plus federal tax. Domestic telegrams are sent via Canadian National–Canadian Pacific Telegraph and may be phoned from your home or hotel room; the charges are added onto your bill. The main telegraph office is located at 1200 Lagauchetière Street West (283-2564).

NEWSPAPERS AND PERIODICALS

Montreal is a lively newspaper town. Its seven major dailies together sell nearly 750,000 copies—five French-language papers, plus the morning *Gazette*, Canada's oldest newspaper (circulation 130,000), and the evening *Montreal Star* (about 190,000). The French-language dailies range from the sober-sided *Le Devoir* (long considered the most influential paper in French Canada) to the political journal *Le Jour* (of the separatist Parti Québécois) to the hot-blooded mass-circulation papers *Le Journal de Montréal* and *Montréal Matin*. The fifth, and most popular, French paper is *La Presse* (circulation 200,000), a generally moderate and middling sort of journal, midway in tone between *Le Devoir* and the racy mass-circulation papers.

Along Boulevard St-Laurent—the ethnic core of the city—you can buy such newspapers as *Magyar Hirlap*, *Il Citadino Canadese*, *Corriere Italiano*, *The Hellenic Postman*, *Greek-Canadian Tribune*, *Montrealer Nachtrichten*, *The Jewish Eagle*, *Glos Polski*, and *Nepriklausoma Lietuva*. Apart, however, from a struggling tabloid, the *Sunday Express*, there are no Sunday papers, only expanded Saturday editions, so a visitor who wants to find out what's going on in Montreal on the weekends is advised to pick up a Saturday paper. Most of the major hotels have newsstands where you can get *The New York Times* and the *Wall Street Journal*. The best place to buy out-of-town newspapers and periodicals is without doubt **Metropolitan News**,

· BIER ET VIN · BAR · NIGHTCLUB

1248 Peel near St. Catherine, just up from Dominion Square. New York, London, and Paris newspapers arrive there by 11 a.m. each day, and by late afternoon the tiny shop is packed to the ceiling with the rest of the world's press. *Paris-Match, Elle, Stern, Punch*, and dozens of other periodicals are also available. Opens at 8 a.m. and stays open until midnight every day of the year. (For more information, see "News Dealers," page 179.)

MATTERS SPIRITUOUS
Liquor

Liquor is easily obtainable everywhere in the city at province-owned package stores—there are no independently owned liquor shops. Prices in Quebec are about 25 percent higher than in the United States for comparable wines and spirits.

The following stores are located in the city center:

Shopping promenade, Place Ville-Marie*
Place Bonaventure*
Place Victoria
1450 Mountain Street near Maisonneuve*
1663 St. Catherine Street West
1439 Bleury Street*
1246 St-Denis Street
29 Notre-Dame Street West

The stores marked with an asterisk are open: Monday, 1 p.m. to 6 p.m.; Tuesday and Wednesday, 10 a.m. to 6 p.m. (Place Bonaventure to 9:30 p.m.); Saturday, 9 a.m. to 5 p.m. The other stores have the following hours: Monday, 1 p.m. to 6 p.m.; Tuesday through Thursday, 10 a.m. to 6 p.m.; Friday, 10 a.m. to 9:30 p.m.; Saturday, 9 a.m. to 5 p.m.

Visitors interested in fine wines might especially wish to drop by the **Maison des Vins** (House of Wines), 600 President Kennedy Avenue, where the greatest wines of France, Italy, and Germany are for sale.

Beer, Ale, and Cider

Canadian beers are comparable to U.S. brands, but are somewhat lighter than the beers of other countries. Cider is extremely popular in Quebec, and well worth savoring. Beer, ale, and cider can be purchased from licensed grocery stores, many of which stay open until 11 p.m. Although some supermarkets (Steinberg's, for instance) carry a cider license, most do not.

GAMBLING

Pari-mutuel betting action will be found at local race tracks (see page 289). There are also several permanent lotteries sponsored by the Quebec government. A chance in any of them begins at 50 cents a ticket; the more you pay for your ticket, the more you stand to gain. Drawings are conducted weekly. Tickets are on sale in innumerable stores and newsstands—wherever you see the LOTO QUEBEC sign. Visitors can take their winnings out of the country.

TIPPING

Service charges are rarely included in restaurant or hotel bills. A waiter or waitress expects 15 percent of the bill in most city restaurants (deduct the 8 percent sales tax before you start figuring). Doubling the tax is the simplest way of arriving at the appropriate tip.

The headwaiter is not tipped unless he provides you with some special service. The hatcheck girl usually gets 25 cents, although in some large hotels the price has jumped to 35 cents. Doormen get 25 cents for helping with baggage or getting a taxi. Porters get between 50 cents and $2, depending on the amount of baggage they carry. Porters at airports and other terminals get 25 cents a bag. Tip a taxi driver 20 percent of what the meter reads for fares under $1.50, and 15 percent of the fare above this figure. At better barber shops and beauty salons, the tip is a minimum of $1 for each separate operation. When you leave your hotel after a week or more, you may wish to leave something for the room maid. Needless to say, you shouldn't feel obliged to tip people who give you rude or grudging service (though that shouldn't happen very often).

RELIGIOUS SERVICES

Montreal is graced with some of the oldest and most beautiful churches in North America. Despite the rising tide of secularism, there remains a strong tradition of religious worship, and in the summer months many city churches provide additional spiritual and musical programs for visitors and Montrealers around

noonday. For hours of worship, see the Friday *Gazette*
or the Saturday *Montreal Star*. A list of Roman Catholic services may be obtained by calling the Catholic
Information Center, at 866-3803.

Roman Catholic

Principal Roman Catholic churches in Montreal include **Notre-Dame Church**, Place d'Armes, notable for
both its music and its magnificent architecture. Notre-
Dame's famous bells sound the Angelus each noon,
and this is followed by the 12:15 Mass, celebrated at
the main altar. **Saint Joseph's Oratory** is easily the
most renowned of Montreal's churches, attracting as
it does nearly 2,000,000 tourists and pilgrims every
year to visit the shrine of Brother André. Another
church of great interest is the **Cathedral of Mary
Queen of the World**, on Dorchester Boulevard near
Dominion Square, a quarter-scale replica of St. Peter's
in Rome, and the see of the Archbishop of Montreal.

Go also to the beautiful **Notre-Dame-de-Bonsecours**,
the mariner's chapel on Bonsecours Street, below
Notre-Dame Street in Old Montreal. Mass is celebrated at 11 a.m. daily and the Sunday service has
organ music. **St. Patrick's**, on Dorchester Boulevard
not far from the Queen Elizabeth Hotel, is the mother
church of local English and Irish Catholic parishes.
The sounding of the Angelus at noon is followed by
a daily 12:10 Mass. Another notable church is the
Jesuits' **Église du Gesù**, at 1202 Bleury Street, built
more than 100 years ago, which offers two services
around the noon hour, at 11:30 a.m. and 12:15 p.m.,
and a Mass at 5:10 each afternoon. The church is
open to visitors from 6 a.m. to 6 p.m.

See also pages 76–78.

Major Protestant Denominations

Christ Church Cathedral, at the corner of St. Catherine and Union, is the leading Anglican church in Montreal—the congregation was founded in 1789. The daily Eucharist is at 12:20 p.m., and during the summer months the church presents outstanding noon-time recitals. A short distance east, at 463 St. Catherine, is **St. James United Church.** Don't be misled by the shops in front: go down the side street (St-Alexandre) and you will find an English country cathedral.

The nearest Baptist church to downtown is **Westmount Baptist Church,** at Sherbrooke Street West and Roslyn. Take a No. 24 bus going west along Sherbrooke to get there. The same bus will also get you to the Lutheran services at **St. Ansgar's,** a friendly, modern church a short walk up Grand Boulevard to Notre-Dame-de-Grace (NDG) Avenue. The principal church of the Presbyterian denomination is the **Church of St. Andrew and St. Paul,** on the corner of Sherbrooke Street West and Redpath in Westmount.

Pentecostal-Gospel

Peoples Church, at Sherbrooke Street West and Union (Métro station: McGill), has the most crowded Gospel services in the city. A Pentecostal assembly that welcomes visitors is the **Evangel Church,** 1235 Closse Street (Métro station: Atwater).

Spiritualist

Spiritualists have plenty of choice, including the **International Temple of Spiritual Revelations,** which holds services in the chapel of the YMCA, 1441 Drummond Street; **Spiritual Healing Church**, 1235 Guy Street; and the **First Spiritual Church of Montreal**, 2186 St. Catherine Street West.

Salvation Army

There is a song service and Christian witness each Sunday at the **Montreal Citadel**, 2085 Drummond Street.

Christian Science

The **First Church of Christ, Scientist**, suggests that visitors first call in at the public reading room, 1416 Crescent Street, or phone 845-5821 or 935-4156.

Muslim

A Muslim mosque, the only one in Quebec, is located on Laval Road in the suburb of Ville St-Laurent. It serves the metropolitan area's 10,000 practicing Muslims. There is community prayer five times daily.

Unitarian

The **Unitarian Church (Church of the Messiah)**, 3415 Simpson, corner Sherbrooke Street West. Services on Sunday at 11 a.m., except during summer. The minister, Leonard Mason, is the man who married the Burtons at the Ritz-Carlton.

Jewish

Temple Emanu-El (Reform), 4100 Sherbrooke Street West; **Congregation Shaar Hashomayim** (Conservative), 450 Kensington Avenue at Côte St-Antoine. Both can be reached by taking a No. 24 bus going west along Sherbrooke. The **Spanish and Portuguese Synagogue** (Orthodox) is at 4894 St. Kevin.

The Bride's Church

In the last twenty years, people have come from miles around to be married in the tiny Anglican church called **St. Francis of the Birds** in the Laurentian village of St-Sauveur. It is popularly known as "The Bride's Church." Services are held each Sunday in the beautiful log-cabin chapel with its stained-glass windows. But it is chiefly the marriage ceremonies (pets allowed to be members of the wedding) that have drawn young people who like the open-mindedness of the service and the attractively simple surroundings.

QUEBEC HOLIDAYS

The major ones are: New Year's Day, Good Friday, Sovereign's Birthday (always the first Monday preceding the 25th of May, regardless of the monarch's actual birthday), Canada Day (which celebrates Canada's Confederation) July 1, Labor Day (first Monday in September), Thanksgiving Day (second Monday in October), and Christmas Day. Two other holidays that to all intents and purposes have become official in the province are Easter Monday and St-Jean Baptiste Day (June 24)—St. John the Baptist being the patron saint of French Canadians. The latter is celebrated by all kinds of well-ordered public activities, enlivened by firework displays arranged by the local authorities.

Language

You certainly don't have to have a working knowledge of the French language to enjoy yourself in Montreal, and even if you have never studied French it's surprisingly easy to drop in a word here and there.

Bonjour! Bonsoir! Très bien, Où? Oui, Non, Combien? Merci, Au revoir, Pardon! Enchanté, Ca va? Here you have a dozen words and phrases that anyone can use: Hello! Good night! Very good, Where? Yes, No, How much? Thank you, Goodbye, Excuse me! Delighted to meet you, How are you?

Parisians don't really speak the same French that Montrealers do. Montrealers speak Quebec French, a vigorous form of the language rich in local mannerisms and idioms. Of course, the higher up the social ladder you climb, the closer is the approximation to European French; the lower down you go, the more local vernacular you will find.

Neighboring Ontario does not have an Office of the English Language, but Quebec spends millions of dollars every year in its Régie de la Langue Française. The fight to save the tongue of Maisonneuve from subversion at the hands of *Les Anglais* is a serious business, and the dread signs of decay are everywhere: American-style drugstores, Western films, American pop music, Coca-Cola edging out Quebec cider, and the growing intrusion of *franglais*, the adoption of English words which are given French pronunciations —*le parking, le quick-lunch, le hot-dog, un triggerman, en blue-jean, le leadership, les bestsellers, le hamburger,* and so on.

Confronting the purists who want to clean up *le parler populaire* and bring it more in line with the French form of French are the nationalists, a loose coalition of writers, teachers, and politicians who refer to their language as *québécois* and who, though opposed to *franglais*, are avid enthusiasts for *joual*, the jargon or street language of urban Quebec.

If you speak some French, you'll find it well worth your while to spend an hour or so in a tavern or brasserie listening to everyday speech. In *québécois*, diphthongs crash into vowels like caroming billiard balls. There is a "wow" sound that turns *père* and *mère* into rhymes for *friar*, and a word like *garage* (which is spelled as in English) comes out *garaouge*. In *joual* —perhaps the most "extreme" dialectal form of Quebec speech—whole syllables are sometimes added, as in *icitte* (*ici*), sometimes dropped at random, as in *j'su* (*je suis*) and *gard* (*regard*).

In Montreal you can buy a *joual*-French dictionary at any bookstore and compare the differences. Here are some examples:

JOUAL	STANDARD FRENCH	
did'cite	*d'ici*	(from here)
itou	*aussi*	(also)
pense-z-y-pu	*n'y pense plus*	(think nothing of it)
toé	*toi*	(yourself, familiar form)

Cursing and swearing, in Quebec as in France, are almost wholly made up of words that deal with sacred objects or the practice of religion, in contrast to the sexual imagery of American or British cuss-words. No barfly in Toronto or New York would get much satisfaction out of such French oaths as *Tabernak!* (Tabernacle), *Calice!* (Chalice), *Hostie!* (Host), and *Calvaire!* (Calvary). *Damn!* has its exact parallel in the French *Maudit*, which in Quebec often has a *z* added, to become *Maudzit!*

If you want to acquaint yourself with the "classic," most cultivated form of Quebec French, you will find it worthwhile to tune to one or another of the French TV stations. Most highly recommended for this purpose is "Téléjournal," the CBC's chief French-language newscast, on Channel 2 at 10:30 p.m. nightly.

STREET FRENCH

Billboards, shop signs, and street directions will help provide you with an instant vocabulary. SENS UNIQUE (One Way), DÉFENSE DE STATIONNEMENT (No Parking), BUVEZ UN COCA-COLA (Drink Coca-Cola), PRENEZ UN PEPSI (Have a Pepsi), MANGEZ BIEN ICI (Eat Well Here), VISITEZ CHEZ EATON'S (Visit Eaton's), CHIENS CHAUDS (Hot Dogs) or HOT-DOGS STEAMÉS (Steamed Hot Dogs), PATATES FRITES (French Fries), J'AIME LE MÉTRO (I Love the Métro).

Among the obviously useful words you might wish to look out for are these:

Dames or *Elle*	Ladies
Messieurs or *Lui*	Men
Libre	Free
Occupé	Occupied, Busy
Sortie	Exit
Ouvert	Open
Fermé	Closed
Caisse	Cash (i.e., Cashier)
Renseignements	Information
Rue	Street
Place	Square
Défense de Fumer	No Smoking
Au Secours!	Help!
Arrét	Stop

Basic commercial and institutional signs

Hotel	*Hôtel*	ott-ell
Restaurant	*Restaurant*	rest-oh-rawn
Inn	*Auberge*	oh-bear-zhh
Barbershop, hairdresser	*Coiffeur*	kwa-fer
Drugstore, pharmacy	*Pharmacie*	far-ma-see
Store, shop	*Magasin*	mag-ga-zah
Supermarket	*Supermarché*	super-mar-shay
Bookstore	*Librairie*	leeb-ra-ree
Library	*Bibliothèque*	beeb-lee-oh-teck
Subway	*Métro*	meh-tro
Lavatory	*Toilette*	twa-lett
Newsstand	*Kiosque*	kee-osk
Museum	*Musée*	moo-zay
Church	*Église*	ay-gleez

Basic words

Yes	*Oui*	wee
No	*Non*	noh
Perhaps	*Peut-être*	puht-etrr
Please	*S'il vous plaît*	see voo play
Thanks	*Merci*	mair-see
Good! Fine!	*Bon!*	boh!
Only	*Seul*	suhl
More	*Plus*	plee
Less	*Moins*	mwah
Wait!	*Un moment!*	awh mo-moh
Where?	*Où?*	oo
Here	*Ici*	ee-see
There	*Là*	lah
When?	*Quand?*	kawhn
How much?	*Combien?*	kawhn-b-en
The (sing.)	*Le (masc.), La (fem.)*	lih, lah

The (pl.)	Les	leh
Time	Temps	tawnh
I	Je	zhih
You	Vous	voo
My luggage	Mes bagages	meh bah-gahzh
Airport	Aéroport	er-ro-por
Railway station	Gare centrale	garr cen-trahl
Occupied	Occupé	oh-kee-pay
Free	Libre	leebrr
Open	Ouvert	oo-vair
Closed	Fermé	fair-may
Tonight	Ce soir	suh swar
Today	Aujourd'hui	oh-zhur-dwee
Tomorrow	À demain	ah deh-meh
Love	Amour	ah-moor
Kiss	Baisser	bay-zay
Smile	Sourire	soo-reer
United States	États-Unis	aytahz-oo-nee
Of (or from)	De	dih
One	Un	awn
Two	Deux	doo (as in "wood")
Three	Trois	trwah
Four	Quatre	kahtrr
Five	Cinq	sahn
Six	Six	sees
Seven	Sept	seht
Eight	Huit	hwee
Nine	Neuf	noof (as in "hoof")
Ten	Dix	dees

Getting About Montreal

SEEING THE SIGHTS

One of the best ways to start your sightseeing in Montreal is to go to the top of the **Bank of Commerce Building** at Dorchester and Peel. You take the elevator to the observation deck and the Galerie Olympique on the forty-fifth floor. Admission is 75 cents for adults, 25 cents for children between six and fourteen; no charge for children under six.

Unless it's a cloudy day, the view before you is breathtaking. From a height of 600 feet you have a panoramic vista of the city. To the north, the wooded slopes of Mount Royal, and in the far distance the Laurentians; to the south and east, the St. Lawrence River; to the west, a maze of streets and overpasses as far as the eye can see. Let's take a closer look:

To the north, what you see is the Mountain, with Peel Street in the foreground. Contrary to guidebook myth and legend, Mount Royal is *not* an extinct volcano. As you can see, it is surrounded by the city. Sherbrooke Street to the south, Park Avenue on the east, Côte St. Catherine on the north, and Westmount to the west. When the glacial Champlain Sea covered the Montreal Plain, Mount Royal constituted the whole island. Away to your right you can see the **Cross of Christ**, which is illuminated at night and is visible for fifty miles. The Cross, which stands where Maisonneuve set his original wooden cross in 1643, is considered the guardian of the city.

Looking east, through a cloud of gasoline fumes, you can survey midtown Montreal—the modern steel-and-concrete center city that is replacing many of the old landmarks. Where you now see Place Ville-Marie, the cross-shaped $100-million office and shopping complex with its acres of walkways and its underground shopping malls, there was once nothing but railroad tracks. Beyond Ville-Marie, the city is growing like proverbial Topsy, spreading out as far as the Olympic site, and rapidly filling in what remains of the old and worn-out East End with modern skyscrapers and shopping malls—in the process, shifting the center of the city farther and farther eastward.

On the south, immediately below you is the **Cathedral of Mary Queen of the World** with its green copper roof, a replica in miniature of St. Peter's in Rome; the **Queen Elizabeth Hotel, Place Bonaventure**, the **Château Champlain, Place Victoria**, and the gaunt, black, modernistic **Montreal Stock Exchange**; and, beyond all these, the great sweep of the St. Lawrence from the **Jacques-Cartier Bridge** to your left, to the old **Victoria Bridge** on your right, with **Man and His World** on the largely man-made islands in mid-river.

To the west, looking down Dorchester Boulevard toward Westmount, the wealthiest residential quarter on the island, and—down close to the river—St-Henri, one of the poorest districts in Montreal, with its ramshackle wood-and-tar-paper dwellings.

Now that you have enjoyed the best view in town, spend a few minutes, if you like, in the Galerie Olympique, with its display of past Olympic highlights and explanation of the 1976 Montreal Games.

Because the sights of Montreal are widely scattered, you are going to need some kind of transportation to get you to most of them. The good news is that you have plenty of choice. No less than three firms offer sightseeing tours, and they are equally respectable, equally good. Whether you use the Métro or rent an air-conditioned Cadillac, take a horse-drawn carriage, or a walking tour (more details on pages 97–122), here are the city's most essential points of interest.

THE MOUNTAIN · Within living memory the Mountain, **Mount Royal**, could be seen from everywhere in the city. But this is no longer true: the downtown high-rises have largely obscured the view. All the same, it remains unique, a maple-covered mountain in the heart of the city—a bird sanctuary, sightseeing lookout, and park, cunningly landscaped to get the maximum effect from minimum space.

Mount Royal has four summits: La Croix (named after the great cross atop it), L'Abre, Westmount, and Outremont. La Croix, the highest, stands 763 feet above the Montreal Plain. In clear weather the view from the Chalet Lookout is unforgettable, a striking panoramic view of the city, the great river, and the countryside as far as Vermont.

On warm summer evenings, Montrealers like to walk or drive up the Mountain and take in the brilliant night-view of the city. You can easily walk to the highest point, the Cross of Christ. This huge illumined cross stands where Maisonneuve planted his wooden votive cross in 1643. In that first winter, when the colony was almost flooded out, Maisonneuve swore that if it were saved, he would carry a wooden cross to the top of Mount Royal. It was, and he did.

One of the pleasantest ways to see the Mountain is by *calèche*, or horse-drawn carriage. *Calèches* can be hired in Dominion Square or Place Jacques-Cartier. You can make the round-trip, or else take leave of your carriage at Beaver Lake, have a picnic or a stroll in the park, and afterward take a bus back to the city from the lake.

Allow a minimum of two hours to really enjoy a visit to the Mountain.

WESTMOUNT LOOKOUT · A 57-acre park and bird sanctuary. Most bus tours stop here for picture-taking. Magnificent city views. In fair weather you can see clear across the silvery St. Lawrence River as far as Vermont's Green Mountains. A stroll down the hill provides you with an opportunity to look at some magnificent homes. This is Montreal's "gold coast," a square mile that contains Canada's single wealthiest community.

PLACE JACQUES-CARTIER · In the heart of the Old City, "Le Vieux Montréal," this cobblestoned square with its flower vendors, street musicians, and outdoor cafes is a must for any visitor. As you explore the narrow, meandering streets around the square— St-Paul, St-Amable, St-Sacrement, St-Thérèse, and, as

a relief from so much sanctity, Rue de la Friponne (Street of the Rascal)—you can easily visualize what Old Montreal must have been like when it was populated by fur traders, missionaries, and explorers. At one time Place Jacques-Cartier was the governor's garden, later it became a marketplace. Today it is one of the liveliest gathering spots in the city. On summer evenings you almost have to push your way into the square; the cafes with their candy-striped awnings are crowded with Montrealers and visitors alike who have come to enjoy a glass of wine or beer and just talk and look over the scene. Dominating the square is a monument to Lord Horatio Nelson, built in 1809. It's the oldest in Montreal and the first tribute to him.

CHÂTEAU DE RAMEZAY · The Château is on Notre-Dame Street, east of Place Jacques-Cartier, in Old Montreal. Originally built by the French governor Claude de Ramezay, it was used by a succession of both French and British governors. It served as headquarters for General Montgomery during the occupation of Montreal by the Continental Army in 1775, and Benjamin Franklin also stayed here.

Churches and Shrines

NOTRE-DAME CHURCH ·
Notre-Dame West, at Place d'Armes

Easily the most outstanding example of church architecture in Montreal, Notre-Dame was built by James O'Donnell, an American architect who is buried here. The church took four years to complete (1825–29), and its construction brought together some of the finest craftsmen of the day. The interior is magisterial. Note especially the magnificent pulpit, the intricately carved High Altar, and the stained-glass windows. The church can seat 5,000 and make room comfortably for 2,000 standees. One of its most noteworthy features is the "Gros Bourdon," a bell weighing 24,780 pounds. When it was in use, it took twelve men to ring it.

Next door is the St-Sulpice Seminary, the oldest building (1685) still in use in Montreal. The belfry clock is the oldest public timekeeper in North America.

CATHEDRAL OF MARY QUEEN OF THE WORLD ·
Dorchester and Dominion Square

Now completely overshadowed by its modern high-rise neighbors, the Cathedral created a public uproar in 1870 with its size and scale. The interior is less impressive than the exterior, which is a small-scale replica of the Basilica of St. Peter's in Rome. The thirteen statues which peer down from its façade represent the patron saints of the thirteen parishes which donated them.

NOTRE-DAME-DE-BONSECOURS ·
400 St-Paul St. East

A hundred years ago, ships coming up the St. Lawrence used to take their bearings from this church, known as "the Sailor's Church." An enormous gold-leafed statue of the Virgin overlooks the harbor. The original chapel was built by Maisonneuve in 1657, but later destroyed by fire. The present building dates from 1771. Noteworthy are the numerous ship models that hang from the ceiling. For those with strong legs, a climb to the roof offers a tremendous view over Old Montreal and the harbor.

CHRIST CHURCH CATHEDRAL ·
635 St. Catherine St. West

This replica of a fourteenth-century English Gothic cathedral was completed in 1859. The Gothic arches are supported by stone pillars decorated with carvings of all the different kinds of foliage that were to be found on Mount Royal at the time the church was being built. A late addition, to the left of the pulpit, is the Coventry Cross: it is made of nails taken from the ruins of the original Coventry Cathedral, which was destroyed by bombs and fire in 1940. Next door to Eaton's Department Store.

ST. JOSEPH'S ORATORY · *3800 Queen Mary Rd.*

Built on the north slope of Westmount Peak, this shrine and sanctuary is visited by an estimated two million pilgrims and visitors a year. Most come as they do to Lourdes—in hope of a miraculous cure. The Shrine, started in 1915, took 40 years to complete. Its construction was largely inspired by the work of Brother André, a lay brother who discovered he possessed extraordinary healing powers. The relic of

Brother André's heart was stolen in 1973 and held for ransom. The Church refused to pay the ransom, and the relic was subsequently returned. There are escalators for the infirm and elderly, souvenir shops, and a cafeteria. Free organ concerts are given each Sunday (see page 250). Near Côte-des-Neiges.

Other Major Points of Interest

PLACE VILLE-MARIE · It was Maisonneuve who transformed the Indian village of Hochelaga into the pious French settlement of Ville-Marie, and it was an American real-estate developer, William Zeckendorf, who turned three city blocks of almost unused land—the old Canadian National Railroad tracks—into the $100-million complex known as Place Ville-Marie. Completed in the late 1950's, this great edifice was the spark which ignited the renovation of downtown Montreal. It is also the heart of Montreal's unique "underground city" (see Walk Four, page 118). Enter from Dorchester and take an elevator down to the lower level. There you may bump into town planners from Japan and the Soviet Union, among the many architects who regularly come to glimpse at the future. The open spaces, split-level terraces, and expanses of glass give the pedestrian the sensation that he is floating rather than walking.

BOTANICAL GARDENS ·
Sherbrooke St. East at Pie IX Blvd.

The 200-acre Botanical Gardens contain the second-largest collection of plants under glass in the world, ranking only behind London's Kew Gardens. The 15,000-plant collection is arranged in a series of large greenhouses that are connected by walkways. You stroll through a lush rainforest filled with exotic wild orchids (the collection of orchids is the world's largest); there is also a desert with an extraordinary variety of cacti, and a fern-house with a stream rippling among the thousand varieties of ferns. The begonia collection is also one of the world's most comprehensive. Outdoors, a miniature train (25 cents) takes you on a tour of the grounds.

There are picnic areas in the Gardens, and a snack bar where you can get hot dogs, soft drinks, and hot beverages. Parking and admission are free. Located next to the Olympic site.

MAISON DU RADIO-CANADA ·

1400 Dorchester Blvd. East

Opened in 1974 by Prime Minister Trudeau, this $75-million building houses the world's most modern broadcasting center. A visit here takes you behind the scenes for a look at Canadian broadcasting. In one hour, you visit the multi-media room for a stunning presentation of the CBC's role in Canadian life; you descend escalators to the TV and radio studios and thread your way among the props and scenery; on to the Master Control Room, nerve center of a multitude of broadcasting operations; finally, backstage to the make-up and costume departments. There is a public restaurant in the building, and a souvenir shop which sells recordings, books, toys, and clothes featured in many of the French TV network's children's programs. Guided tours leave at various times between 9:30 a.m. and 5:00 p.m. Admission is free, although parents are discouraged from bringing children under the age of five. For reservations, phone 285-2692.

THE SEAWAY · One of the greatest engineering feats of all time is the St. Lawrence Seaway, the great commercial water-highway that allows oceangoing vessels to travel nearly 3,000 miles from the Atlantic to the Great Lakes. Built jointly by Canada and the United States, the construction of the Seaway involved moving 50 million tons of earth and rock, and the construction of seven major locks which actually lift the ships 600 feet from the level of the St. Lawrence to that of Lake Superior. You can easily visit the first of these, the St-Lambert Lock, by driving across the Victoria Bridge and following the South Shore route in the direction of Écluse. There is an observatory with maps at St-Lambert, and a photographic display

which describes the Seaway system. Open daily from
10 a.m. to 10 p.m. There is a small admission charge.

CITY HALL (HÔTEL DE VILLE) ·
Notre-Dame St. and Place Jacques-Cartier

Completed in 1877, it is a fine copy of eighteenth-
century French architecture, and was considered in its
day one of North America's most outstanding municipal buildings. Unfortunately, the upper story, which
was added after a disastrous fire in 1922, overwhelms
the original design.

The front doors are usually kept locked, except on
important civic occasions. Visitors may enter by a side
door.

ATWATER MARKET ·
Atwater Ave., below Notre-Dame

One of the few open-air markets remaining in Montreal, and particularly colorful on Saturday, when
hundreds of farmers truck in their produce to display
on dozens of stalls. Springtime brings out acres of
flowers and plants. It's perfectly permissible to haggle
over prices, although it helps to know some French
when doing so. There is an excellent cheese store here
with some of the lowest prices in town, and the grubby-
looking restaurant next door sells splendid *patates frites*
(French fries).

Inside the market building are butcher stalls where,
besides the usual cuts of meat, you can buy homemade patés, *graisse de rôti*—a popular spread made by
reduction of the juice and drippings of a cooked pork
roast—and *cretons*, another kind of pork meat spread.

ST. HELEN'S ISLAND · Not to be missed, this
last piece of French territory in Canada to surrender
to the British is today a favorite place of recreation for

Montrealers. Quebec's past, present, and future are all around you. The island contains the **Montreal Aquarium** (tropical fish, penguins, dolphins) and the **Old Fort**, which houses the Military and Maritime Museum. During the summer months, the Fraser Highlanders perform costume drills, pipers and all. (For more details, see page 126.) **La Poudrière**, the old Powder House, is now home both to an international theatre that presents plays in French and English, as well as in German, Spanish, and Italian, and to **Hélène de Champlain** (see "Eating and Drinking," page 203), the city-owned restaurant with its marvelous view of the river.

Bridges and causeways connect to the site of **Man and His World** (Terre des Hommes) and to **La Ronde**, a 135-acre amusement park that is rivaled only by Copenhagen's Tivoli Gardens.

LA RONDE · The city's main amusement center, owned and operated by the City of Montreal. The 135-acre La Ronde (The Carousel) is in a class by itself. There is a children's fun-fair, lots of rides and sideshows. There are paddle-boats, strolling *chansonniers*, water-skiing demonstrations, a 300-yacht marina, and plenty of outdoor and indoor restaurants.

During the summer months there are nightly firework displays.

Open from mid-May until early September, from noon to 2:30 a.m., seven days a week. Admission is 50 cents for adults; 25 cents for young people between the ages of eight and seventeen; accompanied children under the age of eight are admitted free. There is ample parking at $2 per day. Take the Métro to St. Helen's Island. For 25 cents you can take a thrilling mini-rail ride from La Ronde to Man and His World. Or, for the same charge, you can board a motorized "train" called La Balade, which also goes back and forth between the two sites.

MAN AND HIS WORLD (TERRE DES HOMMES) · Open from about mid-June until early September, from 10 a.m. to 8:30 p.m., seven days a week. Admission to the site is free, but you'll need a "visa"—a general, all-inclusive ticket of admission—to enter the various national pavilions. Visas cost $3 a day during the week, $3.50 a day on weekends, and $5 for the season; children under eight accompanied by an adult are admitted free.

Man and His World covers nearly 1,000 acres of land on a peninsula and two lagoon-laced islands. The British architect Sir Basil Spence has described it as "a modern Venice in the St. Lawrence." A ten-minute Métro ride from downtown (St. Helen's Island station), Man and His World provides instant education and terrific fun for the whole family. It contains parks, pavilions, plazas, lakes, fountains, and plenty of spots to sit and just watch the world go by. There are restaurants, snack bars, and a mini-rail train that glides above the water and grounds, the Village of Yesteryear, Buckminster Fuller's transparent geodesic dome, brass bands, a 360°-screen impressionistic film about Canada, plus a score or so of splendid national pavilions. Here's a listing of some of the chief attractions:

The Biosphere: Imagine, if you can, a soap bubble twenty stories high, and you have Buckminster Fuller's transparent geodesic dome—the world's largest. Originally the U.S. pavilion at Expo '67, it presently enfolds the **Urban Centre,** devoted to the story of man and his environment. Children love the four-story escalator.

International Bandshell: An outdoor amphitheatre for free concerts and folk dancing. You are likely to find almost any kind of group performing here, from a steel band from Trinidad to the Montreal Symphony. For information on performances and schedules, phone 872-6222.

Village of Yesteryear: All the buildings are painstakingly authentic in appearance and detail in this model Quebec village—a three-dimensional snapshot of how life was lived a century ago in *La Belle Province*. A big thrill for the children is the Haunted House.

Mini-rail Train: A 12-minute aerial ride over the water and grounds of Man and His World. Fare 25 cents, children under 3 free.

National Pavilions: Last year Bulgaria, China, Czechoslovakia, France, Haiti, India, Iran, Mexico, Morocco, Pakistan, Switzerland, the USSR, and Yugoslavia were represented. Quebec always has a stunning pavilion, which is refurbished each year.

If you drive, use the Jacques-Cartier Bridge and take the St. Helen's Island exit halfway across the bridge. Parking is $2 for the day. The Métro takes you to the heart of the exhibition (Place des Nations). There are buses from Maisonneuve and Papineau.

PLACE DES ARTS · A magnificent center for fine music and the performing arts located on seven acres of land in the heart of the city. Place des Arts is a nonprofit organization supported by the City of Montreal and the Province of Quebec, so seats are relatively cheap. Be sure to note the magnificent works of art by contemporary Canadian artists. Louis Archambault's impressive 50-foot-long bronze leaf design *Radiant Angels* dominates the grand staircase. The Eskimo sculptor Innukpuk created *The Seal Hunter* for the entrance hall, and Robert LaPalme designed the huge Aubusson tapestry that depicts the meeting of Orpheus and Bacchus on the banks of the River Styx.

Place des Arts is open to the visiting public every

day, including Sundays, during the summer months. During the rest of the year visitors are welcome on Tuesdays, Thursdays, and Saturdays from 1 p.m. to 4 p.m. Tours leave every hour from the hostesses' center of the Salle Wilfrid-Pelletier. Adults 50 cents, students and children 25 cents.

Place des Arts is easily reached by foot, car, taxi, or Métro. For more information, phone 872-2112 or 842-2141.

THE MONTREAL MUSEUM OF FINE ARTS ·
1379 Sherbrooke St. West

Recently reopened after a $15-million face-lift. The pride of the gallery collections is a magnificent Rubens, acquired in 1975. The great strength of the museum is in its extensive collection of pre-Columbian figures. There are also fine collections of Dutch and English portrait and landscape paintings, and of course a wide range of Canadian art. Noteworthy is the Quebec Room, hewn from Canadian pine and containing a superb collection of Quebec art. Admission is free and tours are given daily.

The Neighborhoods

What gives any city its color, vibrancy, and life are its neighborhoods, and in this respect Montreal is as richly endowed as a plum pudding. They are easy to find, well defined, and well worth a visit. What follows is a listing of neighborhoods that interest *me* the most. But any Montrealer could easily create a wholly different and equally interesting list.

CRESCENT, MACKAY, MOUNTAIN, AND BISHOP STREETS · Once the western fringe of Montreal, where the English middle and upper classes lived in tasteful redstones and graystones, these streets have become an intricate tangle of boutiques, bars, discos, and English-style pubs. Most nights it's bumper-to-bumper traffic, and you have to have a good pair of elbows, especially on Crescent Street, to make your way through the sidewalk-to-sidewalk crowds. For specific references on shopping, art galleries, night spots in this area, see pages 146, 173, and 237.

Métro: Peel.

ST-DENIS STREET AND ST-LOUIS SQUARE · The dominant language on Crescent Street is English, that on Rue St-Denis, French—and therein lies the difference. Anyone who knows Montparnasse, who longs to relive the memory of a Pernod sipped at the Dome or the Rotonde, will almost certainly enjoy a visit here. The little strip of Montreal on either side of St-Denis is densely populated by artists and students who study at the nearby University of Quebec. Walk along St-Denis above Maisonneuve. Over there is **Chez**

Achille, a popular local discotheque. Across the street is **L'Ezoterique**, a bookstore that specializes in occult literature. Almost next door is **La Picholette**, one of Montreal's best "little restaurants," and not far away you can drop into **Le Picasso** for a coffee or **La Galoche**, with its cheerful atmosphere, for an inexpensive meal. The clientele is mostly young, bearded, and, if you want to practice your French, friendly. The talk of the cafes is mostly of politics, education reforms, and sport. Nationalism and québécois pride flourish in this *quartier*. Don't miss St-Louis Square (Carré St-Louis), considered by many to be Montreal's most beautiful enclosed green space. (See Walk Three, page 112.)

Métro: Sherbrooke.

"THE MAIN" · St-Laurent (St. Lawrence) Boulevard, popularly known as "The Main," is a fifteen-block-long reminder that, although Montreal is chiefly made up of French- and English-speaking people, there are another forty or fifty nationalities who also call this city home. Most of them shop along St-Laurent, and many of them live in the crowded streets leading off this busy thoroughfare. You visit The Main if you are in need of fifteen live kosher chickens, a large fresh sturgeon, two kilos of *krakowska* sausage, or two dozen fresh-baked bagels. You also come here late at night for a nice home-cooked plate of corned beef with dill pickles, washed down with celery tonic.

The Main begins above Sherbrooke Street. (See Walk Three, page 112.)

"LITTLE ITALY" · With a touch of braggadocio, an Italian-born Montrealer will tell you that more Italians live around Jean-Talon Street and St-Laurent Boulevard than in Naples. It is certainly true that the

Italians form the largest ethnic bloc in the city after the French and English. Some 150,000 of them either live or shop in this area. The best way to get there is to take the Métro to Jean-Talon and walk south down St-Laurent.

At 6714 St-Laurent you come to **Caffè Internazionale.** Well worth a visit for its *cannoli siciliana, baba a crema, millegoglie* eaten with cappucino, or a cup of strong espresso. Farther down the street is the **Casa del Formaggio** (House of Cheese). If you've never seen a 100-pound cheese, you'll get your chance here. If you wish to obtain buttira, the peculiarly delicious breakfast cheese with the butter in the middle, you can buy it at the counter. The smell of all that provolone, locatelli, and mozzarella is enough alone to waft you to Italy. Leaving the shop, return in the direction of Jean-Talon and turn east down Dante Street until you reach Dante Square. There is a neat church, and a statue of the poet, and lots of children who manage to speak French, English, and Italian all at the same time. Complete your visit with a trip to the **Jean-Talon Market** (Marché du Nord). It is open until 9 p.m. on Thursdays and Fridays.

Métro: Jean-Talon.

CHINATOWN · Clark and Lagauchetière is the place to start any visit to Montreal's Chinese section, a neighborhood full of variety and vitality. Within 100 yards of Clark you can buy a wok at the **Leon Jung** supermarket (999 Clark), visit the **China Book Store** (21 Lagauchetière East), dine in any of half a dozen restaurants (there are nearly twenty restaurants in Chinatown all told—see "Eating and Drinking," pages 228-9), or buy a roast duck at **Sun Sing Lung** (72 Lagauchetière West).

Within a slightly larger radius, you can go to church
(Chinese Catholic, Presbyterian, or Pentecostal), purchase a year's supply of noodles at the **Wong Wing**
Noodle Factory, and catch up on the latest from the
People's Republic of China at **Tu Ching** (149 Lagauchetière West). Like San Francisco and New
York, Montreal's Chinatown has Chinese-pagoda-style
telephone booths. The best Chinese restaurant (in the
opinion of many connoisseurs) is the **Tean Hong**, near
the corner of Clark and Lagauchetière, and up a flight
of stairs (see page 229 for more details).

Sunday is the busiest day in Chinatown, since the
Chinese traditionally work six days and take Sunday
off for shopping and relaxation.

Métro: Place Victoria.

PARK AVENUE GREEK ENCLAVE · It's not
Athens, but it might be if you went just by the street
signs and the shops. Stroll down Park Avenue, the
main thoroughfare of Montreal's Greek community,
and you will pass grocery shops stacked high with cans
of olive oil and barrels of gleaming black olives, and
redolent with the pungent smell of feta (goat) cheese.
Across the street from the Olympus Pool Room is the
Psara Taverna (see page 219), a typical Greek seaside
restaurant where you select the fish you want to dine
on from a basket presented at tableside. At **Dionysius**,
you can enjoy *moussaka* (made from eggplant, ground
meat, and spices) and listen to *bouzouki* music; or you
can somehow squeeze your way inside Sara and Stelios
Panayotakopoulos's **Symposium** (see page 218) and
join in the spirited Greek dancing. Park Avenue is the
one street in Montreal that never seems to go to bed
—most of the restaurants stay open until 3 or 4 a.m.

A Drive and
Four Walks

EXPLORING MONTREAL
ON YOUR OWN

There is no way you are going to capture the Gallic charm of this city from the back of a sightseeing bus. You should (as we've said before) take to the streets, rub shoulders with Montrealers, take the necessary time to absorb this crazy patchwork quilt that is half Old France and half North America. Of course, this is a big city, but it is a good deal easier to move around in than, say, Paris or London.

We will use the Métro to reach the starting point for a number of walks, but by way of a beginning, here is a suggestion for a drive around the principal sights. If you do not have a car, you can follow this route by taxi. It will cost around $15 with the tip. First, however, I strongly recommend that (if you haven't done so already) you preface this, or any of the walks below, with the splendid panoramic view from the top of the Bank of Commerce Building—an excellent way to get a feeling for the city as a whole (see page 70).

MONTREAL ON WHEELS
(2 HOURS)

Begin in Dominion Square, the heart of downtown Montreal. Head north up Peel Street, crossing one of the city's main east-west arteries, St. Catherine Street, on the way. On your right is the Sheraton–Mount Royal. Cross Maisonneuve Boulevard, and turn left onto Sherbrooke Street West.

You are now heading west in the direction of West-mount. Sherbrooke Street runs right through the heart of Montreal, and during Queen Victoria's time—from about 1850 until the turn of the century—this was one of the wealthiest streets in the British Empire. According to historians, 70 percent of the entire mate-rial wealth of Canada was controlled by the families who lived between this stretch of Sherbrooke and the Mountain. Although much of the street's charm has since disappeared under the wrecker's hammer, there remains a touch of hauteur about a Sherbrooke ad-dress. The Ritz-Carlton, on your left, is still the city's poshest hotel. On your right is **Le Château**, an apart-ment house in the Scottish baronial style that has long been considered Montreal's most elegant address.

Next on your right is the **Montreal Museum of Fine Arts,** Canada's oldest institution of the arts. Continue westward past Guy Street, and you will see on your right a long, gray stone wall. Behind it is a 30-acre estate that belongs to the Sulpicians, a Parisian lay order founded in 1642. At Fort Street, look to your right. You can see, behind the wall, two stone towers that were built in 1694 as part of the fortifications defending the Order of St-Sulpice against attack by Indians who lived in what is now the city of West-mount.

Keep in the right-hand lane, cross Atwater, and con-tinue to Greene Avenue. On your left is the Canadian "Mother House," or headquarters, of the nuns of the Congregation of Notre-Dame—property coveted by real-estate developers and conservationists alike.

You are now in Westmount, and once past Greene Avenue you will see the *Angel and Soldier* war monu-ment on your right, and immediately after it the ivy-covered **City Hall.**

Westmount: Visitors are apt to take one look at the velvety lawns and spacious houses and say "Westmount isn't part of Montreal at all." In the most literal sense, at least, they are quite correct: Westmount is in fact a separate municipality, and the wealthiest in Canada, with an average per capita income in 1973 of $25,600. Nowadays you can't buy a house north of Sherbrooke for much under $75,000, and there are mansions above the Boulevard that are assessed at more than $250,000.

Westmount is a hilly garden with houses that have somehow survived their century. Hidden behind trees and shrubs, these villas are a solid reminder of the leisured life in Victorian and Edwardian Montreal—here an Italian villa, there a hint of Scottish baronial. Graystones and redstones give way to Flemish-style brick houses with gables and white wood balconies and stained-glass windows.

As you pass through the traffic light at City Hall, still heading west, you will see on your left **Westmount Park**, built to commemorate Queen Victoria's Diamond Jubilee in 1897. It's well worth stopping to take a brief stroll. There is a public library (one of Montreal's best), as well as a conservatory, admission free, that offers seasonal flower shows. Next door is **Victoria Hall**, where Westmounters vote, hold dances, and play bingo. Next to the hall is Westmount's famous **Floral Clock**, made up of hundreds of blooms and blossoms.

Continue west now along Sherbrooke for a couple of blocks, turn right at **Westmount Baptist Church**, and proceed up Roslyn Avenue. Great maple trees here shade houses as strikingly individual as any in Montreal—no two are alike. They were built in an age when there were servants to answer the rows of bells in the cavernous kitchens. Turn right on Westmount Avenue. On your right is **Murray Park** (officially King

George VI Park). A century ago, this was the site of a handsome stone house, West Mount, from which the city took its name. The little park is named after West Mount's owner, William Murray. Turn right at the next traffic light and bear left immediately.

You are now traveling east along a road called simply the Boulevard. About a quarter of a mile along the Boulevard, make a left turn on Belvedere Road— watch carefully because it is not well marked. This is a sharp and winding ascent. Make a sharp right at the stop sign and keep bearing left. Immediately after you have made the turn, you will see across to your left the prettiest rock garden in Westmount, a masterwork of the horticultural art.

Continue on Belvedere until you reach a fork in the road. Bear left at the fork and you are on Summit Road. Make a left at the top of the hill and follow Summit Circle around to the right. You have now reached **Westmount Lookout**, with its spectacular views of the city. Away in the distance you can see the St. Lawrence River; if you look along the stone balustrade, you will find bronze markers indicating the direction of other landmarks. Park here, and perhaps take a walk in the bird sanctuary behind you.

Returning to your car, continue in the same direction. Bear left at Summit Crescent and make a left at Gordon Crescent, which runs into Sunnyside Avenue. In effect, you are following the road in a descent from the summit of Westmount. Sunnyside will bring you to Belvedere Road at the exact point where you made the turn going up. Proceed down Belvedere to the traffic light where Belvedere meets the Boulevard, and turn left. Go east on the Boulevard until you come to two sets of traffic lights. Proceed through the first set of lights and turn left at the second. You are now

heading north on Côte-des-Neiges. Follow it as it
winds up and around the boundary of Mount Royal
Park, keeping in the right-hand lane. Turn right into
the park when you see the sign "Parc Mont-Royal."
This road leads you past Beaver Lake. Follow the sign
"Avenue du Mont-Royal" and continue up the hill.
As the road winds around the mountain, you will have
a spectacular view of Montreal on your right. Here,
if you wish, there is a parking lot you can turn into,
from which you can ascend on foot to the **Cross of
Christ**, the highest point in the city.

If you choose not to, follow the road down to Park
Avenue and take a right turn southward along Park,
which cuts along the lower slopes of Mount Royal.
You will see the **War Memorial** on your right. Stick
with Park Avenue; don't take any turns. You are heading in the direction of Sherbrooke Street through an
area east of McGill University affectionately known
as "the ghetto." Like much of Montreal, the ghetto
is in transition—a good deal of low-cost housing is

being destroyed around here to make way for high-cost, high-rise developments, and the rows of lovely nineteenth-century graystone houses, with their turrets, battlements, and other touches of a Victorian builder's whimsey, may not last much longer. While they remain, keep your eyes open as you cross Prince Arthur and Milton streets. You are now back downtown.

Make a right on Sherbrooke and a left on Aylmer. Cross President Kennedy Avenue and Maisonneuve. **The Bay**, one of Canada's largest department stores, is on your right. Make a left onto St. Catherine Street, and proceed eastward. On your left, at the intersection with Jeanne-Mance, you will see **Place des Arts**. You might care to take a look inside. (See page 84.) As you continue east along St. Catherine, stay in the right-hand lane, and watch out for St-Denis Street, where you should turn right. You will cross Dorchester Boulevard, one of the city's major east-west arteries, and then Lagauchetière Street (which runs into Chinatown). The next thoroughfare is Viger Avenue, which almost immediately becomes Vitre Street East. Make a left at St-Urbain (there is a Métro station on your right as you make the turn). Cross Craig Street, follow the jog in the road up the hill, and directly ahead of you is that splendid example of neo-Gothic architecture, **Notre-Dame Church**, one of the largest churches in North America (see page 76). You are actually in the **Place d'Armes**, one of the city's oldest public places (see page 111). Make a left on Notre-Dame Street.

You are now in the heart of **Old Montreal**, a 100-acre historic district that corresponds closely to the area once enclosed within the fortifications of the Old City. Art galleries, boutiques, restaurants, and outdoor cafes have helped turn Old Montreal into one of the liveliest gathering places in the city, but it is the vivid sense of Montreal's rich past that is its ultimate attraction. Full details on page 103.

Keep in the right-hand lane and watch for **Nelson's Monument** at the head of **Place Jacques-Cartier.** There is a municipal parking lot on the right, just past the monument. You might wish to park here and take a stroll around the square. For more details, see Walk Two, page 103.

Here ends our driving tour. To return to our starting point, make a right turn out of the parking lot and proceed along Notre-Dame Street to Bonsecours Street. Make a right turn down Bonsecours. At the end of this street is **Notre-Dame-de-Bonsecours,** one of Montreal's oldest churches (see page 77). Turn right again and continue west along St-Paul Street, one of the narrowest and most colorful thoroughfares in the city —plenty to look at as you slowly make your way down it. Another right onto McGill, which changes its name here to Beaver Hall Hill, and you very shortly reach Dorchester Boulevard. A left turn on Dorchester, and driving two blocks farther will bring you back to Dominion Square.

WALKS
Walk One: City Center
(1½ HOURS)

STARTING POINT: **Peel and Dorchester**

Before starting off, take a moment to admire the *Reclining Nude,* a statue by the famed sculptor Henry Moore, on the corner of Peel and Dorchester. This is one of several works by Moore on public display in Montreal. Walk north up Peel Street. On your left is the **Windsor Hotel.** Cross the street here and enter the northern half of **Dominion Square,** which is neatly bisected by Dorchester Boulevard. This patch of green, with its century-old elms and maple trees, the many benches along its winding paths, is a favorite summer-

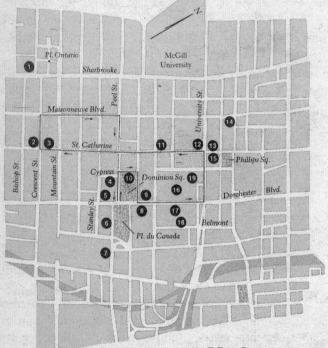

	6 St. George's Church	**12** T. Eaton Co.
1 Museum of Fine Arts	**7** Windsor Stn.	**13** Christ Church Cathedral
2 Classics	**8** Mary Queen of the	**14** The Bay
3 Ogilvy's	World Cathedral	**15** Henry Birks
4 Windsor	**9** Sun Life Building	**16** Place Ville-Marie
5 Canadian Imperial	**10** Tourist Information	**17** Queen Elizabeth (Hotel)
Bank of Commerce	**11** Simpson's	**18** Central Terminal (Gare Centrale)
		19 Tourist Information

time rendezvous for Montrealers. Notice the statuary. One gets the impression that every time the city was donated a monument and didn't quite know where to put it, some official said, "Why not Dominion Square . . . ?" I particularly like the small statue of Scotland's greatest poet, Robert Burns—directly opposite the Windsor—whose plinth bears the poet's words:

> *It's comin' yet for a' that*
> *That man to man the world o'er*
> *Shall Brithers be for a' that.*

Cross Dorchester to the south side. Here's another statue, a grand piece of Victorian chisel-work honoring the man many Canadians consider the very greatest of their prime ministers, "the Father of Confederation," Sir John A. Macdonald. All around you are sightseeing buses, tourist guides, balloon sellers, *calèches*, and hot-dog vendors. Between May and September the city usually mounts an outdoor art exhibit here, and weekdays there are band concerts. Visitors in search of free city maps and other useful information can find these in the log-cabin tourist office in the northeast corner of the square.

The east side of the square is taken up with the beam and bulk of the **Cathedral of Mary Queen of the World,** a scaled-down copy of St. Peter's in Rome (see page 76). Note the floral display in front of the Cathedral spelling out LOVE and its French equivalent, AIME.

Glance across to the west side of Dominion Square; almost dwarfed by its neighbors is the red-roofed **St. George's Centennial Church.** Built in 1870, it is the last survivor of five Protestant churches that once surrounded the square. At noontime you are welcome to enter for rest and meditation.

Leaving the square, turn right and proceed east along Dorchester. Facing the Cathedral of Mary Queen of the World is the block-long **Sun-Life Building**—a palace of nineteenth-century British commerce staring down French Montreal's tribute to the Mother Church in Rome. Ahead of you and on your right is the **Queen Elizabeth Hotel,** which is literally built on top of the Canadian National's **Central Station** (Gare Centrale). Past the hotel we come to Mansfield Street, and on your left now is one of Montreal's best-known landmarks, **Place Ville-Marie** (see page 78). Looking across it, you can see the Cross on the Mountain, a motif repeated in the aluminum-sheathed, cruciform Royal Bank Building which dominates this great plaza.

Continue east along Dorchester. At the corner of University, pause for a few moments, and take a look down toward the river. From the river to the Mountain, Montreal is geographically a succession of plateaus or terraces, Dorchester Boulevard forming the Lower Terrace, and Sherbrooke Street the Upper Terrace.

A hundred years ago, river floods of the most formidable kind were an annual event. As the spring sun melted the frozen St. Lawrence, the great river would burst its banks and extend its dominion beyond what is now the Boulevard. In the spring flood of 1861, one-quarter of all Montreal was under water, and the only way to reach the upper parts of town was by boat.

Cross the boulevard here to its north side and continue eastward. Turn left on Union Street, and the first intersection will be St. Catherine Street—Montreal's busiest shopping thoroughfare, and (like Dorchester) a major east-west artery. It is usually choked with traffic and shoppers. Not long ago a group of architects proposed an elevated pedestrian mall that would be enclosed in clear plastic. The cars would go below on the street and the people would walk above. The result would be the world's longest enclosed shopping concourse. So far no one official has accepted the idea, but no doubt its time is going to come.

Montreal's five major department stores are all located on this street, four of them within a few blocks of where you are presently standing. At the corner of Union and St. Catherine is **Henry Birks & Sons Ltd.**, Canada's best-known jewelry store. Across the street is the **T. Eaton Company**, the largest store in town, and a block to your right is **The Bay** (shorthand for "Hudson's Bay Company"). Directly in front of you across the street is **Christ Church Cathedral**, seat of the Anglican diocese, and a brilliant example of Gothic revival architecture (see page 77).

Walk west now along St. Catherine Street. Construction on your right is for a $20-million retailing-and-office complex called **Les Terrasses**. The multi-level terraces and outdoor restaurants are a key element in the underground city north of St. Catherine, which is already rivaling the existing network to the south. By the 1980's, pedestrian walkways will link the two.

Continuing westward, you come to **Simpson's**, another huge department store, on your right at No. 977. Between Mansfield and Crescent on St. Catherine is the "home stretch" for Montreal shoppers. Lamps from China, Italian shoes, Japanese paper lights, Eskimo sealskin slippers, handwoven basket chairs from Mexico are all available here. At 1196 St. Catherine is **Mister Steer**, a good place to stop for the second-best-tasting hamburger in the city (the best is a Di Lallo burger—see page 155).

Jas. Ogilvy's at 1307 St. Catherine, at Mountain Street, is a genteel department store, heavily patronized by tweedy ladies in search of imported shortbread and stout walking shoes. Strong Scottish influence—don't be surprised to find a bagpiper walking the aisles, or to have your purchases wrapped in a tartan box. The store stocks twenty-five clan colors, and there is a wide choice of jams and jellies from Scotland on the ground floor. Next door to Ogilvy's, at 1327, is **Classics**, the world's largest paperback bookstore, and next to Classics, **Henri Poupart's** tobacconist's shop, a mecca for the serious pipe or cigar smoker. Nearly 300 varieties of pipe tobacco are available, cigarettes from the world over, and Cuban cigars of every known brand.

Make a right turn on Crescent Street. The chief attraction on this stretch of the tour is the neighborhood: you are now in the heart of swinging Montreal —the "Crescent Strip," a streetscape made up of *boîtes*, bars, boutiques, and good restaurants. The real action, of course, starts after dark. (For more details, see page 196.)

Turn right again on Maisonneuve Boulevard, and keep walking east until you reach Peel Street. Turn right on Peel Street, which takes you to our starting point in Dominion Square.

Walk Two: Old Montreal
(2 HOURS)

STARTING POINT: **Place Jacques-Cartier**
MÉTRO: **No. 2 line to Champs-de-Mars station**

Enter **Place Jacques-Cartier** from Notre-Dame Street. As you look down the cobbled square with its *calèche* stands, flower vendors, and outdoor cafes, you are surrounded by the richest evidence of Montreal's historical past. It was on the waterfront close by that

7   Palais de Justice
8   John Astor's Fur Warehouse
9   Rasco's Hotel
10 Château de Ramezay
11 City Hall (Hôtel-de-Ville)

4   Old Stock Exchange   12 Papineau House
   (Centaur Theatre)   13 Bonsecours Market
1   Place d'Youville   5   Notre-Dame Church   14 Dusavelt House
2   Old Customs House   6   St-Sulpice Seminary   15 Notre-Dame-de-Bonsecours
3   Lotbinière House

Maisonneuve stepped ashore in 1642 to found his settlement of Ville-Marie. Notre-Dame, laid out in 1672, was the main street, and the chief road of entry by land. St-Paul, at the foot of the square, is the oldest street in Montreal, a narrow, winding thoroughfare that was just a path through the woods in Maisonneuve's day. Immediately to your right, on the corner, the building now occupied by a tobacconist was formerly the **Silver Dollar Saloon**, so named because of the 350 silver dollars that were then inlaid in the floor tiling.

Immediately to your left, beyond the municipal parking lot, is the **Château de Ramezay**, built in 1705 as a manor house by the eleventh governor of Montreal. The British used it for a time as Government House. Benedict Arnold slept under its roof during the American occupation of Montreal in 1775. It was also Benjamin Franklin's residence during his abortive attempt to persuade French Canadians to join the American revolutionary cause. It is now a historic and numismatic museum, and well worth a visit. At the head of the square is **Nelson's Monument**, the oldest monument in Montreal, dating back to the year 1809. Facing Lord Nelson (who for some odd reason has his back turned to the river) is a small square with a fountain named

after another great naval hero, Jean Vauquelin, a French
officer who fought bravely in the battles of Louisbourg
and Quebec. To the right of **Place Vauquelin** is **City
Hall,** or shall we say the **Hôtel de Ville.** Built in 1877,
it is a resplendent example of French neo-Renaissance
architecture—stuffy, pompous, and fearfully official-
looking. To the left of Place Vauquelin is the old court-
house, the **Palais de Justice,** a cut-stone Victorian
building in the Greek style.

Take a brief stroll around Place Jacques-Cartier. For
generations it served as an outdoor vegetable market,
attached to the Bonsecours Market on St-Paul Street.
On the left side of the square, as you face south
toward the river, is the **Hotel Nelson,** a lively gathering spot for artists and writers. Across the square is
the **Hotel Iroquois,** another popular watering spot.
Toward the south end of the square are two of Montreal's finest restaurants (owned by the same management), **La Marée** and **Le St-Amable.** Both are located
in beautifully restored eighteenth-century houses.

Return to Nelson's Monument and bear right along
Notre-Dame Street. City Hall will be on your left, and
the Château de Ramezay on your right. Here, more
old buildings of dressed limestone of the period 1780–
1830, a time when Montreal was growing rich and
prosperous from the fur trade. Now turn right down
Bonsecours Street. Immediately on your right is the
austerely beautiful, gray-painted **Papineau House,** more
than two centuries old. Today, it is the home of Eric
McLean, music critic of the *Montreal Star,* and one
of the leading figures in the restoration of Old Montreal.

As you walk down Bonsecours Street, glance at the
house on the northeast corner of St-Paul and Bon-

secours. This is the **Du Calvet House**, a magnificent example of a merchant's home around the beginning of the English regime. It dates back to 1731 and is named for Pierre du Calvet, a French Huguenot who found himself sentenced to a prison term for aiding the Americans during the invasion of Canada.

From Bonsecours Street, turn right and proceed west along St-Paul. On your left is the **Bonsecours Market**, with its finely proportioned dome and classical portico. It was completed in 1845. Its original function was as an assembly hall and a ballroom for lavish social affairs. By the turn of the century, it had become the central market, filled with farmers selling their produce. Restored to its former splendor a few years ago, the building now houses the City Planning Department. In the days of sail, the river at this point just behind the Bonsecours Market was a gathering place for ships waiting for a favorable wind to set sail.

A little farther along St-Paul, on the right, is the now-boarded-up façade of **Rasco's Hotel**. Built in 1835, and advertised as a "British-American" hotel, it was considered in its time one of the finest hostelries in North America. In 1842, Charles Dickens stayed here following his calamitous American tour.

When you reach Place Jacques-Cartier once again, cross to the west side of the square, and turn down Rue St-Amable (just around the corner from the restaurant La Marée). Street artists sell their wares along the walls, and you can pick up some fine watercolors of Old Montreal for a modest sum. Take particular note of the private courtyard on the left-hand side of the street. Such enclosures are a special architectural feature of Old Montreal. In contrast to the English tradition of surrounding the house with a garden, the early French settlers chose to build their houses right up to the street line, leaving space within for an interior courtyard. Thus the four walls protected the garden against the severe winter weather and, in addition, provided a source of safety against possible Indian attacks.

Turn left at the end of St-Amable. Across St-Vincent Street is the **Boîte à Chanson,** which offers folk-singing and wine by the carafe. Turn left on St-Vincent, return to St-Paul Street, and go right, heading westward once again. (Only Rome compares to Montreal in the extraordinary catalogue of saints that have lent the city's streets their names!) The street at this point has a lovely curve. Glance up at the rooftops. Two centuries ago, after a series of disastrous fires, the French regime compelled householders to cover their roofs with tin, and banned the use of shingles. Each house had to have two ladders and a supply of buckets on the roof. Most windows had sheet-iron blinds which were closed at night, not only as a fire precaution but because of the prevalent belief that night air was unhealthy. In many of the walls, you can still see the iron hooks that held back the steel shutters.

If you wish to make a small detour, you can cut up St-Jean-Baptiste Street to your right. Here, on the right-hand side, you will find the fur warehouse that once belonged to John Jacob Astor. It is said that Astor bought almost half of Manhattan Island out of his Montreal fur profits. Go back now to St-Paul.

Cross St-Laurent and turn left at **Place Royale,** with its obelisk commemorating the founding of the city. Built in 1676, this is the city's oldest public square. An open-air fruit and vegetable market flourished for a hundred years here, and the square was the site of the gallows and pillory in the days when hanging was a common punishment for minor crimes. The neoclassical building is the old **Custom House**, built in 1836 according to plans by John Ostell. On the east side of the square is Rue Capitale, a street that was crowded with taverns in the fur-trading era. Here lived Fleury de Mesplet, a propagandist who was brought up to Montreal from Philadelphia by Benjamin Franklin, and who stayed behind to found in 1778 *La Gazette de Commerce et Littéraire*, the forerunner of Montreal's present-day *Gazette*.

· Turn right at the end of Rue Capitale and proceed along Commissioners Street. You have a view of the waterfront on your left. Now you will again pass Place Royale. As you do so, glance across at **Pointe à Callières**, a pie-shaped plot of ground named after Louis-Hector, Chevalier de Callières, a governor of Montreal in the late seventeenth century. It was here that the first landings were made by Cartier and Champlain, and the city's first fort stood on this site. A few minutes' walk on Commissioners Street will bring you to **Place d'Youville,** named after Marie Marguerite d'Youville, founder of the Order of Grey Nuns. The St-Pierre River once occupied a great part of this area, but over the centuries it was gradually covered over. When you reach the middle of the square, you will be facing the **Old Firehouse,** a splendid example of Victorian fancy, built as it is in the manner of a Tuscan villa.

It was on this exact spot that Canada's Parliament building stood until it was burned down in 1849. After a brief sojourn in the Bonsecours Market, Parliament left Montreal forever, the legislators apparently preferring the tranquility of Ottawa to the noisy and wayward ways of Montreal.

On the south side of the square is **Youville Stables,** a long, low building with gables at each end, each of

them with a distinctive *oeil-de-boeuf* ("bull's eye") window. The stables were built between 1825 and 1860 on land owned by the Grey Nuns. Cross the street and enter through a low carriageway that leads to one of the most beautiful courtyards in Old Montreal. In recent years the building has been magnificently restored, and now provides office space for various groups active in the arts. **Gibby's** restaurant and bar occupies part of the ground floor.

St-Paul Street is one block north. Take any side street out of Place Youville and turn right on St-Paul, keeping your eyes open for Rue St-Nicholas—turn left on St-Nicholas and start walking north.

Next, turn right along St-Sacrement (not a saint this time—the name means "Holy Sacrament"), and when you reach the corner of St-Sacrement and St-Eloi, be sure to look at the house on your left. This was the townhouse of the **Marquis de Lotbinière**, chief engineer to General Montcalm, the French general who confronted Wolfe at Quebec in 1759. The house has been lovingly restored by the shipping company that now occupies it. Note the tiny dormer windows, very much a distinctive feature of Quebec domestic architecture.

When you reach the end of St-Sacrement, turn left along St-François-Xavier. A wonderful bit of Old Montreal, this was one of the first streets laid out in the new colony, and dates back to the 1690's. It leads from the harbor to the St-Sulpice Seminary, and, though choked with traffic today, it's not difficult to imagine how it looked two centuries ago when it was filled with fur traders and French soldiers, priests from the seminary and farmers looking to exchange a salted pig for a few yards of cloth.

On your right is the **Centaur Theatre**, Montreal's leading English-language playhouse. It is housed in the **Old Stock Exchange**, a fine example of late-Victorian architecture in the classic style. Now turn right along Notre-Dame Street, a street as straight as St-Paul is crooked. On your right is the beautiful **St-Sulpice Seminary**, which dates back to 1685, one of the oldest extant structures in Montreal and one of the few buildings in the Old City that is still used for its original purpose. There is supposed to be all manner of secret

passages beneath the seminary, some of them said to reach as far as the river itself. Note in particular the beautiful 1710 clock, a little to the right of the main gates, regarded as the oldest timepiece of its kind in North America. To your left, the street opens into **Place d'Armes**, with its monument to Montreal's founder, Paul de Chomedey, Sieur de Maisonneuve.

Across the street is the old **Bank of Montreal**, headquarters for Canada's oldest bank (1817), and worth a brief detour to visit its collection of coins, documents, and other memorabilia of nearly two centuries of financial history. Beside St-Sulpice Seminary stands **Notre-Dame Church**, with its twin towers named Temperance and Perseverance. One of the largest and most beautiful churches in North America, it was designed by the Irish-American architect James O'Donnell and opened in 1829. Especially noteworthy are its bells, whose peals can be heard for miles around—among them, the **Gros Bourdon**, eight feet high and weighing 24,780 pounds, one of the largest church bells in the world. Even more impressive is Notre-Dame's richly decorated interior. The church can seat 5,000 and accommodate another 2,000 standees. The art of the Quebec wood-carver can be seen at its best here, from the magnificently carved pulpit to the dozens of intricately chiseled statues and decorations. Don't overlook the Sacred Heart Chapel, to the side of the High Altar. Its ornate interior is finished in Canadian white wood and adorned with enormous religious paintings. There is no charge for visiting the church, although a small fee is asked if you wish to visit the museum beside the chapel.

To return to Place Jacques-Cartier, turn right on leaving the church and walk east along Notre-Dame Street toward City Hall.

Walk Three: St-Louis Square and "The Main"
(1½ HOURS)

STARTING POINT: St-Louis Square
MÉTRO: No. 2 line to Sherbrooke station

This walk takes you through a flourishing section of Montreal's "Left Bank," up and down several of the colorfully painted streets in the Portuguese community, and winds up on "The Main" (St. Lawrence Boulevard)—Montreal's immigrant corridor—a shopping street notable for its low prices and the lively argumentativeness and *Gemütlichkeit* of its shopowners. Take the Métro to the Sherbrooke station, which will put you a scant two minutes' walk away from **St-Louis Square** (Carré Saint-Louis). Walk west to busy St-

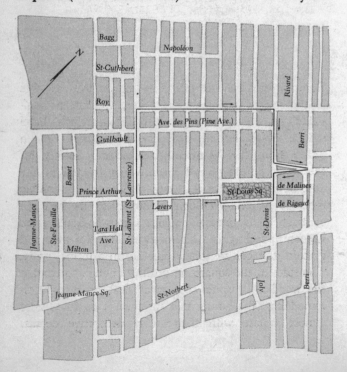

Denis Street. You are now standing on the east side of the square, and the block where you are is dominated by the Quebec Tourist Department's hotel school, which recently won the *prix citron* (lemon prize) from the Montreal Architectural Society for the worst building most recently constructed in the city. St-Louis Square is a cozy, shabby, all-of-a-jumble mélange of mid-Victorian Montreal at its best. In contrast to Dominion Square, Carré St-Louis is as French in feeling as a bite of Brie. The elm trees and graceful terraces are joined together in a formal unity. The sides of the square are positive enough to contain the middle. In spite of a great deal of thoughtless remodeling, the houses that surround it on three sides almost vibrate with their richly decorative details:

Gothic towers and turrets of every variety, gingerbread woodwork, painted balconies, brick cornices, arched windows, and outside staircases that connect the up-stairs lodger to the street below.

The magnificent fountain and water basin that once graced the center of the square is, alas, in disuse. It has been replaced by a somewhat forlorn-looking children's play area. Cross the park, taking care not to disturb the regulars feeding the pigeons, and you will find yourself on **Laval Street**, a reminder of that *Belle Époque* when Scottish bankers controlled this city and their French-Canadian office managers lived the comfortable bourgeois life on streets such as this.

Walk west along **Prince Arthur Street,** and you enter a neighborhood somewhat akin to New York's East Village, a place where poets and painters and aspiring writers can still find an apartment for $60 a month. Most of the buildings here date from the late Victorian era; there has been little or no rebuilding in this area for at least half a century. New immigrants—energetic, sunny individualists, chiefly Portuguese—have taken over such side streets as de Bullion, Coloniale, and St-Dominique, streets that were until very recently fetid slums. The result has been an incredible explosion of color, with houses now painted every hue of the rainbow—reds, chrome yellows, brilliant greens, and so on.

Prince Arthur is the main stem. A vivid wall mural declares the neighborhood to be St-Louis Village. With St-Louis Square behind you, you see on your left a row of Greenwich-Village-style boutiques, with a heavy emphasis on old clothes. Among the best of these is *Mucha*, on the corner of Hôtel-de-Ville Street: it sells fans, bags, clothes, and a wonderful assortment of hats (and hatpins) dating back to 1900. Next door, **Joail-**

lerie Molle specializes in rings, pendants, and bracelets fashioned from old tableware. Continuing westward down Prince Arthur, you will find **Titikaka**, a boutique that deals in South American Indian artifacts, and next door to it, the **Mazurka**, a Polish restaurant highly recommended for its home cooking and reasonable prices (see page 227). All of the streets to your left— Hôtel-de-Ville, de Bullion, Coloniale, St-Dominique— are worth a detour, for the happy transformation wrought by their newest inhabitants. Today the neighborhood is alive with children and laughter, old people enjoying the sunshine on their balconies, and some of the liveliest street life in Montreal.

Return to Prince Arthur and proceed in a westward direction to St. Lawrence (St-Laurent) Boulevard. You are now on "The Main," Montreal's ethnic melting pot, where at least twenty-four nationalities are represented. St. Lawrence is Montreal's chief north-south artery. Sociologists generally agree that The Main has historically represented a kind of cultural dividing line, separating French-speaking (everything east of St. Lawrence) from English-speaking Montreal (everything to the west). It should be pointed out, however, that this distinction is becoming increasingly blurred with the ever-increasing migration of upwardly mobile French Canadians into the old *anglophobe* communities. The Main itself is Jewish and Italian and Greek and Portuguese and Hungarian and German—it is truly international. Peter Vizel, a local woolen merchant, notes that "there isn't a chain store or a department store on the street." The street is dilapidated, yes, and the amenities of space and greenery are almost nonexistent. But the neighborhood is in every other respect a planner's dream of community. Only the outsiders have cars, the local folks walk to work. People

Rue St AMABLE

on The Main live, work, play, and shop in the neighborhood.

As you turn right along St-Lawrence, you are in the heart of a marvelous block-long marketplace. Let's examine this one block more closely. Between Prince Arthur and Pine Avenue (Avenue des Pins) you will discover old-fashioned dry-goods emporiums that sell buttons, ribbons, and cloth by the yard. The latest Greek hits can be bought at the Athens Music store, and a copy of the Greek-language paper *Hellenic Postman* can be purchased next door.

The last couple of years have seen the arrival of two Portuguese restaurants on this block. On the east side of St. Lawrence is the **Solmar** (see page 226), and across the street the **Old Lisbon**. The **4 Frères** (Brothers) **Supermarket**, next door to the Solmar and just off the intersection of Pine and St. Lawrence, is a cozy neighborhood establishment. It is without question the largest retail Greek grocery in Montreal, with the richest variety of goods.

You are now at the corner of St. Lawrence and Pine. If you wish to return to the city center, walk two blocks west to St-Urbain and catch a No. 55 bus going south (don't forget to ask for a transfer). At Sherbrooke you can get another bus going west which will take you to Peel Street, within a few blocks of Dominion Square; or you can stay on the bus to within a few minutes' walk of Old Montreal (see Walk Two).

If you want to continue your walk, however, the most fascinating section of The Main is directly ahead: the food-market area. For sheer variety and color, there is nothing in the heart of Montreal to beat it, a six-block marketplace where you can buy everything from pig's snouts to live chickens to octopus. Keeping to the east side of St. Lawrence, cross Pine. The next street on your right will be Roy. Turn down Roy, past **Sam's Poultry Market**, all flying feathers, excited clucking, and fresh eggs, and the next store will be **Waldman's**, the best fish market in Montreal. Fresh salmon, oysters, cod, scallops, octopus, conch, rainbow trout, crabs, clams, and turtles adorn the counters, or float around in tanks. You might ask for Canadian black-sturgeon caviar, a rare treat when available. There's plenty for a visitor to the city, because Waldman's has all manner of prepared shellfish—perfect for a picnic or for dinner in your hotel room.

It would be a shame to leave The Main without at least a mention of a beloved Montreal institution, the weekend visit to the bagel shop, an unpretentious hole-in-the-wall at 263 Viateur (see page 170). You can watch the bagels being prepared and then pushed on long wooden boards into the oven. It's a short bus or car ride away from where you are now standing, in the 550 block of St. Lawrence.

To return to the city center, go west a couple of blocks to St-Urbain Street, a thoroughfare made famous the world over by Montreal writer Mordecai Richler. From here, take the No. 55 bus heading south to Sherbrooke Street, and catch any bus heading in a westward direction.

Walk Four: Exploring Montreal's Unique Indoor City
(3–4 HOURS)

STARTING POINT: **Place Bonaventure**
MÉTRO: **No. 2 line to Bonaventure station**

Five hundred years ago, Leonardo da Vinci devised a plan for a multilevel city that would separate urban transportation from the people, thus allowing pedestrians to walk and shop without having to worry about weather or traffic. In our own time, Leonardo's dream is coming true in Montreal. You'll certainly want to explore this extraordinary subterranean city. There is nothing quite like it anywhere else in the world.

Fifteen years ago, Montreal's downtown was just another glum example of the failure of town planning. Then came $3-billion worth of urban renewal, a

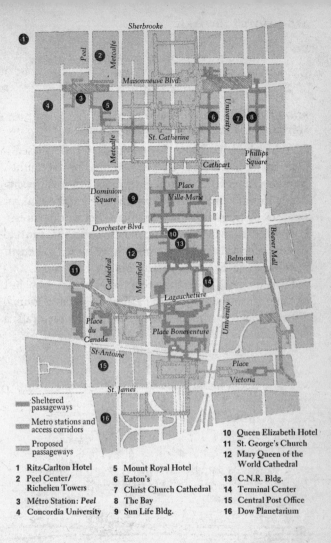

Sherbrooke

Peel

Metcalfe

Maisonneuve Blvd.

University

St. Catherine

Metcalfe

Phillips
Square

Cathcart

Dominion
Square

Place
Ville-Marie

Dorchester Blvd.

Beaver Mall

Cathedral

Mansfield

Belmont

Lagauchetière

University

Place
du
Canada

Place Bonaventure

St-Antoine

Place

St. James

Victoria

Sheltered
passageways

Metro stations and
access corridors

Proposed
passageways

1 Ritz-Carlton Hotel
2 Peel Center/
   Richelieu Towers
3 Métro Station: *Peel*
4 Concordia University

5 Mount Royal Hotel
6 Eaton's
7 Christ Church Cathedral
8 The Bay
9 Sun Life Bldg.

10 Queen Elizabeth Hotel
11 St. George's Church
12 Mary Queen of the
    World Cathedral
13 C.N.R. Bldg.
14 Terminal Center
15 Central Post Office
16 Dow Planetarium

process that began with the completion of Place Ville-
Marie in 1962. Almost like a jig-saw puzzle, the new
and old railroad terminals, hotels, and high-rise office
towers were connected to one another by underground
walkways. Today the miles of shop-lined promenades

and malls begin at Westmount Square to the west and connect, via Métro, as far east as Berri-de-Montigny. Together with the downtown core, they establish the world's first weatherproof city. Without so much as getting your nose cold, you can enjoy a concert; see half a dozen movies; check into any of four hotels; have a Turkish bath; go for cocktails 737 feet above-ground; do business with the head offices of most leading Canadian corporations; dine in fifty-four different restaurants; take a train to Miami; get a visa to Pakistan; visit a choice of supermarkets; buy a diamond necklace or a white rabbit; take a subway ride; go to an international trade fair; see the Stock Exchange at work; or take a taxi to the airport. In short, you can live the life of a pampered mole.

Follow the signs from the Métro into **Place Bonaventure**, the third largest commercial building in the world. Like a skyscraper turned upside down, this enormous office and merchandise mart spreads sideways and downwards on 1,000,000 square feet of midtown Montreal. From the outside it looks like a huge, brown, near-windowless cube. Inside you find a 1,500-car underground garage, a 600-seat cinema, a two-level, 100-store shopping mall, plus **Le Viaduc**, an international bazaar. Above all this activity is **Concordia Hall**, the city's largest convention center, which can seat 18,000 at a convention, and more than 10,000 for a banquet. Above the hall, the five-story **Merchandise Mart and International Trade Center**. On top of all this, like a cherry on a chocolate cake, is the **Bonaventure**, one of Montreal's finest hotels. Many of the rooms look out onto the rooftop garden, which provides a green setting for the hotel's bars and restaurants.

A few hundred feet south from Place Bonaventure stands the **Place Victoria** complex, which houses the

Montreal Stock Exchange. It has a 47-story tower, and a second, the 33-story Hyatt Regency Hotel, is due for completion in December 1976. This second tower will link up with Place Bonaventure, thus extending the southern limits of the sheltered city.

After exploring Place Bonaventure, descend to the Métro level. Re-enter the Métro and follow the signs to the **Place du Canada**, a $40-million complex that houses both a 26-story office block and the **Château Champlain**, another of the city's great hotels, owned by the Canadian Pacific. The hotel is 38 stories high, and its curved bay windows have caused local wags to refer to the building as "the Cheese Grater." It's worth a quick ride up to **L'Escapade**, the bar on the top floor, for a superb view of the city. On the ground floor there are boutiques and a cinema, along with several restaurants and a handy coffee shop. There are toilets near the coffee shop, a noteworthy point since toilets are one item conspicuously hard to find in Montreal's sheltered city.

To the west, Métro corridors lead you to the Canadian Pacific's magnificent **Windsor Station**, a historical landmark once threatened by demolition. Current plans are to incorporate Windsor Station into a new architectural scheme. Proceeding east, via the Bonaventure Métro station, follow the signs and head north along the pedestrian walkway that leads to the **CN Building**, head offices of Canadian National, Canada's other great rail system. From the CN Building,

another walkway brings you to Canadian National's **Central Station** (Gare Centrale).

Head for the **Queen Elizabeth Hotel**, but ignore the escalators, which lead to the hotel's lobby. Instead, follow the signs for **Place Ville-Marie**.

As you enter Place Ville-Marie, crossing beneath Dorchester Boulevard, you will be joining some of the 90,000 people a day who make the same journey. Within the next few years, pedestrian malls will connect P.V.M. to the great department stores—Simpson's, Eaton's, and The Bay—along St. Catherine Street to the north, and then beyond, to the McGill Métro station. (For more on Place Ville-Marie, see page 78.)

You have now walked the equivalent of a dozen football fields, and done so without seeing a single automobile or a traffic light. Outside it may be 90° in the shade or 20° below zero; inside you will feel quite comfortable wearing a jacket, or scarcely need one. Already 30 of Montreal's 200 downtown acres are air-conditioned and climate-controlled, and more are being added to the total every working day. Time for a quick drink, and a fast exit to the more familiar world of traffic, smog, and honking horns, an escalator ride away.

Children's Montreal

Montreal is an unusually good town for a family with youngsters. Quite apart from there being plenty of things to see and do, there is a very great deal of fascinating history and pageant—all part of the daily life of this wonderful city. No one with children should miss a visit to the Old Fort on St. Helen's Island (page 82), to watch a demonstration of musket firing and hear the bagpipers of the Fraser Highlanders (page 126). And a *calèche* ride through the ancient and narrow streets of Old Montreal is a delight that can be shared by all the family. There are boat rides on the St. Lawrence, and most youngsters would be entirely happy to spend their whole vacation in La Ronde (page 82), the city's great amusement park. And be sure not to pass up a visit to Ogilvy's (page 140) candy counter—groaning with such imported suckable delights as barley sugar, lemon drops, butterscotch, and peppermints.

As for baby-sitting, most of the big downtown hotels, and many of the motels, have an in-house baby-sitting service. Rates are in the $1.25–$1.50 range, plus transportation. (Check also under "Domestic Help," page 165.)

What follows is a listing of ideas, places, and expeditions.

STELLAR ATTRACTIONS

LAFONTAINE PARK · A 10-minute bus or taxi ride from the city center, the chief attraction here is the **Garden of Wonders**, a children's zoo set in fairytale surroundings. Within are found Hansel and

Gretel's sugar candy house, Jonah and the Whale, Noah's Ark, Babar's House, and nearly a hundred colorful settings from the Bible and from famous children's stories. There are ponies, a couple of wise old donkeys, ducks and geese, a llama or two, a house full of brilliantly hued parrots and macaws, and, in a nearby cage, what seems like two dozen owls. All told, more than 250 child-size animals to feed or pet, plus a special penguin pool with performances on the hour.

The Garden of Wonders is open from May to September, daily between 10 a.m. and sundown. There is a small admission charge.

From downtown, take any eastbound bus along Sherbrooke. When you get off at the park, head for the northwest corner, where you will find the Garden of Wonders.

MONTREAL AQUARIUM · The Aquarium, one of the best in North America, is divided into two main buildings: the Alcan Pavilion and the Alcan Dolphin Pool.

In the Alcan Pavilion will be found hundreds of different kinds of fishes and invertebrates from almost every ocean and river in the world. There are gigantic sturgeon, ferocious-looking tropical sharks, coral reef fish the colors of the rainbow, electric eels, and a family of cheerful penguins from Antarctica.

Next door, at the Alcan Dolphin Pool, you can see these remarkable sea mammals perform a 20-foot-high jump.

Alcan Pavilion, Tuesday to Sunday 10 a.m. to 5 p.m. Admission: 25 cents for children, 75 cents for adults.

Alcan Dolphin Pool, Tuesday to Sunday 1:30, 2:30, 3:30 and 4:30 p.m. Tuesday to Friday show at 11 a.m. Sunday show at noon. Admission: 50 cents for children, 75 cents for adults. For more information, phone 872-3455. Métro: St. Helen's Island.

LA RONDE · The City of Montreal's magnificent pleasure ground. For details, see page 82.

MAN AND HIS WORLD · On the site of Expo '67, which some parents will remember as the biggest (and, some say, the best) world's fair in history. Today the stunning Expo site is devoted to a permanent exhibition, Man and His World. A marvelous family outing. For more details, see page 83.

MILITARY AND MARITIME MUSEUM · Housed in the Old Fort on St. Helen's Island, the museum is a small boy's delight, with its display of ancient and modern weapons and descriptions of military heroics from 1500 to the present day. All summer there are costume drills with the bagpipers of the Fraser Highlanders and the bright uniforms of Les Compagnies Franches de la Marine, the first permanent militia in Canada (1683).

There is a tour of the Old Fort, a demonstration of musket- and cannon-firing, a slide show, and of course the sound of bagpipes, and it's all free. From May to mid-October, between the hours of 10 a.m. and 5 p.m. every day of the week. The military parades are from June 24 to September 3, throughout the day from 10:30 a.m. to 5 p.m. There is a small charge for the parades: 25 cents for children, 50 cents for adults. Phone 872-3561 for more information. Métro: St. Helen's Island.

MONTREAL WAX MUSEUM · The **Musée Historique Canadien** has just the right element of spookiness to enthrall your youngsters. The main emphasis is on early Christian and Canadian history, and the wax sculptures are arranged in a series of 3-D tableaux. Open daily in summer from 9 a.m. to 9:30 p.m. and in winter from 9 a.m. to 5:30 p.m.

You might wish to combine a visit here with a trip to St. Joseph's Oratory across the road (see page 250). Adults $2.50, students (with cards) $1.65, children $1.00. For more information, phone 738-5929. You can reach the museum by taking Bus No. 65, going west on Dorchester.

BOTANICAL GARDENS · This is a good bet any time, but especially useful for those what-shall-we-do rainy days, and it's really a sequence of treats rather than a single event. With children, you shouldn't try to take in absolutely everything. I would opt for the miniature desert in the cacti house, then move briskly along to the tropical rainforest with its fantastic orchids. There is a monastery garden that looks like a page from a story book, a snack bar where the kids can get ice cream and hot dogs, and a miniature train ride that tours the grounds. Can be combined with a visit to the site of the 1976 Olympics, which you will find at the end of Pie IX Boulevard, a few minutes' walk away.

To reach the Gardens, take a No. 24 eastbound bus along Sherbrooke Street to end of line, then transfer to a 185 bus; alternatively, Métro to Pie IX.

DOW PLANETARIUM ·

1000 St-Jacques St. West at Peel

A fantastic experience to walk from the bright outdoors into the planetarium, where you sit beneath 9,000 stars. A lively program follows, in which the various star clusters, nebulae, and galaxies are pointed out. There are all kinds of special effects—rainbows, clouds, thunderstorms, the northern lights, and even a panoramic view of the moon's surface. There is a bookstore where you can buy astronomy books, toys, and scientific games.

The planetarium is closed Mondays. English presentations are at 12:15 p.m. and 8:15 p.m., Tuesday through Friday; 1:00 p.m., 3:30 p.m., and 8:15 p.m. on Saturday; and 2:15 p.m. and 8:15 p.m. on Sunday. For details of French-language presentations and up-to-the-minute information, phone 872-4210. Admission: $1 for adults, children under sixteen 40 cents. Métro: Bonaventure.

MCCORD MUSEUM · *690 Sherbrooke St. West*

A museum small enough not to exhaust youngsters. There is a fascinating collection of nineteenth-century costumes on display, as well as a toy collection, a three-story totem pole in the lobby, and a marvelous display of Eskimo and Indian artwork. The McCord, which is just opposite McGill University, is open Friday, Saturday, and Sunday only, 11 a.m. to 6 p.m. Admission is free. For more information, phone 392-4778.

ST-LAMBERT LOCK · The first lock of the incredible St. Lawrence Seaway system. There's an observation tower to look down at the enormous oceangoing ships as they make their way to or from the Great Lakes. There are charts of shipping flags to help a child iden-

tify where the ships come from. Open 9 a.m. to 9:30 p.m. Cross the Victoria Bridge and take the South Shore route in the direction of Écluse. See also page 80 for more information.

ST. LAWRENCE RIVER CRUISE · A marvelous way to spend part of a summer's day—can be combined with a tour of the waterfront. Board the *Miss Montreal* at the foot of McGill Street. There is a bilingual commentary as the *Miss Montreal* takes a 12-mile cruise among the islands of the St. Lawrence from the Harbour to Boucherville. Refreshments are available on board. Daytime cruises at 9:30 a.m., 11:30 a.m., 1:30 p.m., and 3:30 p.m. Children $2.50, adults $4.00. Evening cruises at 5:30 p.m. and 8:30 p.m. Children $2.50, adults $5.00. For reservations, phone 842-8841.

BEAVER LAKE · Located in Mount Royal Park, this is a great place for a picnic while the children sail their boats. There is a refreshment pavilion nearby, and a miniature train to take a ride up to the chalet and the famous lookout for a view over the city. To reach the park, drive up Côte-des-Neiges and turn right at Boulevard Camilien-Houde. Various city buses go to the park. Phone 877-6260 for information.

VIEW OF THE CITY · One of the best vantage points in the downtown area is from the observation deck of the Canadian Imperial Bank of Commerce, 1155 Dorchester West. (See page 70.)

SPECIAL OR OUT OF THE WAY

For children who've exhausted the more familiar possibilities, or those with special interests, here is a brief listing of some alternative attractions:

BANK OF MONTREAL MUSEUM · There is a replica of Canada's first banking office, and a fascinating collection of old coins and paper bills. Open Monday to Friday from 10 a.m. to 3 p.m. Admission is free. Telephone 877-6892. Might be combined with a visit to Notre-Dame Church (page 76). The museum is in the bank's main office at 129 St-Jacques Street West, on the north side of Place d'Armes.

REDPATH MUSEUM · The Carpenter Shell Collection is one of the best in the world, as is the Redpath's collection of fossils and rocks. Other attractions include an armadillo the size of a small car, giant skeletons of prehistoric beasts, cases of stuffed animals (including George, a gorilla from the Congo). The Redpath is part of McGill University. Go to Sherbrooke Street, walk through the main gate, and bear left. Open 9 a.m. to 5 p.m. Monday to Saturday. Admission is free. For more information, phone 844-6311, extension 314.

CANADIAN RAILWAY MUSEUM · There are locomotives of every vintage here, as well as Montreal's first streetcar. There is Sir William van Horne's private coach, passenger and freight engines, and all kinds of streetcar memorabilia. On weekends you can enjoy a ride on a streetcar, and on Sundays there's even a train ride available. Weekdays 9 a.m. to 5 p.m., Saturday and Sunday 10 a.m. to 6 p.m. Admission adults $1.25, children six to twelve 75 cents, children under six free.

At 122A Rue St-Pierre on the South Shore at St-Constant. Take Route 209, about 4 miles south of the Mercier Bridge. For more information, phone 632-2410.

PANORAMA OF TELEPHONE PROGRESS · As every Canadian schoolchild knows, the telephone was invented by a Canadian, Alexander Graham Bell, and Canadians are the world's greatest users of the telephone. This fascinating museum traces the story of man's attempts to communicate. There are telephones from the earliest days to present times, along with a glimpse into the twenty-first century. Admission is free. Open weekdays 9 a.m. to 4 p.m. Bell Telephone Company, 1050 Beaver Hall Hill.

SEAPLANE RIDES · What better way to see Montreal Island, the St. Lawrence River, and the Lake of Two Mountains than in a seaplane? A half-hour ride in a Cessna or Beaver costs $5 for adults, $2.50 for children. For more information, contact: Pierre Champoux's Air Charters, À Ma Baie Yacht Club, 101 Rose, in Pierrefonds, or phone 631-3597.

NATURE WALKS · Operated by the Nature Conservation Centre at Mont St-Hilaire. Families are welcomed on a three-hour guided walking tour (in both French and English) around the mountain. Summer months only. For more information, call 672-7771. The Gault Estate, 422 des Moulins, Mont St-Hilaire.

CAUGHNAWAGA INDIAN RESERVE · Home of the Mohawk Indians, many of whom were converted to Catholicism in the seventeenth century. There is a Catholic Church on the reservation, **St. Francis Xavier**, where services are celebrated in the Mohawk tongue, and also a museum of Indian history. Best way to visit the Reserve is to take a limousine service (see page 51).

CHILDREN'S SUNDAY CONCERTS · Enormously popular with Montreal parents are the "Son et Brioche" ("Sound and Pastry") concerts that run all winter long in **Place des Arts**. The concert is followed by cakes and coffee, which adds to the informal atmosphere. Phone 842-2141 for more information.

PARC SAFARI AFRICAIN · Located at Hemmingford, this is one of the finest animal parks in Canada. There are more than 200 exotic and domestic animals that you may feed, pet, and photograph in their natural habitat. Picnic tables, barbecue pits, recreational and games areas are also provided. Open every day from 10 a.m. To get there, take Champlain Bridge, then Route 15 to Exit 4, and follow the signs. Phone 247-2727 for more information.

See also the chapter "Sports."

CHILDREN'S THEATRE

LE PETIT THÉÂTRE DE MARIONETTE ·
La Poudrière, St. Helen's Island
A company that works with large marionettes. A delight to look at, beautiful costumes, and a repertoire that always pleases young children make a visit here a pleasure. Tuesday, Thursday, Friday, and Saturday during holiday seasons. French version 2 p.m., English

at 4 p.m. Adults $1.50, children $1. Information: 526-0821. Métro: St. Helen's Island.

YOUTHEATRE · 1585 *St-Laurent*

Housed at Theatre on the Main, this company specializes in plays and musicals for children four to eleven. One of their best is *Aesop's Fables*, staged in "black light," a unique invention that creates some dazzling effects. Unfortunately, Youtheatre is usually closed during the summer. For more information, phone 844-8781.

THE CHILDREN'S THEATRE ·
5626 *Sherbrooke St. West*

Westmounters take their children as regularly as clockwork to these productions staged in Victoria Hall by Dorothy Davis and Violet Waters. Best, though, to phone 484-6620 to find out what their plans are.

EATING OUT

Here are a few places for dining out with the family. They are all modestly priced, and baby chairs are available.

THE OLD SPAGHETTI WAREHOUSE ·
29 *St-Paul (Old Montreal)*

An appealing place with palm trees, Tiffany lamps, and, on the downstairs level, school-desk tables. Upstairs, the children can look down at the passing street parade. The food is filling and prices reasonable. Spaghetti with tomato sauce $1.85, spaghetti with meatballs $2.50. Children under twelve are served at half the regular price.

CURLY JOE'S STEAK HOUSES · 1453 Metcalfe;
   1221 University; 3636 Côte-Vertu

The usual choice of steaks and chops for the adults,
plus a salad bar. There is a children's menu that includes a choice of either a steerburger platter or spaghetti with milk and ice cream for 99 cents.

O-PTI-ZOIZO · 27 Ontario St. West

Not far from Place des Arts, this is a friendly, informal
health food restaurant with self-service and low prices.
The name is the owner's play on Au Petit Oiseau
(At the Little Bird).

MISTER STEER · 486A St. Catherine St. West;
   1196 St. Catherine St. West; 6647 St-Hubert

Friendly service, plenty of seating, and extremely tasty
hamburgers. All the relish, pickles, tomato ketchup,
etc., are stacked up on the table.

À LA CRÊPE BRÉTONNE · 2080 Mountain St.;
   808 St. Catherine St. East

Cheerful atmosphere, and Brittany-style, paper-thin
pancakes with a choice of over eighty kinds of filling.

MURRAY'S · 962 St. Catherine St. West;
   457 St. Peter St.; 5011 Sherbrooke St. West;
   6556 Sherbrooke St. West

Among Montreal's reasonably priced restaurants, Murray's rank among the best. The menus run to such English standbys as chicken pot pie and roast beef. The
service is good and the bill won't break the bank.

Shopping
and Services

You'll enjoy shopping in Montreal, a city where fine detail is prized, and where European flair is seen at every level of design and display. There's less hustle here than in most big cities, shop assistants take a genuine interest in helping you, and, of course, there is the Gallic touch that turns an everyday purchase into a bit of adventure. What follows is a selective listing of some of the better (though not necessarily the best-known) shops and services available in Montreal.

Sherbrooke Street between Mountain and Guy, and the side streets south to St. Catherine, represent midtown luxury shopping.

St. Catherine Street, tacky and somewhat down-at-heel these days, is where you will find the major department stores—four within a few blocks of each other—as well as Canada's best-known jewelry and gift store, Henry Birks & Sons.

St-Laurent (St. Lawrence) Boulevard, above Sherbrooke, is full of dozens of European delicatessens and bakeries, along with an amazing variety of stores that cater to Montreal's immigrant population. Polish, Portuguese, Italian, and a dozen other languages are spoken here.

St-Hubert, north of Rachel, is almost entirely French, ruggedly working-class—a thoroughfare more interesting to the neighborhood than to visitors.

Notre-Dame Street. Try this narrow street of two- and three-story buildings, between Atwater and Mountain streets, for antiques. And in Old Montreal, between Place Royale and Bonsecours, you'll find Quebec handicrafts, Canadiana, and any number of boutiques and souvenir shops.

St-Denis above Maisonneuve, and **Prince Arthur** between St-Laurent and St-Louis Square, are both areas with a Greenwich Village flavor. Most Montreal stores are open from 9 or 9:30 a.m. to 6 or 6:30 p.m. Monday through Saturday, and till 9 p.m. Thursday and Friday.

WHERE TO SHOP
Department Stores

Montreal has six of them, including the "Three Graces" of Canadian retailing—Eaton's, Simpson's and The Bay (La Baie). They are all sensible places to shop, a bit short on adventure perhaps, but long on content. Like Harrods, whose cable address, EVERYTHING, LONDON, says it all, Montreal department stores offer you the convenience of one-stop shopping. You can spend a day in any one of them and not be tired. Restaurants, restrooms, public telephones, and other amenities make them comfortable places to visit with children.

EATON'S · *677 St. Catherine West*

Eaton's, the city's largest store, was founded by Timothy Eaton in 1869 as part of a nationwide chain that is still owned by his descendants. It has a well-deserved reputation for selling reliable goods, and it continues to stand by its motto: "Goods Satisfactory or Money Refunded." Noteworthy are the fashion floors, the coin and stamp shop on the main floor, and the fine-food department, with one of the most extensive selections of cheeses to be found anywhere. You'll need cash, traveler's checks, or an Eaton's credit card; no other credit cards are accepted.

SIMPSON'S · *977 St. Catherine West*

It's hard to tell the difference between Eaton's and Simpson's. In almost every respect they look alike, offering much the same merchandise at much the same prices. Simpson's does, however, have one especially outstanding department: the **Dunhill Humidor**, where a fine selection of Cuban cigars is to be found in cedar-lined cabinets. Price range: 75¢ to $5.00.

As can be said of Eaton's, an immense amount of goods from the most inexpensive in the bargain basement to good-medium elsewhere in the store; and, as also with Eaton's, only the store's own credit card is accepted, or cash or traveler's checks.

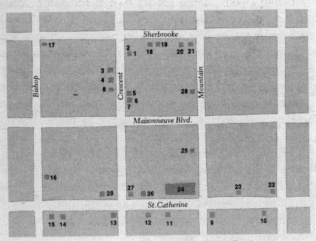

1	Michel Robichaud	16	John Warden Boutique
2	Pol Martin's Kitchen Counter	17	Peel Cycle Centre
3	Clubissimo	18	Corinne de France, clothes
4	Laura Ashley Boutique	19	The Mountain Hut
5	Eric-Yane Boutique	20	Michel Taschereau, antiques
6	Croque-Monsieur	21	Holt Renfrew
7	Elle, boutique	22	Dionne Fils
8	Lady Madonna, maternity clothes	23	Betty's, shoes
9	Rive Gauche	24	Jas. Ogilvy's Department Store
10	China Resource Products	25	Old Europe, delicatessen
11	Le Château, mod clothes	26	Classic Bookstore
12	Dutchy's Record Cave	27	Henri Poupart, tobacco
13	Hick's Oriental Rugs	28	Vogel Health Foods
14	Roots, shoes	29	Eliot-Duncan Ltd., books
15	Barber, Newsstand		

THE BAY (LA BAIE) ·
St. Catherine West at Phillips Square

Some years back, Henry Morgan and Company, Montreal's oldest department store (1845), was taken over by the Hudson's Bay Company. Since then, The Bay (as the place is universally called) has undergone a $15-million face-lift. The Hudson's Bay Company is now entering its fourth *century* of retailing in Canada, and what began in the seventeenth century as a handful of fur-trading posts is now one of Canada's biggest retailing chains, noted for its own brand-name goods (many of them manufactured in Great Britain), and especially for its furs and winter clothing. Unique are the famous Hudson's Bay all-wool blankets, which are sold according to the number of "points"—points being the short stripes that originally represented a blanket's value in beaver skins. A two-point blanket, 54 by 72 inches, costs around $35. The largest, six points, are 90 by 100 inches and cost around $100.

The Bay also features plenty of restaurants, ranging from self-service to the posh Regency Room. In the basement you'll find "Bon Marché," an excellent place to hunt for bargains.

The only credit card accepted is The Bay's own.

OGILVY'S · 1307 *St. Catherine West*

Staid Old World atmosphere and a great emphasis on
things English and Scottish, especially the latter. The
day begins and ends at Ogilvy's with a kilted and
sporanned bagpiper marching up and down the shopping aisles playing Scottish medleys, and every purchase
is wrapped and packed in green, red, and yellow tartan
boxes. There's a good antique department on the top
floor and an excellent china department that stocks
both English and French pottery and porcelain. English
and Scottish knitwear, Nova Scotia handmade quilts,
and European chocolates and candies are among
Ogilvy's special items. All in all, the store has the
warmest atmosphere of any Montreal store, and the
shop assistants are just great. It's great fun to take tea
in the Tartan Room, all very British.

Accepts American Express, Chargex, and own credit
card.

HOLT RENFREW · 1300 *Sherbrooke West*

Posh, perfumed, and pricey. Excellent in all departments. First-rate men's shop on the ground floor. One
of the few Canadian department stores that stock
original models from leading French and Italian coutu-
riers. There is a tiny Yves St-Laurent boutique on the
second floor (see page 160). The fourth floor features
handbags and accessories, and the store also has a
gourmet shop with epicurean specialties from Fauchon's
in Paris.

Accepts American Express, Chargex, and own credit
card.

DUPUIS FRÈRES ·
865 *St. Catherine Street East at St-Hubert*

A short Métro ride from downtown, and well worth

the visit, is the brand-new version of the oldest established French department store in Canada, and Montreal's only major department store east of St. Lawrence Boulevard. It's good to have some French, but you'll find the staff extremely helpful even if you don't. The store is bright and cheerful, and has some great values, especially in medium-priced fashions and accessories such as handbags, gloves, scarves. Excellent bookstore, outstanding stationery department, and the men's-wear department seems light years ahead of the competition. Pierre Cardin shirts are cheaper here than in downtown stores. Features bargain counters and special sales too. There's a good restaurant licensed for beer and wine.

Accepts all major credit cards.

Underground Shopping

In a paragraph or two each, here are a few useful details about the major shopping areas in Montreal's underground city. Besides Sherbrooke to St-Antoine (see Walk Four, page 118), you most certainly ought to take a brief Métro ride to the luxury shops and stores in Westmount Square, if only to window-shop.

PLACE VILLE-MARIE · The granddaddy of Montreal's underground shopping concourses, it remains one of the pleasantest to visit. P.V.M. caters chiefly to the people who work or do business in and around this giant complex—150,000 people a day, ebbing and flowing in synch with the office hours. If you don't care for crowds, avoid the noon–2:30 p.m. crush.

Besides **Marks and Spencer's** ("Marks and Sparks" to its devoted customers), the high-quality, medium-priced British store famous for its own "St Michael's" brand merchandise, and a branch of the fashionable **Holt Renfrew**, there are more than 200 shops where you will find children's toys, crystal and china, leather goods, women's and men's wear (with the accent on the career person), bookstores, and a number of fix-it-while-you-wait repair shops. Dorchester Boulevard opposite Queen Elizabeth Hotel.

PLACE DU CANADA · In sharp contrast to P.V.M., the tone here is quiet—and expensive. Primarily this promenade provides handy gift shopping for guests of the **Château Champlain**, and the shops offer a range of high-priced souvenirs, Canadiana, fine clothes, and jewelry. There's a big, comfortable, medium-priced restaurant, a movie house, lots of bars, and access to **L'Escapade**, the Château's penthouse bar and restaurant—great for lunch or dinner (see page 232).

PLACE BONAVENTURE · The city's largest convention hall is located here, and provides many of the customers for this area's shops. You can roam and browse through two levels of medium-priced-to-expensive shops, plus **Le Viaduc**, an international bazaar.

PLACE-DESJARDINS ·
Dorchester East at Jeanne-Mance
The newest and certainly the flashiest of Montreal's shopping centers. Opened to the public in 1976, Place-Desjardins is notably French in feeling—part of the city's eastward shift. You'll enjoy the open galleries, trees, plants, and feeling of space. Nearest Métro is Place Des Arts, or a ten-minute stroll if you walk east along Dorchester from Place Ville-Marie.

ALEXIS NIHON PLAZA · A satellite of the downtown underground, only a few minutes from the *centreville*, Alexis Nihon is next door to the **Forum**, home of ice hockey and rock music concerts. It takes on some of the same atmosphere—a big, brassy shopping and entertainment happening. There's always some kind of entertainment taking place in the central mall, and on weekends the management provide a variety of events that keep the youngsters happy while the family shops. There are lots of boutiques that sell clothes and shoes, a "Miracle Mart," a huge supermarket, a movie theater, and half a dozen snack bars and restaurants. Métro: Atwater.

WESTMOUNT SQUARE · Same Métro stop (Atwater) as Alexis Nihon, just follow the signs. If Alexis Nihon Plaza is for the *hoi polloi*, Westmount Square is for folks with deep, deep pockets. All that is chic, fashionable, and *à la mode* can be found here. You can shop for Ungaro, Yves St-Laurent, Cardin, Hermès fashions, along corridors lined with travertine marble. There's an outpost of Bally Shoes, and nearby is Lucas, the city's most glittering jeweler. If you're famished, Westmount Square boasts a first-rate steak house, and a delicatessen which has both take-out service and a considerable sit-down-and-eat trade.

WHAT'S WHERE

For Quebec handicrafts, Eskimo and Indian sculpture and drawings, go to Peel Street, St-Paul East, St-Denis Street; secondhand furniture, Victorian bric-a-brac, old china and antiques: Notre-Dame Street (off Atwater), Old Montreal, Greene Avenue; Chinese drygoods and groceries: Lagauchetiére Street; delicatessen: St. Lawrence (St-Laurent) Boulevard above

Pine Avenue (Avenue des Pins); outdoor equipment: St. Catherine Street; live poultry: Roy Street; *haute couture* and designer fashions: Crescent Street, Bishop Street, Westmount Square; bookshops: St. Catherine Street, Bishop Street, Mansfield Street, St-Denis Street; leather goods: Prince Arthur Street East, St-Denis Street, St. Catherine Street West; art galleries: Sherbrooke Street West, St-Denis Street.

ANTIQUES AND BRIC-A-BRAC

For high-quality antiques, china, and glass try Sherbrooke Street West, between Mountain and Guy, Mountain Street between Sherbrooke and Maisonneuve, and Greene Avenue in Westmount. For more modest budgets, the best street in town is Notre-Dame West, between 1500 and 1800. Begin your search from the corner of Atwater. There is also a cluster of reasonably priced antique dealers on Sherbrooke Street West between Grosvenor and Vendôme.

Notre-Dame West Area

Napoleon Antiques: English and Canadian stock. Lots of china and porcelain figures. Dolls, tea sets, religious objects from Quebec churches, some furniture. Reasonable prices. 1535 Notre-Dame West (932-6844).

La Toile d'Araignée (The Spider's Web): Grandmother's attic. Hundreds of things to poke over and examine. Jukeboxes, war souvenirs, old mirrors, bicycles, postcards, photographs, pine furniture. Reasonable. 1418 Notre-Dame West (935-3933).

Marché aux Puces (Flea Market): Crammed with Quebec furniture from floor to ceiling. Reasonable. 1960 Notre-Dame West (937-7695).

Circa 1880: Late-Victorian and Edwardian pieces. Some furniture. 1654 Notre-Dame West and 1886 Notre-Dame West (849-9670).

Martin Antiques: Quebec pine furniture. 1874 Notre-Dame West (932-6213).

Le Kaleidoscope Boutique: Old clothes, Victorian bric-a-brac, jewelry, postcards. Reasonable prices. 1810 Notre-Dame West (935-3204). For better-quality antiques with emphasis on Art Deco, Art Nouveau, cameos, and old valentines, try their other shop, at 1198 Bishop Street (861-5069).

Greene Avenue and Westmount

Breitman's Antiques: The place for museum-quality Canadian furniture (with prices to match). Samuel Breitman is one of the grand old men of Canadiana. He always has something out of the ordinary—a Quebec carved church statue of the nineteenth century, say ($1,000), or an eighteenth-century butternut bow-front commode ($2,500). Also pine furniture and Canadian prints. Expensive but authentic. 1353 Greene (937-0275).

Sotell Felicia: Irish glass and English porcelain. 1 Westmount Square (845-2410).

Victoria Furniture: Lead soldiers, dolls, penny banks, and furniture. Reasonable prices. 4875a Sherbrooke West (484-5882).

Past and Present: A mixed bag, with many a bargain to be found. Stock changes as fast as the customers. From 50 cents up—silver, china, lighting fixtures, kitchen gadgets from the thirties, soup tureens, and the odd piece of furniture. 353 Prince Albert (around the corner from Steinberg's on Sherbrooke Street) (488-0746).

Found Objects: A great place to hunt for old clothes. Emphasis is on *haute couture* of 1900–1940. Hats, ball gowns, feather boas, and accessories. Children's wear too. 4886 Sherbrooke West, up the stairs (481-3304).

The Collector's Corner: Owner has one of the best collections of ginger-beer bottles in Canada, but he trades rather than sells. Prints, furniture, bric-a-brac, and war souvenirs. 5126 Sherbrooke West (481-2012).

Georgian Antiques: English furniture of the Georgian and Regency periods. Pre-1850 china. 4924 Sherbrooke West (489-2075).

St-Denis, Above Rachel

Here you'll find a group of antique dealers who specialize in Quebec pine furniture. Lowest prices in town.

Puces Libres Antiques: Large, cluttered shop. Washstands, bread hutches, small tables, and chairs of every description. 4274 St-Denis (842-5931).

La Galerie des Ancêtres: Three floors of tables, armoires, chests, and chairs. If you're lucky, you may find a *habitant* (rural Quebec) spool-bed. 4743 St-Denis (843-6106).

Aux Trouvailles St-Denis: Some real bargains in *tel quel*—"as is"—pine furniture. You'll have to refinish the stuff yourself. 7370A St-Denis (276-4991).

Sherbrooke—Mountain to Guy

Here, and on the side streets south to St. Catherine, is where you find high-quality antiques with prices to match.

John Russell: English and Canadian stock, from china to early Canadian silver. 1504 Sherbrooke West (935-2129).

Michel Taschereau: European and early Canadiana. Top-quality and expensive. 1316 Sherbrooke West (288-4630).

Irene Walton: Eighteenth- and ninteenth-century English furniture, silver, Irish glass, carpets, paintings, brass, and copper. 1390 Sherbrooke West, Suite 35, third floor (288-9959).

Petit Musée: Arms and armor jewelry, ivory, primitive art, and archeological antiquities. 1494 Sherbrooke West (937-6161).

Ogilvy's: Don't ignore the antique galleries on Ogilvy's fifth floor. Impressive collection of Canadiana prints, and unusual pieces. Ogilvy's, St. Catherine at Mountain (842-7711).

Old Vic Pine Shop: Early Quebec and Ontario furniture. Reasonable prices, considering the quality. 2190 Crescent (288-8948).

Obsession: Art Nouveau, Art Deco, and collectibles. 1431 Mackay (845-1503).

Old Montreal and Vicinity

Another growing area for antique stores.

Architectural Antiques: A stained-glass window or a chandelier? Everything you can imagine from some of Montreal's finest homes is here—fireplaces, doors, window's, doorknobs, etc. Well worth a visit. 119 St-Pierre (849-3344).

Aux 1000 Trouvailles: An enormous stock of Quebec furniture and antiques. Wholesale and retail. 112 St-Paul (692-0581).

Bonsecours Antiques: Quebec church and *habitant* furniture. Everything from a convent table to armoires. Bottle collectors should also make a stop here. 441 St-Claude (861-4375).

L'Atelier: Eclectic stock. Never know what you will discover here. Reasonable prices. 515 Bonsecours (844-0360).

Jacoby's House of Antiques: One of the oldest dealers in the city—carries everything from Quebec pine to English Chippendale. Great for browsing. 480 St-François-Xavier (842-1803).

Midtown

Scattered around the midtown shopping district are the following:

Canadian National's Nostalgia Shop: Open from July 1 to Labor Day, an Aladdin's cave of delights for the railroad buff. Everything from Limoges china to lamps and lanterns. Catalogue available. Write to: Canadian National, 935 Lagauchetière West. Shop located at Central Station, Dorchester Boulevard.

CP Bygones: The rival railroad has its own nostalgia shop, and what a delight it is. Beautifully organized, with a wide range of choice—silverware, glassware, lamps, hardware of all kinds, signs and posters. For catalogue, write CP Rail, Windsor Station. The shop will be found inside Windsor Station, Place du Canada.

The Nostalgia Factory: What your mother and father threw out as junk in the Thirties and Forties has been dusted off and given a price tag. A fascinating store, crammed floor to ceiling with pop culture's artifacts—Mickey Mouse watches, Coca-Cola collectibles, movie posters, political buttons and campaign literature ("Nixon's the One"). Definitely worth two visits. Le Viaduc, Place Bonaventure (845-8002).

Blue Pillow Antiques: Victorian and Georgian jewelry. 620 Cathcart, near Phillips Square (871-0225).

Auctions

Ripley's Auctioneers: Auctions every other Thursday at 8 p.m. Mostly household furniture. 1426 McGill College (845-9712).

Fraser Bros., Auctioneers: Auctions every Monday from 10 a.m. Antiques, works of art, household furnishings, office equipment. Mostly dealers. 8010 Devonshire near Jean-Talon (342-0050).

Jacoby's: Antiques and fine furniture. Recognized by *aficionados* as one of the best auctions in the city. Irregular schedule, best to phone 842-1803. 480 St-François-Xavier.

Christie, Manson & Woods (Canada) Ltd.: A branch of the world-famous London firm that sells antique furniture, pictures, carpets, silver, china, jewelry, and books, and specializes in the sale of fine Canadiana. The sales are mostly attended by dealers but the public is welcome. Auctions are held at the Ritz-Carlton Hotel. No regular schedule, although sales are announced in the Montreal press. Printed catalogues and a list of forthcoming auctions can be obtained by writing their office, at 1115 Sherbrooke West (842-1527).

Montreal Book Auctions Ltd.: Bernard Amtmann has built a worldwide reputation as a book dealer who specializes in Canadiana. No regular schedule. For catalogue, write 1529 Sherbrooke West (932-6261).

City of Montreal: Every few weeks or so, the city auctions off what it no longer needs—used cars, trucks, heavy machinery, office equipment, etc.: Municipal Yard, 1700 Sauve East and 969 De Louvain East. Details are announced in city newspapers.

BARBERSHOPS

See "Hairdressers—Men."

BOOKS, NEW AND SECONDHAND

Classic: Canada's biggest paperback chain, with branches everywhere. The largest of these (in fact, the owners claim it is the world's biggest paperback store) is at 1327 St. Catherine West. The help is knowledgeable and courteous, and the range is enormous (844-1721). Check out also 1430 St. Catherine West, where the emphasis is on hardcovers, art books, and a strong children's section. Other branches: Westmount Square (931-8501), Place Ville-Marie (866-1323), Alexis Nihon Plaza (933-4336), Place Bonaventure (861-4037), 2020 University (843-4788). Also in several shopping centers.

Coles: Nationwide chain has outpost in Montreal. Convenient for West End shoppers. Cavendish Mall (482-2163).

Eliot-Duncan Ltd.: Paperbacks, hardcovers, used books. Recommended for anyone searching for out-of-print titles (849-3201).

THE
OLYMPIC GAMES
MONTREAL
1976

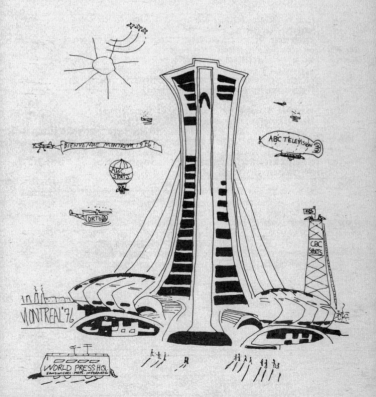

SCHEDULE

July

17 | OPENING CEREMONY 3 pm

18
MODERN PENTATHLON 8 am, 10:15 am SHOOTING 9 am
BASKETBALL 9 am, 2 pm, 7 pm HOCKEY 10 am, 3 pm
GYMNASTICS 8:30 am, 12:30 pm, 3:30 pm, 7:15 pm
SWIMMING 9:30 am, 2:30 pm, 7 pm CYCLING 10 am
ROWING 10 am YACHTING 11 am BOXING 1 pm, 7 pm
VOLLEYBALL 1 pm, 7:30 pm WEIGHT-LIFTING 2:30 pm, 7 pm
FOOTBALL 3 pm, 5 pm HANDBALL 7 pm

19
BASKETBALL 9 am, 2 pm, 7 pm MODERN PENTATHLON 9 am
SHOOTING 9 am SWIMMING 9:30 am, 2 pm, 3 pm, 7 pm
HOCKEY 10 am, 3 pm ROWING 10 am
YACHTING 11:20 am BOXING 1 pm, 7 pm
VOLLEYBALL 1 pm, 7:30 pm GYMNASTICS 1 pm, 7 pm
FOOTBALL 4 pm, 6 pm WEIGHT-LIFTING 2:30 pm, 7 pm

20
FENCING 8 am, 6 pm BASKETBALL 9 am, 2 pm, 7 pm
MODERN PENTATHLON 9 am SHOOTING 9 am
SWIMMING 9:30 am, 2:30 pm, 7 pm ROWING 10 am
HOCKEY 10 am, 3 pm CYCLING 10 am, 3 pm
YACHTING 11:20 am BOXING 1 pm, 7 pm
FOOTBALL 3 pm, 4 pm, 6 pm, 7 pm GYMNASTICS 3 pm, 7 pm
HANDBALL 5:30 pm WEIGHT-LIFTING 2:30 pm, 7 pm
WRESTLING 10 am, 7 pm VOLLEYBALL 1 pm, 7:30 pm

21
FENCING 8 am, 6 pm BASKETBALL 9 am, noon, 7 pm
SHOOTING 9 am SWIMMING 9:30 am, 2 pm, 7 pm
WRESTLING 10 am, 7 pm HOCKEY 10 am, 3 pm ROWING 10 am
MODERN PENTATHLON 10:45 am YACHTING 11:20 am
VOLLEYBALL 1 pm, 7:30 pm BOXING 1 pm, 7 pm
WEIGHT-LIFTING 2:30 pm, 7 pm CYCLING 3 pm
FOOBALL 4 pm, 6 pm GYMNASTICS 4 pm, 6 pm

22
FENCING 8 am, 6 pm EQUESTRIAN SPORTS 8 am SHOOTING
9 am BASKETBALL 9 am, 2 pm, 7 pm SWIMMING 9:30 am,
12:30 pm, 7 pm ROWING 10 am HOCKEY 10 am, 3 pm
WRESTLING 10 am, 7 pm YACHTING 11:20 am
VOLLEYBALL 1 pm, 7:30 pm BOXING 1 pm, 7 pm
WEIGHT-LIFTING 2:30 pm, 7 pm CYCLING 3 pm
HANDBALL 5:30 pm MODERN PENTATHLON 6:15 pm
GYMNASTICS 7:30 pm FOOTBALL 3 pm, 4 pm, 6 pm, 8 pm

23
EQUESTRIAN SPORTS 8 am FENCING 8 am, 6 pm SHOOTING 9 am
BASKETBALL 9 am, 2 pm, 7 pm SWIMMING 9:30 am, 7 pm
TRACK & FIELD 10 am ROWING 10 am HOCKEY 10 am, 3 pm
WRESTLING 10 am, 7 pm VOLLEYBALL 1 pm, 7:30 pm
BOXING 1 pm, 7 pm CYCLING 2 pm
FOOTBALL 4 pm, 6 pm, 9 pm GYMNASTICS 7:30 pm

LOCATIONS

ARCHERY–Joliette Archery Club
BASKETBALL–Etienne Desmarteau Centre,
    Montreal Forum
BOXING–Maurice Richard Arena, Montreal Forum
CANOEING–Ile Notre-Dame Basin
CYCLING–Olympic Velodrome, Fairview
    Circuit, Mount Royal Circuit

EQUESTRIAN SPORTS–Bromont; Olympic
    Stadium
FENCING–Winter Stadium, University of Montreal
FOOTBALL–Montreal, Toronto, Ottawa,
    Sherbrooke
GYMNASTICS–Montreal Forum
HANDBALL–Montreal Forum:
    Claude Robillard Centre; Laval University,
    Quebec City; Palais des Sports; Sherbrooke

OF EVENTS

24
FENCING 8 am, 6 pm EQUESTRIAN SPORTS 8 am
BASKETBALL 9 am, 2 pm, 7 pm
SWIMMING 9:30 am, 2 pm, 3 pm, 7 pm ROWING 10 am
WRESTLING 10 am, 7 pm HOCKEY 10 am, 3 pm
TRACK & FIELD 10 am, 3 pm VOLLEYBALL 1 pm, 2:30 pm
BOXING 1 pm, 7 pm WEIGHT-LIFTING 2:30 pm, 7 pm
CYCLING 3 pm HANDBALL 5:30 pm

25
TRACK & FIELD 9:30 am, 3 pm SWIMMING 9:30 am, 7 pm
ROWING 10 am BASKETBALL noon, 8 pm
YACHTING 11:20 am BOXING 1 pm, 7 pm
EQUESTRIAN SPORTS 2 pm VOLLEYBALL 1 pm, 7 pm
WEIGHT-LIFTING 2:30 pm, 7 pm HOCKEY 3 pm
FOOTBALL 4 pm, 6 pm, 9 pm FENCING 6 pm

26
FENCING 8 am SWIMMING 9:30 am, 3 pm, 8 pm
TRACK & FIELD 10 am, 2 pm CYCLING 10 am YACHTING
11:20 am BASKETBALL noon, 8 pm BOXING 1 pm, 7 pm
VOLLEYBALL 1 pm, 7:30 pm JUDO 2 pm, 8 pm
WEIGHT-LIFTING 2:30 pm, 7 pm HANDBALL 7:30 pm

27
FENCING 8 am, 6 pm EQUESTRIAN SPORTS 8 am
SWIMMING 9:30 am, 3 pm, 10 pm VOLLEYBALL 10 am, 6:30 pm
ARCHERY 10 am, 2 pm WRESTLING 10 am, 7 pm
YACHTING 11:20 am BASKETBALL noon, 7 pm
BOXING 1 pm, 7 pm HANDBALL 2 pm, 7 pm
JUDO 2 pm, 8 pm WEIGHT-LIFTING 7 pm FOOTBALL 5 pm

28
EQUESTRIAN SPORTS 8 am FENCING 8 am, 6 pm
ARCHERY 10 am, 2 pm WRESTLING 10 am
CANOEING 10 am, 4 pm TRACK & FIELD 10 am, 2 pm
YACHTING 11 am HOCKEY 10 am, 3 pm
HANDBALL noon, 5 pm BOXING 1 pm, 7 pm JUDO 2 pm, 8 pm

29
FENCING 8 am, 6 pm TRACK & FIELD 10 am, 2 pm
CANOEING 10 am HOCKEY 10 am, 3 pm WRESTLING 10 am,
7 pm ARCHERY 10 am, 2 pm VOLLEYBALL 1 pm, 7:30 pm
BOXING 1 pm, 7 pm JUDO 2 pm, 8 pm
EQUESTRIAN SPORTS 2 pm FOOTBALL 9 pm

30
TRACK & FIELD 9 am, 3 pm ARCHERY 10 am, 2 pm
HOCKEY 10 am, 3 pm CANOEING 10 am, 4 pm
VOLLEYBALL 1 pm, 7:30 pm JUDO 2 pm, 8 pm
WRESTLING 1 pm, 7 pm EQUESTRIAN SPORTS 2 pm

31
CANOEING 10 am WRESTLING 10 am, 3 pm, 7:30 pm
JUDO 2 pm, 8 pm TRACK & FIELD 3:30 pm BOXING 6 pm
FOOTBALL 9 am

August

1
EQUESTRIAN SPORTS 9 am CLOSING CEREMONY 5 pm

FIELD HOCKEY–Molson Stadium, McGill
  University
JUDO–Olympic Velodrome
MODERN PENTATHLON–(riding, fencing,
  pistol-shooting, swimming, and the
  4,000-meter cross-country race) several sites
ROWING–Ile Notre-Dame Basin
SHOOTING–L'Acadie Sports Centre
SWIMMING–Olympic Pool; Claude Robillard Centre

TRACK & FIELD–(running, walking, hurdling,
  jumping and throwing events) Olympic
  Stadium
VOLLEYBALL–Paul Sauvé Centre;
  Montreal Forum
WEIGHT-LIFTING–St. Michael Arena
WRESTLING–Maisonneuve Sports Centre,
  Maurice Richard Arena
YACHTING–Kingston, on Lake Ontario

FINALS AT
(Selected

July 18

CYCLING– 100-km. team road race GYMNASTICS– Team exercises, women–team exercises, men PENTATHLON– Equestrian event SHOOTING– Free pistol– trap shooting
SWIMMING & DIVING– 200 b'fly, men–
400 medley relay, women WEIGHT-LIFTING– Flywt. class

19

GYMNASTICS – Team optional exercises, women PENTATHLON–
Fencing SHOOTING– Smallbore rifle–trap shooting
SWIMMING & DIVING– 100 free, women– 100 back, men–
200 b'fly, women– 200 free, men
WEIGHT-LIFTING– Bantamwt. class

20

CYCLING– 1000-m. time trial GYMNASTICS– Team optional exercises, men PENTATHLON– Shooting SHOOTING–
Trap shooting SWIMMING & DIVING– 1500 free, men–
400 free, women– 100 breast, men– 3-m. springboard, women

21

FENCING– Ind. foil, men GYMNASTICS– Ind. all-around, women–
ind. all-around, men PENTATHLON– Swimming
SHOOTING– Smallbore rifle SWIMMING & DIVING–
100 b'fly, men– 100 back, women– 200 breast, women–
800 free relay, men

22

CYCLING– Ind. pursuit FENCING– Ind. sabre PENTATHLON–
Cross-country running SHOOTING– Running target–
skeet shooting– rapid-fire pistol SWIMMING & DIVING–
400 free, men– 100 b'fly, women– 200 free, women–
400 medley relay, men WEIGHT-LIFTING– M'dlwt. class

23

CYCLING– Sprint– team pursuit FENCING– Ind. épée
TRACK & FIELD– Long jump, women– 20 km. walk, men

24

FENCING– Ind. foil, women ROWING–Fours w. coxwain, women–
double sculls, women– pairs w/o coxwain, women–
single sculls, women– quad. sculls w. coxwain, women–
eights w. coxwain, women SWIMMING & DIVING–
100 breast, women– 200 breast, men– 400 ind. medley, women–
200 back, men TRACK & FIELD– Javelin, women– shot put, men–
100 m., men WEIGHT-LIFTING– Lt-h'vywt. class
WRESTLING– Greco-Roman, round robin

25

FENCING– Team foil, men ROWING– Fours w. coxwain, men–
double sculls, men– pairs w/o coxwain, men– single sculls, men–
pairs w. coxwain, men– fours w/o coxwain, men–
quad. sculls w/o coxwain, men– eights w/o coxwain, men
SWIMMING & DIVING– 800 free, women– 400 ind. medley, men–
200 back, women– 100 free, men– 400 free relay, women–
platform dive, women TRACK & FIELD– Discus, men–
800 m., men– 400 m. hurdles, men– 100 m., women
WEIGHT-LIFTING– M'dl. h'vywt. class

A GLANCE
Events)

26
BASKETBALL– 11th place, men
CYCLING– Ind. road race
PENTATHLON– Long jump, women– 200 m., women
TRACK & FIELD– Pole vault, men– Javelin, men– 200 m., men–
10,000 m., men– 800 m., women

27
BASKETBALL– 9th, 7th, 5th, 3rd, 1st place, men
FENCING– Team sabre
HANDBALL (TEAM)– 11th, 9th, 7th, 5th place, men
JUDO– Lt. h'vy wt. class
SWIMMING & DIVING– Platform dive, men
VOLLEYBALL– 9th, 7th, 5th place, men– 7th, 5th place, women
WEIGHT-LIFTING– Super-h'vywt. class

28
FENCING– Team foil, women
HANDBALL (TEAM)– 3rd, 1st place, men   JUDO– M'dlwt. class
TRACK & FIELD– Hammer throw, men– high jump, women–
110 m. hurdles, men– 200 m., women–
3000 m. steeplechase, men

29
EQUESTRIAN SPORTS– Team dressage
FENCING– Team épée   FOOTBALL (SOCCER)– 3rd place
HOCKEY (FIELD)– 11th, 9th place   JUDO– Lt. m'dlewt. class
TRACK & FIELD– 100 m. hurdles, women– long jump, men–
discus, women– 400 m., women– 400 m., men–
DECATHLON, men– 100 m.– long jump– shot put–
high jump– 400 m.

30
CANOEING– 500-m. kayak, men– 500-m. canoe, men–
500-m. kayak, women   EQUESTRIAN SPORTS– Ind. dressage
HOCKEY (FIELD)– 7th, 5th, 3rd, 1st place
JUDO– Ltwt. class   TRACK & FIELD– Triple jump, men–
1500 m., women– 5000 m., men–
DECATHLON– 110 m. high hurdles– discus– pole vault–
javelin– 1500 m.   VOLLEYBALL– 3rd, 1st place, men–
3rd, 1st place, women

31
BOXING– finals
CANOEING–1000-m. kayak, men– 1000-m. canoe, men
FOOTBALL (SOCCER)– 1st place
JUDO– Open   TRACK & FIELD– High jump, men–
shot put, women– 1500 m., men–
400 m. relay, women– 400 m. relay, men–
1600 m. relay, women– 1600 m. relay, men– marathon, men
WRESTLING– Freestyle, round robin

August

1 | EQUESTRIAN SPORTS– Team jumping, Grand Prix

CONTENTS

SCHEDULE OF EVENTS   2

FINALS AT A GLANCE   4

THE MONTREAL GAMES   7

IF YOU'RE COMING TO MONTREAL   12

MUNICH AND MONTREAL: THE ATHLETES   14

MONTREAL '76—THE QUEST FOR GOLD   19

CHART: MUNICH 1972—OLYMPIC MEDAL WINNERS—
    MONTREAL 1976   23

A COMMUNICATIONS TRIUMPH: THE ARMCHAIR
    OLYMPICS   41

A BRIEF HISTORY OF THE GAMES   43

OLYMPIC PROTOCOL   61

In 1896, when the Olympics were revived as a sports and cultural festival after an interval of 2,500 years, only 311 athletes from thirteen countries showed up to perform in the brand-new stadium in Athens. On hand to watch were some 80,000 people. The Games were won by Greece—no surprise, since over two-thirds of the competitors were Greek, and five countries sent only one representative each.

Eighty years later, a record 10,000-odd athletes from 132 countries are gathering in Montreal, and via television an estimated one billion people on five continents will view the most widely seen sports spectacular in history—the Twenty-first Olympiad. From July 17 to August 2, they will see the world's finest athletes stretching the human body to the outer limits of its capacities, in competition of a white-hot intensity.

This first Olympics on Canadian soil was originally meant to be a relatively modest affair. But as things have turned out, it will be in its scope and facilities the biggest and costliest ever. Athletes and officials will arrive at Mirabel International, the world's largest airport; will be housed in one of the world's most grandly conceived apartment complexes, the multimillion-dollar **Olympic Village;** and will compete, many of them, in the world's most expensive stadium, in **Olympic Park.** Of the 300-odd events scheduled, not quite half will take place in this stadium, while such activities as handball, volleyball, basketball, weight-lifting, fencing, hockey, rowing, and canoeing will be held at other locations in the city (see general map in the front of the book).*

Olympic Park is actually a section of Maisonneuve

* A number of events will also be held outside the city (see page 10).

Park, Montreal's largest, which also contains the city's renowned Botanical Gardens and the former municipal golf course—now called Viau Park—where Olympic Village is located. The Olympic site, as you can easily see if you fly over the city, lies about five miles east of downtown Montreal. It covers 125 acres overall, which makes it relatively small compared, say, to Munich's Brobdingnagian 740. There's nothing modest in scale, though, about the main stadium, a soaring sculpture that suggests in outline an enormous clamshell. Designed by French architect Roger Taillibert (who is believed to have received a fee in excess of $15-million for his work), the stadium has an estimated final price tag of more than $564-million. By comparison, Houston's famed Astrodome—called "the eighth wonder of the world" when it was opened eleven years ago—cost a piddling $31.6-million, and Munich's controversial Olympic Stadium, $63-million.

Visible for miles around, the stadium is dominated by a skyscraping 622-foot "mast": a tower containing eighteen stories of training facilities, capped by a restaurant with a panoramic view. The stadium will accommodate 70,000 spectators. Just below the tower is the **Swimming Center**, which contains a warmup pool and two pools for competition. One of the most novel features of Taillibert's design is a parachute-like membrane roof that covers the stadium in bad weather. The roof will probably not be used during Olympic competitions, since International Amateur Athletic Federation rules require that performances must be held out of doors to qualify as world records.

Next to the stadium is the **Velodrome**, a $60-million cycling stadium with a canted track. The shield-backed building will be turned into a Convention Center after the Games. Also close by are two existing sports installations, the **Maurice Richard Arena** and the **Maisonneuve Sports Center**. A 4,000-car underground garage

and a 400-meter synthetic training track complete the park.

Over a nearby ridge is the heavily guarded Olympic Village, home for the 10,000 athletes and team officials while they are the city's guests; to reach their living quarters the athletes have to pass through a tightly patrolled viaduct that will be closed off to the public. Not even representatives of the news media will be allowed into the Village on less than 24 hours' notice, and then only after passing through a rigid security check.

Inside their "golden ghetto," athletes will take up residence in a series of seventeen-story, pyramid-shaped apartment houses. And for the first time at any Olympics, men and women will share the same facilities (though not the same floors), so that each national team will have all its members under the same roof. There will be 24-hour room service, free milk-bars, and "quiet zones" where the competitors can listen to classical music, talk, and relax. Another innovation will be the twenty-one TV viewing rooms, one for each major sport, where in the evenings athletes will be able to catch up on their performances of the day.

Across a pedestrian walkway is the "international zone," located in the **Marguerite-de-Lajemmerais School**. Two discotheques, a 400-seat restaurant to which outside guests may be invited, a shopping center, a library, and art galleries are just a few of the facilities to be available to athletes here.

Once the Olympic torch has been extinguished, the Village is scheduled to be turned into middle- and upper-income housing.

Events Outside Montreal

In addition to Montreal, the host city, the Organizing Committee has chosen other locations to share in the staging of the Games.

The yachting events (July 19–30) will take place in Portsmouth Harbour at Kingston on Lake Ontario. The harbor has been dredged, the seawall extended 400 feet, and the breakwater rebuilt to a distance of 600 feet. Student residences at Queen's University in Kingston will provide housing for the 400 competitors and 800 officials.

Shooting events (July 18–24) will take place at the L'Acadie Range, 20 miles from Olympic Village. Archery will be held (July 27–30) at Joliette, a city 35 miles from Montreal.

The Bromont Equestrian Center in Bromont, 50 miles from the Olympic Village, will be the site of the equestrian sports competitions for the Three Day Event, Grand Prix Dressage (July 28–30) and individual Grand Prix jumping (July 27). The Grand Prix jumping team competitions will take place at Olympic Stadium (August 1).

In team sports, football (soccer) preliminaries will take place at Varsity Stadium in Toronto (July 18–23, 25, 27), Lansdowne Park, Ottawa (July 18–23, 25), and Sherbrooke Stadium in Sherbrooke (July 18, 19, 21, 23, 25). In the handball competitions, preliminaries will be held at Laval University, Quebec City (July 18, 20, 22, 24, 26) and at Claude Robillard Center, Montreal (July 18, 20, 22, 24, 26, 27, 28). Handball finals will be held at the Montreal Forum (July 28).

From June to August, Montreal will mount a multi-million-dollar cultural extravaganza in honor of the Olympics. The city's magnificent **Place des Arts** will be host to some of Canada's finest concert and dance groups, including Les Grands Ballets Canadiens and the Montreal Symphony Orchestra. There will be jazz concerts, folk dance festivals, art exhibits (including an artist's outdoor fair in the Botanical Gardens) and a number of special events that relate the Olympic movement to the world of art. All tickets will be sold at a subsidized price as part of the program. Sherbrooke Street, the main access route to the Olympic site, is to be transformed into what one project organizer has described as "a modern Via Appia." Banners, sculpture, and photographs enlarged to billboard size will line the street. This will be the first such Olympic arts program to be strictly national. Previous host countries were required to hold international events, but for Montreal the International Olympics Committee changed its bylaws—reportedly at the insistence of Mayor Jean Drapeau.

Some 1,200 young people from seventy-one countries are expected to attend an international Olympic youth camp from July 13 to August 4. These visitors, all between 17 and 20 years of age, will gather in **Lafontaine Park**, about a mile-and-a-half west of the Olympic site. Many of them are members of their respective countries' "B" (second-string) teams, and the camp's organizers say that between visits to the Games (and ringside seats), there will be a full schedule of athletic activities. The public is invited to visit the park during the Games.

The Organizing Committee, called in French **Comité Organisateur des Jeux Olympiques** (COJO for short), has gone flat out to make this the most splendid Olympics of all time. Visitors to the Montreal Games— and more than 4,000,000 tickets have been printed —should enjoy a very good time indeed.

IF YOU'RE COMING TO MONTREAL

Montreal is a great greenhouse of a city in summertime, certainly one of the most beautiful in North America. You can expect an average temperature of 70.8° F. (21.6° C.) and an average humidity of 58 percent. The advance meteorological forecast for the Games (a projection based on historical records) envisages five or six days of rain. Historically, July is the rainiest month of the year in Montreal; but the summer of 1975 was unusually dry, as well as being extremely hot, with the mercury well above 90° F. on many days. For what it's worth, local tradition has it that whenever Montreal has a celebration, good weather joins the party.

Tickets

You should definitely get your tickets as far in advance as possible; it is extremely unlikely that you will find any available after your arrival in the city. The official agents for the sale of tickets are:

IN CANADA:
T. Eaton & Company, which has sales offices in all of its stores throughout the country.
COJO 388 St. James St. W. Montreal.

IN THE U.S.: Montgomery Ward Inc.

These are the *only* places in Canada and the United States where tickets can be bought. What you will receive is a voucher which you can exchange in Montreal for an actual ticket or tickets on or after June 1, 1976.

Prices range from a low of $2, for the equestrian events at Bromont, to a high of $32, for the opening ceremonies in Olympic Stadium on July 17.

Accommodations

For out-of-town visitors, **Hébergement Québec,** the official Quebec lodging agency, will reserve rooms at rates pegged by law. Prices range from $1 for a place to park a sleeping bag to $80 for a deluxe hotel room. Organizers are reckoning on finding accommodations for 125,000 visitors a day. Hotels, motels, and tourist rooms provide roughly 50,000 beds in and around Montreal—though this total includes thousands of rooms in the best hotels which have already been reserved for dignitaries and officials. Hébergement staff members expect private homes to accommodate everyone else, much as they did during Expo '67. All rooms available for this purpose have been inspected by Hébergement staff.

Accommodations are also available for events outside Montreal. Hébergement will make reservations for those who wish to watch the equestrian events at Bromont in the Eastern Townships, or for archery fans in the resort district of the Laurentians north of Montreal.

Visitors are required to make a 20-percent deposit within twenty-one days of receipt of response from Hébergement Québec. The money will be held in a trust fund. The remaining 80 percent must be paid before the start of the Games. If reservations are canceled, the money is refundable provided the accommodations are rentable to other visitors. *Hébergement Québec*, 201 Crémazie St. East, Montreal, Qué., H2M 1L2.

Getting to Olympic Park

The official advice is, don't take your car unless you absolutely must—you will reach the park a lot faster via public transportation. Best bet is to take the Métro (Line No. 1) to either the Pie IX or the Viau station;

both are only a little more than five minutes' ride from downtown and will leave you within a hundred yards or so of the main stadium. If you are driving, finding your way will be simple. Sherbrooke Street is the main access route, and all city thoroughfares will be posted with signs carrying the Olympic symbol and a directional arrow.

On-site parking is severely limited. There are places for around 4,500 cars, but most of this space is reserved for officials, and public parking is virtually nonexistent in the surrounding residential area.

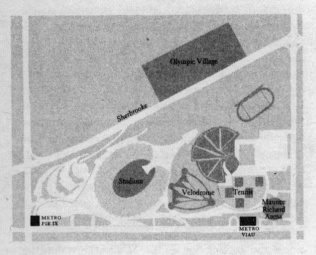

MUNICH AND MONTREAL: THE ATHLETES

For two decades, a major feature of successive Olympiads has been the intense rivalry between the USA and the Soviet Union. But at Munich in 1972, a couple of new contenders thrust themselves into the spotlight—and Soviet and American athletes frequently found themselves trailing behind the entrants from both East and West Germany. It will be worth seeing if the two Germanies can repeat their performance in Montreal. To be sure, the USSR came in first in 1972, with 99 medals, and the U.S. was second with 94; but the East and West German teams piled up an impressive 106 medals between them, and their women athletes won almost every title in a dazzling sweep.

East Germany's Renate Stecher, 22, dominated the field in the 100- and 200-meter dashes, to become the world's fastest female, and West Germany's Ulricke Meyfarth equaled the world record set by Ilona Gusenbauer of Austria for the high jump. Fräulein Meyfarth, a 16-year-old schoolgirl, became the youngest athlete ever to win a gold in track and field with a jump of 6 feet 3½ inches.

The East German athletes also made a spirited bid to break the Russian and Japanese monopoly on the gymnastic bars and swings. Karin Janz initially won a silver medal in the women's all-round individual competition. She went on to win two golds in the individual long-horse and uneven-bar competitions. Another East German, Wolfgang Nordwig, won the pole vault over the American Bob Seagren, thus becoming the first non-American ever to triumph in this event.

The U.S.: Disappointment and Triumph

As will also be the case at the Montreal Games, the swimming events were first on the Munich program. The U.S. swimming team quickly turned the water in the *Schwimmhalle* to steam in a string of spectacular victories. Sandra Neilson, 16, clocked a new Olympic record of 58.59 in the 100-meter freestyle. Later the U.S. team of Sandra, Shirley Babashoff, Jennifer Kemp, and Jane Barkman flashed to an arm's-length finish over the East German team in the 400-meter relay, with a time of 3:55.19 to claim another world record. Micki King, 28, an Air Force captain, triumphed in the

15

3-meter springboard competition over Sweden's favored Ulrika Knape. But all eyes were on 22-year-old Mark Spitz—the most sensational swimmer in the history of the Games. Spitz not only won a gold medal for each event he entered, he also established seven new world records: in the 100-meter and 200-meter freestyle, the 100-meter and 200-meter butterfly, and three relay races, including the difficult 400-meter medley (four different strokes).

If the U.S. team could do no wrong in the swimming events, the opposite proved true in track and field. Since the modern Games began in 1896, Americans have won thirteen of seventeen 100-meter dashes, twelve of fifteen 200-meter sprints, and all but one pole vault. At Munich, however, they did not gain a single gold medal in these events. Pole-vaulter Bob Seagren, a 1968 gold-medalist, found himself caught in a squabble over his new pole: the International Amateur Athletic Federation first banned, then unbanned, and finally rebanned its use. Seagren went into the finals with an unfamiliar pole, and got over in not quite 17 feet 10½ inches, while Nordwig of East Germany topped 18 feet ½ inch to win the gold. Two 100-meter dashmen, Rey Robinson and Eddie Hart—both of whom had equaled the world record of 9.9 seconds—were disqualified from running because a coach had used the wrong schedule, and they failed to get to their qualifying heats on time. In the qualifying heat for the 1,500-meter, the Olympics' most prestigious race, Jim Ryun, 25, who was favored to take the gold, tangled legs with another runner, and was also disqualified.

In boxing, the Russian-coached Cuban team outpointed the Americans. But perhaps the most crushing defeat of all was the U.S. basketball team's 51–50 loss to the Soviet Union, the first defeat suffered by a U.S. team since basketball became an Olympic sport in 1936.

The Russians Win Again

At Munich, the Soviet Union again piled up more points than any other competing nation, and for the fourth time since the Helsinki Games of 1952, the USSR outpointed the USA.

Among their best, gold-medal weight-lifter Vasily Ivanovich Alexeyev, a holder of fifty-four world records, earned the title of world's strongest human. Nikolai Avilov broke Bill Toomey's 1968 Decathlon record by collecting 8,454 points in the grueling two-day, ten-event competition, and became the finest all-round athlete. Then there was Valery Borzov, from the Ukrainian town of Novaya Kakhovka, who qualified as the world's fastest human by winning the 100-meter dash and then flashing to a 200-meter victory in 20.0 seconds. The Soviets also won the gold and bronze medals in the women's all-round individual competition. Victor in this event was 19-year-old Ludmilla Turishcheva, who put on a dazzling performance on the uneven bars with such extraordinary maneuvers as 360° swings and somersaults underneath the bars.

The crowd favorite, however, was unquestionably another Soviet gymnast, Olga Korbut. She was 17, only 4 feet 11 inches high, and weighed 84 pounds. After a poor start in the all-round event, Olga overcame her nervousness to take two gold medals, in the balance beam and floor exercises. She will certainly be worth watching during the Montreal Games.

17

The Finns and the Japanese Show Great Form

Tiny Finland, with a population less than half that of New York City, had won most of the middle- and long-distance races until 1936 in Berlin. The Finnish tradition of excellence began with Hannes Kolehmainen at the Stockholm Games of 1912, and was carried on in the 1920's by Ville Ritola and Paavo Nurmi, and by Iso-Hollo in the 1930's. Just as it appeared that the tradition had died out, the Finns revived it at Munich: Lasse Viren breezed home in the 10,000-meter race in 27:38.4, for a new world record. He also won a gold for the 5,000-meter, setting a new Olympic record of 13:26.4. Another Finn, Pekka Vasala, won the coveted 1,500-meter, a race that had been expected to go to either Ryun of the USA or Keino of Kenya.

Japanese men dominated the gymnastic bars, swings, and rings with an awesome display of airborne maneuvers that decisively outpointed the strong Russian competition. The Japanese also won all three medals in the all-round individual competition. Soviet athletes, however, garnered golds in the floor exercises and the long-horse event. The Montreal Games are almost certain to see a replay of this Japanese-Russian rivalry.

Canajan, eh?

The Canadians sent their biggest squad—more than 300 athletes and team officials—in the history of the Olympics. The results were a disappointment. By the time the tournament was over, Canada's athletes had captured only five medals: two silver and three bronze. As in the 1968 Mexico Games, swimming was Canada's strongest suit. Bruce Robertson won a silver, behind Mark Spitz in the 100-meter butterfly, and Leslie Cliff also gained a silver in the women's 400-meter medley; Donna Marie Gurr picked up a bronze for the 200-meter backstroke, and the Canadian team of Eric Fish, William Mahony, Bruce Robertson, and Bob Kasting won another bronze, finishing third after the U.S. and East Germany in the 400-meter medley. Canada's final bronze was won in yachting in the Soling category.

MONTREAL '76—THE QUEST FOR GOLD

Ask a dozen experts who are the likely gold-medalists at the '76 Games, and you'll get a dozen different answers. No one really knows—chance, for one thing, seems to play an extraordinary role in the tense, hothouse atmosphere of Olympic competition; and firm favorites often fail to do their best, sometimes through their own errors, occasionally through the mistakes of team officials, coaches, or judges.

Sports experts, moreover, will tell you that winning margins in the Olympics—always narrow—have become razor-thin in recent times. In only five of twenty-one events in Olympic track-and-field competition does the margin of superiority now exceed 1 percent. The average margin overall is 1.13 percent, and if you leave out the long jump, it drops to 0.79 percent.

Try gulping a breath of air. If you did it very fast, it probably took you only a second—that's by how much time Canadian Bruce Robertson lost the 100-meter butterfly event to American Mark Spitz. Sweden's Gunnar Larrson won his gold by hitting his electronic touch-plate at the end of the 400-meter individual medley swim just 2/1000 of a second before Tim McKee.

And then there are those once-in-a-lifetime achievements that astound even the experts—for example, the 29-foot 2½-inch winning long jump of America's Bob Beamon in Mexico in 1968, which shattered the world record by nearly two feet; no other athlete has even come close to that extraordinary leap, and few expect the record to be broken in Montreal. But who knows?

Swimming is the first major sport in the Montreal schedule, and because it encompasses so many separate events (though there are fewer this year than at Munich) it offers the best opportunity for medal-collecting. The leading medal winner, judging from past records of national preeminence in this sport, is likely to be an Australian, an American, or an East German.

From time to time, of course, in swimming as in other sports, a nation that has not figured prominently in past Olympics will come to the fore. Japan and Canada, which won gold and silver swimming medals, respectively, at Munich, will be two nations to watch at Montreal.

In track and field, which will dominate the second part of the schedule, the United States will certainly make a strong bid to regain the title of "world's fastest human" in the 100-meter dash—a title lost to the USSR's Valery Borzov at Munich. Look out for Houston McTear (pronounced McTeer), a 19-year-old from the backwoods hamlet of Milligan, Florida, who in nine seconds flat tied the world 100-yard dash record in 1975.

If recent form prevails, the final in another outstanding event, the 1,500-meter race, should bring about a tight race between Filbert Bayi of Tanzania and John

Walker of New Zealand. After two years of chasing Bayi, Walker ran "the perfect race" at the 1975 Göteborg Games in Sweden, covering the mile in 3:49.4—a set of stopwatch numbers that hardly seemed real. Finland, which has over the years produced a battalion of long-distance athletes, has a hot contender for the 20-kilometer walk in tall Pekka Paivarinta. Last year, Paivarinta lowered two world marks, first cruising through 15 miles in 1:11:16.8, and then continuing to 25 kilometers in 1:14:16.8.

In the shotput, a traditional domain of the U.S. but lost to Poland at Munich, the Americans have a powerful contender in Brian Oldfield, who in 1975 bettered Poland's Olympic record by an astonishing 5 feet. And if Oldfield does not bring the stadium to its collective feet, it is near-certain that a West German soldier, Karl-Hans Riehm, will do so in the hammer throw (not a hammer at all, but a 16-pound shot attached to a grip and a length of wire)—an event dominated since 1948 by Hungary and the USSR. Riehm has already surpassed the Olympic record of the USSR's Anatoly Bondarchuk by nearly 10 feet!

The pole vault is generally regarded as the most difficult event in the realm of track and field. The first gold-medalist, in Athens in 1896, was an American, William Hoyt, who vaulted just under 11 feet, using a hickory pole. Until Munich, the United States had an unbroken string of victories in this event, and vaulters using flexible fiberglass poles surpassed heights of more than 18½ feet in 1975. The Americans have high hopes of winning the Olympic title back from East Germany, and there's a fair chance we'll see the 19-foot barrier broken for the first time at Montreal.

The Decathlon is an all-round test of sprinting, hurdling, middle-distance running, and other types of track-and-field events, ten in all. Although the Russians won at Munich, the USA's Bruce Jenner broke the world

Decathlon record in 1975, and he'll be the athlete to watch during the Montreal Games.

In team events, there's going to be quite a fight between India and Pakistan, the world's two top nations in field hockey, to see which of them will win back the Olympic title from—of all countries—West Germany, who was the surprise victor in 1972. Of the nine previous gold medals in this sport, beginning in 1928, seven had gone to India and two to Pakistan.

The Russians, Hungarians, and Yugoslavs will probably put up the biggest struggle for the gold in water polo, but there are plenty of strong contenders this year. As much a surprise as Asians losing in field hockey to a European team was the staggering blow to American pride when the Russians took the Munich gold medal in basketball. Until 1972, the Americans had never lost a contest, let alone a gold medal, in this sport.

That's tough, of course, but traditions and records are (to coin a phrase) made to be broken. Few of them nowadays last more than a year or two. If we look back at the old record books, it is astonishing to discover that Patrick Ryan's hammer throw was not surpassed for twenty-five years; that Cornelius Warmerdam's pole-vault record lasted for fifteen years; and that Jesse Owens's phenomenal long jump stood from 1936 to 1960. Munich provided dozens of upsets and startling victories, and there is little reason to doubt that Montreal will have its share as well.

MUNICH 1972—OLYMPIC MEDAL WINNERS—MONTREAL 1976

Note: *An asterisk indicates that the performance thus marked constitutes the Olympic record in that event. In all other cases, the Olympic record appears in parentheses following the winning performance.*

Track & Field–Men

100 METERS

	GOLD MEDAL–WINNING PERF.	SILVER	BRONZE
1972	Borzov (USSR)–10.14 (9.9)	Taylor (USA)	Miller (Jamaica)
1976			

200 METERS

1972	Borzov (USSR)–20.00 (19.8)	Black (USA)	Mennea (Italy)
1976			

400-M. RELAY

1972	USA–38.19*	(USSR)	(West Germany)
1976			

400 METERS

1972	Matthews (USA)–44.66 (43.8)	Collett (USA)	Sang (Kenya)
1976			

1,600-M. RELAY

1972	Kenya–2:59.8 (2:56.1)	(Great Britain)	(France)
1976			

800 METERS

1972	Wottle (USA)–1:45.9 (1:44.3)	Arzhanov (USSR)	Boit (Kenya)
1976			

1,500 METERS

1972	Vasala (Finland)–3:36.3 (3:34.9)	Keino (Kenya)	Dixon (New Zealand)
1976			

5,000 METERS

1972	Viren (Finland)–13:26.4*	Gammoudi (Tunisia)	Stewart (Great Britain)
1976			

10,000 METERS

1972	Viren (Finland)–27:38.4*	Puttemens (Belgium)	Yifter (Ethiopia)
1976			

MARATHON

1972	Shorter (USA)–2:12:19.8 (2:12:11.2)	Lismont (Belgium)	Wolde (Ethiopia)
1976			

23

STEEPLECHASE (3,000 METERS)

	GOLD MEDAL—WINNING PERF.	SILVER	BRONZE
1972	Keino (Kenya)–8:23.6*	Jipcho (Kenya)	Kantanen (Finland)
1976			

110-M. HURDLES

1972	Milburn (USA)–13.24*	Drut (France)	Hill (USA)
1976			

400-M. HURDLES

1972	Akil-Bua (Uganda)–47.82*	Mann (USA)	Hemery (Great Britain)
1976			

HIGH JUMP

1972	Tarmak (USSR)–7'3.75" (7'4.5")	Junge (East Germany)	Stones (USA)
1976			

LONG JUMP

1972	Williams (USA) 27'0.5" (29'2.5")	Baumgartner (West Germany)	Robinson (USA)
1976			

TRIPLE JUMP

1972	Saneev (USSR)–56'11" (57'0.75")	Drehmel (East Germany)	Prudencio (Brazil)
1976			

POLE VAULT

1972	Nordwig (East Germany)–18'0.5"*	Seagren (USA)	Johnson (USA)
1976			

SHOTPUT

1972	Komar (Poland)–69'5.75"*	Woods (USA)	Briesenick (East Germany)
1976			

DISCUS

1972	Danek (Czechoslovakia)–211'3.5" (212'6.5")	Silvester (USA)	Bruch (Sweden)
1976			

HAMMER

1972	Bondarchuk (USSR)–247'8.5"*	Sachse (East Germany)	Khmelevski (USSR)
1976			

JAVELIN

1972	Wolfermann (West Germany)–296'10.25"*	Lusis (USSR)	Schmidt (USA)
1976			

DECATHLON

	GOLD MEDAL—WINNING PERF.	SILVER	BRONZE
1972	Avilov (USSR)–8,454 pts.*	Litvinenko (USSR)	Katus (Poland)
1976			

20-KM. WALK

	GOLD MEDAL—WINNING PERF.	SILVER	BRONZE
1972	Frenkel (East Germany)–1:26:42.4	Golubnicki (USSR)	Reimann (East Germany)
1976			

Track & Field–Women

100 METERS

1972	Stecher (East Germany)–11.07 (11.0)	Boyle (Australia)	Chivas (Cuba)
1976			

200 METERS

1972	Stecher (East Germany)–22.40*	Boyle (Australia)	Szewinska (Poland)
1976			

400-M. RELAY

1972	(West Germany)–42.81*	(East Germany)	(Cuba)
1976			

400 METERS

1972	Zehrt (East Germany)–51.08*	Wilden (West Germany)	Hammond (USA)
1976			

1,600-M. RELAY

1972	(East Germany)–3:23.0*	(USA)	(West Germany)
1976			

800 METERS

1972	Falck (West Germany)–1:58.6*	Sabaite (USSR)	Hofmeister (East Germany)
1976			

1,500 METERS

1972	Bragina (USSR)–4:1.4*	Hofmeister (East Germany)	Cacchi (Italy)
1976			

100-M. HURDLES

1972	Ehrhardt (East Germany)–12.59*	Bufanu (Romania)	Balzer (East Germany)
1976			

HIGH JUMP

1972	Meyfarth (West Germany)–6'3.75"*	Blagoeva (Bulgaria)	Gusenbauer (Austria)
1976			

LONG JUMP

	GOLD MEDAL—WINNING PERF.	SILVER	BRONZE
1972	Rosendahl (West Germany)–22'3" (22'4.5")	Yorgova (Bulgaria)	Suranova (Czechoslovakia)
1976			

SHOTPUT

	GOLD MEDAL—WINNING PERF.	SILVER	BRONZE
1972	Chizhova (USSR)–69'0"*	Gummel (East Germany)	Christova (Bulgaria)
1976			

DISCUS

	GOLD MEDAL—WINNING PERF.	SILVER	BRONZE
1972	Melnik (USSR)–218'6.75"*	Menis (Romania)	Stoyeva (Bulgaria)
1976			

JAVELIN

	GOLD MEDAL—WINNING PERF.	SILVER	BRONZE
1972	Fuchs (East Germany)–209'7"*	Todten (East Germany)	Schmidt (USA)
1976			

PENTATHLON

	GOLD MEDAL—WINNING PERF.	SILVER	BRONZE
1972	Peters (Great Britain)–4,801 pts.*	Rosendahl (West Germany)	Pollak (East Germany)
1976			

Swimming–Men
100-M. FREESTYLE

	GOLD MEDAL—WINNING PERF.	SILVER	BRONZE
1972	Spitz (USA)–51.22*	Heidenreich (USA)	Bure (USSR)
1976			

200-M. FREESTYLE

	GOLD MEDAL—WINNING PERF.	SILVER	BRONZE
1972	Spitz (USA)–1:52.78*	Genter (USA)	Lampe (West Germany
1976			

400-M. FREESTYLE

	GOLD MEDAL—WINNING PERF.	SILVER	BRONZE
1972	Cooper (Australia)–4:0.27*	Genter (USA)	McBreen (USA)
1976			

1,500-M. FREESTYLE

	GOLD MEDAL—WINNING PERF.	SILVER	BRONZE
1972	Burton (USA)–15:52.58*	Windeatt (Australia)	Northway (USA)
1976			

100-M. BREASTSTROKE

	GOLD MEDAL—WINNING PERF.	SILVER	BRONZE
1972	Taguchi (Japan)–1:04.94*	Bruce (USA)	Hencken (USA)
1976			

200-M. BREASTSTROKE

	GOLD MEDAL—WINNING PERF.	SILVER	BRONZE
1972	Hencken (USA)–2:21.55*	Wilkie (Great Britain)	Taguchi (Japan)
1976			

	GOLD MEDAL—WINNING PERF.	SILVER	BRONZE
1972	Spitz (USA)–54.27*	Robertson (Canada)	Heidenreich (USA)
1976			

200-M. BUTTERFLY

1972	Spitz (USA)–2:0.70*	Hall (USA)	Backhaus (USA)
1976			

200-M. INDIVIDUAL MEDLEY

1972	Larsson (Sweden)–2:07.17*	McKee (USA)	Furniss (USA)
1976			

100-M. BACKSTROKE

1972	Matthes (East Germany)–56.58*	Stamm (USA)	Murphy (USA)
1976			

200-M. BACKSTROKE

1972	Matthes (East Germany)–2:02.82*	Stamm (USA)	Ivey (USA)
1976			

400-M. INDIVIDUAL MEDLEY

1972	Larsson (Sweden)–4:31.98*	McKee (USA)	Hargitay (Hungary)
1976			

400-M. FREESTYLE RELAY

1972	(USA)–3:26.42	(USSR)	(East Germany)
1976			

800-M. FREESTYLE RELAY

1972	(USA)–7:35.78*	(West Germany)	(USSR)
1976			

400-M. MEDLEY RELAY

1972	(USA)–3:48.16*	(East Germany)	(Canada)
1976			

SPRINGBOARD DIVE

1972	Vasin (USSR)–594.09 pts.	Cagnotto (Italy)	Lincoln (USA)
1976			

PLATFORM DIVE

1972	DiBiasi (Italy)–504.12 pts.	Rydze (USA)	Cagnotto (Italy)
1976			

100-M. FREESTYLE

	GOLD MEDAL—WINNING PERF.	SILVER	BRONZE
1972	Neilson (USA)–58.59*	Babashoff (USA)	Gould (Australia)
1976			

200-M. FREESTYLE

1972	Gould (Australia)–2:03.56*	Babashoff (USA)	Rothammer (USA)
1976			

400-M. FREESTYLE

1972	Gould (Australia)–4:19.04*	Calligaris (Italy)	Wegner (East Germany)
1976			

800-M. FREESTYLE

1972	Rothammer (USA)–8:53.68*	Gould (Australia)	Calligaris (Italy)
1976			

100-M. BREASTSTROKE

1972	Carr (USA)–1:13.58*	Stepanova (USSR)	Whitfield (Australia)
1976			

200-M. BREASTSTOKE

1972	Whitfield (Australia)–2:41.71*	Schoenfield (USA)	Stepanova (USSR)
1976			

100-M. BUTTERFLY

1972	Aoki (Japan)–1:03.34*	Beier (East Germany)	Gyarmati (Hungary)
1976			

200-M. BUTTERFLY

1972	Moe (USA)–2:15.57*	Colella (USA)	Daniel (USA)
1976			

100-M. BACKSTROKE

1972	Belote (USA)–1:05.78*	Gyarmati (Hungary)	Atwood (USA)
1976			

200-M. BACKSTROKE

1972	Belote (USA)–2:19.19*	Atwood (USA)	Gurr (Canada)
1976			

200-M. INDIVIDUAL MEDLEY

1972	Gould (Australia)–2:23.07*	Binder (East Germany)	Vidali (USA)
1976			

400-M. INDIVIDUAL MEDLEY

	GOLD MEDAL—WINNING PERF.	SILVER	BRONZE
1972	Neall (Australia)–5:02.97*	Cliff (Canada)	Calligaris (Italy)
1976			

400-M. FREESTYLE RELAY

1972	(USA)–3:55.19*	(East Germany)	(West Germany)
1976			

400-M. MEDLEY RELAY

1972	(USA)–4:20.75*	(East Germany)	(West Germany)
1976			

SPRINGBOARD DIVE

1972	King (USA)–450.03 pts.	Knape (Sweden)	Janicke (East Germany)
1976			

PLATFORM DIVE

1972	Knape (Sweden)–390.00 pts.	Duchkova (Czechoslovakia)	Janicke (East Germany)
1976			

Archery—Men

1972	Williams (USA)–2528 pts.	Jarvil (Sweden)	Laasonnen (Finland)
1976			

Archery—Women

1972	Wilder (USA)–2424 pts.	Szydlowska (Poland)	Gaptchenko (USSR)
1976			

Basketball

1972	(USSR)	(USA)	(Cuba)
1976			

Boxing
LIGHT FLYWEIGHT

1972	Gedeo (Hungary)	Kim (North Korea)	Rodriguez (Spain) Evans (Gr. Br.)
1976			

FLYWEIGHT

1972	Kostadinov (Bulgaria)	Rwarwogo (Uganda)	Rodriguez (Cuba) Blazynski (Poland)
1976			

BANTAMWEIGHT

1972	Martinez (Cuba)	Zamora (Mexico)	Turpin (Gr. Br.) Carreras (USA)
1976			

	GOLD MEDAL—WINNING PERF.	SILVER	BRONZE
1972	Kousnetsov (USSR)	Waruinge (Kenya)	Rojas (Colombia) Botos (Hungary)
1976			

LIGHTWEIGHT

1972	Szczepanski (Poland)	Orban (Hungary)	Mbugua (Kenya) Perez (Colombia)
1976			

LIGHT WELTERWEIGHT

1972	Seales (USA)	Anghelov (Bulgaria)	Vujin (Yugoslavia) Daborg (Niger)
1976			

WELTERWEIGHT

1972	Correa (Cuba)	Kajdi (Hungary)	Murunga (Kenya) Valdez (USA)
1976			

LIGHT MIDDLEWEIGHT

1972	Kottysch (West Germany)	Rudkowski (Poland)	Minter (Gr. Br.) Tiepold (E. Ger.)
1976			

MIDDLEWEIGHT

1972	Lemechev (USSR)	Virtanen (Finland)	Amartey (Ghana) Johnson (USA)
1976			

LIGHT HEAVYWEIGHT

1972	Parlov (Yugoslavia)	Carillo (Cuba)	Ikhouria (Nigeria) Gortat (Poland)
1976			

HEAVYWEIGHT

1972	Stevenson (Cuba)	Alexe (Romania)	Hussing (W. Ger.) Thomsen (Sweden)
1976			

Canoeing—Men

KAYAK SINGLES SLALOM

1972	Horn (East Germany)	Sattler (Australia)	Gimpel (East Germany)
1976			

CANADIAN SINGLES SLALOM

1972	Eiben (East Germany)	Kauder (West Germany)	McEwan (USA)
1976			

CANADIAN PAIRS SLALOM

1972	(East Germany)	(West Germany)	(France)
1976			

KAYAK SINGLES

	GOLD MEDAL—WINNING PERF.	SILVER	BRONZE
1972	Shaparenko (USSR)–3:48.06	Peterson (Sweden)	Czapo (Hungary)
1976			

KAYAK PAIRS

1972	(USSR)–3:31.23	(Hungary)	(Poland)
1976			

KAYAK FOURS

1972	(USSR)–3:14.02	(Romania)	(Norway)
1976			

CANADIAN SINGLES

1972	Patzaichin (Romania)–4:8.94	Wichmann (Hungary)	Lewe (West Germany)
1976			

CANADIAN PAIRS

1972	(USSR)–3:52:60	(Romania)	(Bulgaria)
1976			

Canoeing—Women
KAYAK SINGLES SLALOM

1972	Bahmann (East Germany)	Grothaus (West Germany)	Wunderlich (West Germany)
1976			

KAYAK SINGLES

1972	Ryabchinskaya (USSR)–2:03.17	Jaapies (Netherlands)	Pfeffer (Hungary)
1976			

KAYAK PAIRS

1972	(USSR)–1:53.50	(East Germany)	(Romania)
1976			

Cycling
1,000-M. TIME TRIAL

1972	Fredborg (Denmark)–1:06.44	Clark (Australia)	Schuetze (East Germany)
1976			

1,000-M. SCRATCH

1972	Morelon (France)	Nicholson (Australia)	Phakadze (USSR)
1976			

2,000-M. TANDEM

1972	(USSR)	(East Germany)	(Poland)
1976			

	GOLD MEDAL—WINNING PERF.	SILVER	BRONZE
1972	Knudsen (Norway)–4:45.74	Kurmann (Switzerland)	Lutz (West Germany)
1976			

TEAM PURSUIT

1972	(West Germany)–4:22.14	(East Germany)	(Great Britain)
1976			

INDIVIDUAL ROAD RACE

1972	Kuiper (Netherlands)–4:14:37.0	Sefton (Australia)	Huelamo (Spain)
1976			

TEAM ROAD RACE

1972	(USSR)–2:11:17.8	(Poland)	(Belgium)
1976			

Equestrian
THREE DAY

1972	Meade (Great Britain)–57.73 pts.	Argenton (Italy)	Jonsson (Sweden)
1976			

THREE-DAY TEAM

1972	(Great Britain)–95.53 pts.	(USA)	(West Germany)
1976			

DRESSAGE

1972	Lisenhoff (West Germany)–1,229 pts.	Petushkova (USSR)	Neckermann (West Germany)
1976			

DRESSAGE TEAM

1972	(USSR)–5,095 pts.	(West Germany)	(Sweden)
1976			

INDIVIDUAL PRIX DES NATIONS (JUMPING)

1972	Mancinelli (Italy)–8 faults	Moore (Great Britain)	Shapiro (USA)
1976			

TEAM PRIX DES NATIONS (JUMPING)

1972	(West Germany)–32 faults	(USA)	(Italy)
1976			

Fencing–Men
FOIL

1972	Woyda (Poland)	Kamuti (Hungary)	Noel (France)
1976			

FOIL TEAM

	GOLD MEDAL—WINNING PERF.	SILVER	BRONZE
1972	(Poland)	(USSR)	(France)
1976			

SABER

1972	Sidiak (USSR)	Maroth (Hungary)	Nazlymov (USSR)
1976			

SABER TEAM

1972	(Italy)	(USSR)	(Hungary)
1976			

EPÉE

1972	Fenyvesi (Hungary)	La DeGaillerie (France)	Kulcsar (Hungary)
1976			

EPÉE TEAM

1972	(Hungary)	(Switzerland)	(USSR)
1976			

Fencing—Women
FOIL

1972	Lonzi (Italy)	Bobis (Hungary)	Gorokhova (USSR)
1976			

FOIL TEAM

1972	(USSR)	(Hungary)	(Romania)
1976			

Field Hockey

1972	(West Germany)	(Pakistan)	(India)
1976			

Gymnastics—Men
TEAM

1972	(Japan)—571.250 pts.	(USSR)	(East Germany)
1976			

ALL-ROUND

1972	Kato (Japan)—114.650 pts.	Kenmotsu (Japan)	Nakayama (Japan)
1976			

FREE EXERCISES

1972	Andrianov (USSR)—19.175 pts.	Nakayama (Japan)	Kasamatsu (Japan)
1976			

	GOLD MEDAL—WINNING PERF.	SILVER	BRONZE
1972	Klimenko (USSR)–19,125 pts.	Kato (Japan)	Kenmotsu (Japan)
1976			

RINGS

1972	Nakayama (Japan)–19.350 pts.	Voronin (USSR)	Tsukahara (Japan)
1976			

LONG HORSE

1972	Koeste (East Germany)–18.850 pts.	Klimenko (USSR)	Andrianov (USSR)
1976			

PARALLEL BARS

1972	Kato (Japan)–19.475 pts.	Kasamatsu (Japan)	Kenmotsu (Japan)
1976			

HORIZONTAL BAR

1972	Tsukahara (Japan)–19.725 pts.	Kato (Japan)	Kasamatsu (Japan)
1976			

Gymnastics–Women

TEAM

1972	(USSR)–380.500 pts.	(East Germany)	(Hungary)
1976			

ALL-ROUND

1972	Turishcheva (USSR)–77.025 pts.	Janz (East Germany)	Lazakovich (USSR)
1976			

LONG HORSE VAULT

1972	Janz (East Germany)–19.525 pts.	Zuchold (East Germany)	Turishcheva (USSR)
1976			

UNEVEN PARALLEL BARS

1972	Janz (East Germany)–19.675 pts.	Korbut (USSR)	Zuchold (East Germany)
1976			

BALANCE BEAM

1972	Korbut (USSR)–19.400 pts.	Lazakovich (USSR)	Carlin (East Germany)
1976			

FREE EXERCISES

1972	Korbut (USSR)–19.575 pts.	Turishcheva (USSR)	Lazakovich (USSR)
1976			

Judo

	GOLD MEDAL—WINNING PERF.	SILVER	BRONZE
1972	Kawaguchi (Japan)	Buidaa (Mongolia)	Kim (North Korea) Mounier (France)
1976			

WELTERWEIGHT

		SILVER	BRONZE
1972	Nomura (Japan)	Zajkowski (Poland)	Hoetger (E. Ger.) Novikov (USSR)
1976			

MIDDLEWEIGHT

		SILVER	BRONZE
1972	Sekine (Japan)	Oh (South Korea)	Jacks (Gr. Br.) Coche (France)
1976			

LIGHT HEAVYWEIGHT

		SILVER	BRONZE
1972	Chochoshvili (USSR)	Starbrook (Gr. Britain)	Ishi (Brazil) Barth (W. Ger.)
1976			

HEAVYWEIGHT

		SILVER	BRONZE
1972	Ruska (Netherlands)	Glahn (West Germany)	Onashvili (USSR) Nishimura (Japan)
1976			

OPEN

		SILVER	BRONZE
1972	Ruska (Netherlands)	Kuznetsov (USSR)	Brondani (France) Parish (Gr. Br.)
1976			

Modern Pentathlon

INDIVIDUAL

		SILVER	BRONZE
1972	Balczo (Hungary)–5,412 pts.	Onishenko (USSR)	Leonev (USSR)
1976			

TEAM

		SILVER	BRONZE
1972	(USSR)–15,968 pts.	(Hungary)	(Finland)
1976			

Rowing

SINGLE SCULLS

		SILVER	BRONZE
1972	Malishev (USSR)–7:10.12	Demiddi (Argentina)	Gueldenpfennig (East Germany)
1976			

DOUBLE SCULLS

		SILVER	BRONZE
1972	(USSR)–7:01.77	(Norway)	(East Germany)
1976			

PAIRS

		SILVER	BRONZE
1972	(East Germany)–6:53.16	(Switzerland)	(Netherlands)
1976			

	GOLD MEDAL—WINNING PERF.	SILVER	BRONZE
1972	(East Germany)–7:17.25	(Czechoslovakia)	(Romania)
1976			

FOURS

1972	(East Germany)–6:24.27	(New Zealand)	(West Germany)
1976			

COXED FOURS

1972	(West Germany)–6:31.85	(East Germany)	(Czechoslovakia)
1976			

EIGHTS

1972	(New Zealand)–6:08.94	(USA)	(East Germany)
1976			

Shooting
FREE RIFLE

1972	Wigger (USA) 1,155 (1,157)	Melnik (USSR)	Pap (Hungary)
1976			

SMALL-BORE: PRONE

1972	Li (North Korea)–599 pts.*	Auer (USA)	Rotaru (Romania)
1976			

SMALL BORE: THREE POSITIONS

1972	Writer (USA)–1,166 pts.*	Bassham (USA)	Lippoldt (East Germany)
1976			

FREE PISTOL

1972	Skanakar (Sweden)–567 pts.*	Iuga (Romania)	Dollinger (Austria)
1976			

RAPID-FIRE PISTOL

1972	Zapedzki (Poland)–595 pts.*	Faita (Czechoslovakia)	Torshin (USSR)
1976			

MOVING TARGET

1972	Zhelezniak (USSR)–569 pts.*	Bellingrodt (Colombia)	Kynoch (Great Britain)
1976			

TRAP

1972	Scalzone (Italy)–199 pts.*	Carrega (France)	Bassagni (Italy)
1976			

	GOLD MEDAL—WINNING PERF.	SILVER	BRONZE
1972	Wirnhier (West Germany)– 195 pts. (198 pts.)	Petrov (USSR)	Buchheim (East Germany)
1976			

Soccer

1972	(Poland)	(Hungary)	(USSR) (East Germany)
1976			

Team Handball

1972	(Yugoslavia)	(Czechoslovakia)	(Romania)
1976			

Volleyball–Men

1972	(Japan)	(East Germany)	(USSR)
1976			

Women

1972	(USSR)	(Japan)	(North Korea)
1976			

Water Polo

1972	(USSR)	(Hungary)	(USA)
1976			

Weight-Lifting

FLYWEIGHT

1972	Smalcerz (Poland)–337.5 kg.* (742.5 lb.)	Szuecs (Hungary)	Hodczreiter (Hungary)
1976			

BANTAMWEIGHT

1972	Foldi (Hungary)– 377.5 kg.* (830.5 lb.)	Nassiri (Iran)	Chetin (USSR)
1976			

FEATHERWEIGHT

1972	Nourikian (Bulgaria)– 402.5 kg.* (885.5 lb.)	Shanidze (USSR)	Benedek (Hungary)
1976			

LIGHTWEIGHT

1972	Kirzhinov (USSR)– 460 kg.* (1,012 lb.)	Koutchev (Bulgaria)	Kaczymarek (Poland)
1976			

MIDDLEWEIGHT

1972	Bikov (Bulgaria)– 485 kg.* (1,067 lb.)	Trabulsi (Lebanon)	Silvino (Italy)
1976			

	GOLD MEDAL—WINNING PERF.	SILVER	BRONZE
1972	Jenssen (Norway)– 507.5 kg.* (1,116.5 lb.)	Ozimek (Poland)	Horvath (Hungary)
1976			

MIDDLE HEAVYWEIGHT

1972	Nikolov (Bulgaria)– 525 kg.* (1,155 lb.)	Chopov (Bulgaria)	Bettembourg (Sweden)
1976			

HEAVYWEIGHT

1972	Talts (USSR)– 580 kg.* (1,276 lb.)	Kraitchev (Bulgaria)	Gruetzner (East Germany)
1976			

SUPER HEAVYWEIGHT

1972	Alexeyev (USSR)– 640 kg.* (1,408 lb.)	Mang (West Germany)	Bonk (East Germany)
1976			

Wrestling–Freestyle

PAPERWEIGHT

1972	Dmitriev (USSR)	Nikolov (Bulgaria)	Javadpour (Iran)
1976			

FLYWEIGHT

1972	Kato (Japan)	Alakhverdiev (USSR)	Kim Gwong (North Korea)
1976			

BANTAMWEIGHT

1972	Yanagida (Japan)	Sanders (USA)	Klinga (Hungary)
1976			

FEATHERWEIGHT

1972	Abdulbekov (USSR)	Akdag (Turkey)	Krastev (Bulgaria)
1976			

LIGHTWEIGHT

1972	Gable (USA)	Wada (Japan)	Ashuraliev (USSR)
1976			

WELTERWEIGHT

1972	Wells (USA)	Karlsson (Sweden)	Seger (West Germany)
1976			

MIDDLEWEIGHT

1972	Tediashvili (USSR)	J. Peterson (USA)	Jorga (Romania)
1976			

	GOLD MEDAL—WINNING PERF.	SILVER	BRONZE
1972	B. Peterson (USA)	Strakhov (USSR)	Bajko (Hungary)
1976			

HEAVYWEIGHT

1972	Yarygin (USSR)	Baiamunkh (Mongolia)	Csatari (Hungary)
1976			

SUPER HEAVYWEIGHT

1972	Medved (USSR)	Douraliev (Bulgaria)	Taylor (USA)
1976			

Wrestling—Greco-Roman
PAPERWEIGHT

1972	Berceanu (Romania)	Aliabadi (Iran)	Anghelov (Bulgaria)
1976			

FLYWEIGHT

1972	Kirov (Bulgaria)	Kibayama (Japan)	Bognanni (Italy)
1976			

BANTAMWEIGHT

1972	Kazakov (USSR)	Veil (West Germany)	Bjoerlin (Finland)
1976			

FEATHERWEIGHT

1972	Markov (Bulgaria)	Wehling (West Germany)	Lipien (Poland)
1976			

LIGHTWEIGHT

1972	Khisamutdinov (USSR)	Apostolov (Bulgaria)	Ranzi (Italy)
1976			

WELTERWEIGHT

1972	Macha (Czechoslovakia)	Galaktopoulos (Greece)	Karlsson (Sweden)
1976			

MIDDLEWEIGHT

1972	Hegedus (Hungary)	Nazarenko (USSR)	Nenadic (Yugoslavia)
1976			

LIGHT HEAVYWEIGHT

1972	Rezantsev (USSR)	Corak (Yugoslavia)	Kwiecinski (Poland)
1976			

	GOLD MEDAL—WINNING PERF.	SILVER	BRONZE
1972	Martinescu (Romania)	Iakovenko (USSR)	Kiss (Hungary)
1976			

SUPER HEAVYWEIGHT

1972	Roshin (USSR)	Tomoff (Bulgaria)	Dolipschi (Romania)
1976			

Yachting
SOLING

1972	(USA)	(Sweden)	(Canada)
1976			

TEMPEST

1972	(USSR)	(Great Britain)	(USA)
1976			

DRAGON

1972	(Australia)	(East Germany)	(USA)
1976			

STAR

1972	(Australia)	(Sweden)	(West Germany)
1976			

FLYING DUTCHMAN

1972	(Great Britain)	(France)	(West Germany)
1976			

FINN

1972	(France)	(Greece)	(USSR)
1976			

A COMMUNICATIONS TRIUMPH:
THE ARMCHAIR OLYMPICS

Beginning on the third Saturday afternoon in July 1976, and for two weeks thereafter, it is expected that more than *one billion* people in almost every corner of the globe—from storm-lashed drilling rigs in the Canadian Arctic to sun-baked trailers in Saudi Arabia, from Bogota to Kyoto to Irkutsk to Khartoum and back to Montreal —will be following the Olympic Games on their radios and TV sets. What will make this possible will be five telecommunications satellites in stationary orbits, 22,375 miles above the Equator: two over the Atlantic, one over the Pacific, one over the Indian Ocean, and one, "Anik," over the Canadian North. The Montreal Games will thus become the most widely seen and heard sports spectacular in history.

To put it all together, some 200 broadcasting organizations representing more than a hundred nations will be in attendance at the Games. And leading the pack will be the **Canadian Broadcasting Corporation**, the designated host-broadcaster to the world, and the **American Broadcasting Company**, which has exclusive broadcast rights to the Games in the United States.

What the Canadian Viewer Will See

CBC has been confronted with the awesome task of scheduling 1,300 hours of sports in some 180 hours maximum of program time, and Gordon Craig, head of Television Sports, has promised the greatest TV coverage of any Olympics. For two weeks, both of the CBC's television networks, French and English, will virtually preempt regular programming for dawn-to-dusk coverage of the Games. For eleven to twelve hours each day, the viewer will get what amounts to the best seat in the stadium for *every* event. As might be expected from the public network, there will be a definite focus on Canadian contestants—and, not incidentally, Canada will be sending the largest sports delegation to the Games in its history. The stations of the privately owned CTV Network will limit their coverage to one hour a day selected from the full coverage ORTO will be producing.

ABC: *America's Olympic Network*

When COJO sold the U.S. rights to the American Broadcasting Company, they got a lot more in return than the record $25-million ABC paid for the deal. They got the best television sports department in the world. Under the leadership of Roone Arledge, president of ABC Sports, ABC revolutionized sports coverage in the 1960's. In an interview with Gilbert Rogin of *Sports Illustrated* some years ago, Arledge noted that "When I got into it in 1960, televising sports amounted to going out on the road, opening three or four cameras, and trying not to blow any plays. . . . What we set out to do was to get the audience involved emotionally."

ABC Sports under Arledge has pioneered such devices as the rifle-type mike (you can hear the thud of the football when it is punted), hand-held cameras for close-up action, underwater cameras for the coverage of swimming and diving, split-screen techniques for further analysis of events, and instant replay.

At Montreal, ABC is determined to produce the most comprehensive Olympic coverage in history.

What the U.S. Viewer Will See

If you live anywhere within 50–100 miles of the long U.S.-Canadian border, chances are you will have your choice between the CBC's marathon coverage and ABC's daily presentation of the Olympics. Because the

Montreal Games will take place in the Eastern Time Zone, ABC plans to present more live television coverage than ever before. In 1972, it provided 64 hours of satellite coverage of the Munich Games; for 1976 it is planning upwards of 75 hours of total coverage, including prime time and weekends.

A BRIEF HISTORY OF THE GAMES

The Olympic Games originated in Greece more than 2,500 years ago. They were held for the first time in the year presently denoted as 776 B.C.; and the Greeks took this year as a point of departure for their own chronology, dating the passage of time thereafter in terms of successive four-year periods, or Olympiads. Olympia, the site of the Games, was located in the plain of Elis at the foot of Mount Olympus. The games of the first Olympics lasted only one day and consisted of one event only, the *Dromos*, or "race of the Stadium"—running from one end of the stadium to the other. Gradually the Olympics were expanded to include other forms of contests. Among these were a race "in arms," fervently recommended as a preparation for military service; chariot races; discus throwing; and the *Dolichos*, a race of twenty-four lengths of the stadium. The *Pentathle*, the origin of the present-day Decathlon, represented a combination of five events: racing, the long jump, discus-throwing, javelin-throwing, and wrestling.

The motivating idea behind these early Olympics was to put an end to the fratricidal warfare that so long and so constantly ravaged Greece. During the Games a general truce would be declared, and all athletes given safe conduct through what was at other times mutually hostile territory. Unfortunately, the Olympiads did not succeed in this primary purpose. Perhaps equally unfortunately, all kinds of chicanery came to be associated with the Games—a perhaps inevitable result of the temptations created by the practice of loading down Olympic winners with manifold honors, including lifetime pensions and tax exemptions. Slaves started cheating when their masters promised them freedom if they snatched victory in the chariot races. In *The Iliad*, Homer recounts how the winner of the chariot race was given "A magnificent prize, a captive girl to take with him, as well as a tripod of 22 measures with handles."

It was the Roman emperor Theodosius who finally put an end to the Games in A.D. 393, in fulfillment of a promise to St. Ambrose to do away with these "pagan" exhibitions.

The Modern Era Begins

While the exact circumstances under which interest in the Olympics was revived are a matter of some dispute, most authorities generally credit Baron Pierre de Coubertin of France with being the energizing genius behind the modern Games. A great believer in physical fitness and competition, de Coubertin was enormously impressed with the methods of the famous Dr. Arnold, headmaster of Rugby School in England, who espoused a merger of sports and academic studies as the best means of teaching discipline, manliness, and self-reliance.

De Coubertin's writings on the subject of physical fitness attracted wide attention in France, where they eventually led to the addition of sports in teaching programs. In 1889 he helped in the expansion of the Union of French Athletic Sports Associations, and it was in that same year, at a gathering in the Sorbonne, that he first unveiled his idea of reviving the Olympic Games. Five years later, in June 1894, the representatives of thirteen nations met—also at the Sorbonne—and unanimously voted to reinstitute the Games.

The Baron envisioned *"Olympisme"* as a worldwide movement, one that would bring amateur athletes from every continent together to compete every four years, without consideration of race, religion, social class, or wealth. It was on his initiative that the International Olympic Committee was founded in Paris in 1894. Of the thirty-four nations who approved de Coubertin's plan, however, only thirteen were represented in Athens two years later: Australia, Bulgaria, Chile, Denmark, Germany, France, Greece, Great Britain, Austria, Sweden, Switzerland, Hungary, and the United States. George Averoff, a wealthy Greek whose enthusiasm had been sparked by de Coubertin's ideas, donated a million drachmas to rebuild the original Athens stadium—which thereby became the first great athletic arena of modern times.

Athens 1896

The Olympic motto, *Citius, Altius, Fortius* ("Swifter, Higher, Stronger"), was used for the first time at Athens in 1896, and fittingly, it was a Greek who won the first Olympic marathon. To ensure a Greek winner, all kinds of inducements were provided. Mr. Averoff promised the hand of his daughter in marriage and a dowry of one million drachmas to any of his countrymen who might win the race; a chocolate manufacturer put forward 2,000 lbs. of free confectionery, a barber offered a lifetime of free shaves and haircuts, a tailor offered to clothe the winner for life, and scores of

45

other people offered gifts that ranged from domestic cattle and sheep to barrels of vintage wine. The winner was Spyridon Louis, a postal worker from Athens area, and he collected most of the gifts. Unfortunately, he could not collect Mr. Averoff's gift—he was already a married man with two children.

Compared to Montreal in 1976, the first Games of the modern era were extremely modest in scale. Slightly over 300 athletes attended, and they competed in only nine events. The majority of the contestants entered on an individual basis; many of them were tourists who happened to be in Europe at the time. Typical were the Paine brothers, two wealthy young Americans who became the first to win Olympic medals for shooting. The Paines heard about the event in Italy, where they were vacationing, and after chartering a train to Brindisi they boarded a boat for Greece. They got there only just in time. The Greeks had omitted to tell the other countries that they followed the Julian calendar, which differed from the Gregorian calendar by 11 days.

The Athens Games were a relaxed affair, with competitors walking about the stadium in their regular street clothes between events. The sprinters started from an upright stance—only one contestant adopted the kneeling position, somewhat to the bemusement of other athletes.

Although the Greeks were the overall victors, it was the Americans who became the sensation of the 1896 Games by winning almost every track-and-field event. The very first Olympic gold medal was awarded to a Harvard man, James Connolly, in the triple jump (hop, skip, and jump), for a leap of 44 feet 11¾ inches. Robert Garrett of the United States won a silver in the broad jump, a gold medal in the shotput, and took another gold in the discus, much to the dismay of the Greek organizers, who had been hoping that one of their own countrymen might prevail in this traditional

Greek event. The victory was all the more surprising in that Garrett had never seen a proper discus before entering the Games.

In spite of all the confusion surrounding the first Olympic Games of modern times, they did succeed in attracting worldwide interest in sports as a spectacle. The Athens arena was only the first of many Olympic stadiums that were subsequently to be built in many other major cities throughout the world.

1900–1908: *The Keystone Comedy Era*

At the first Games there were no cinder tracks, no starting blocks, no jumping pits; and, more often than not, a race official held up an event until a colleague could bring over a stopwatch or a starter's pistol. They must have been fun to watch, but spectators could just as easily turn into participants by the simple act of signing up for a race. Regrettably perhaps, such free-lance enterprise ended with the Stockholm Games of 1912. Since then, entry has been permitted only via membership in a national team.

Both the Paris Games of 1900 and the St. Louis Games of 1904 were little more than side-shows to national expositions. The French took a particularly light-hearted approach to the Olympics, including among the events such items as an angling competition on the Seine, three-legged races, and leapfrog.

Organization was clearly not the forte of the organizers of the Paris Games. Someone somehow forgot to strike Olympic medals, and there was considerable annoyance on the part of competitors who found themselves presented instead with gifts of umbrellas and books. Perhaps the most embarrassing episode came when Rudolf Bauer of Hungary won the discus event. As he was being led to the rostrum for the victory ceremony, the band struck up the U.S. national anthem and officials solemnly raised the Stars and Stripes. In response to Bauer's strenuous and quite understandable objections, a Hungarian flag was found, and the band promptly launched into the Austrian national anthem.

President Theodore Roosevelt opened the 1904 Games in St. Louis with one of his rousing speeches, but from then on, it was all downhill. The U.S. organizers had promised to send a liner to Europe to bring competitors over, but no one in St. Louis followed through on the promise. As a result, only six overseas nations competed, and the Games turned into an American athletic meet, with Americans winning 209 medals out of a total of 250.

In an attempt to attract bigger crowds—the total attendance for all the Games' events put together came to less than 2,000—the organizers created an "Ethnographical Olympics" largely comprised of foreigners who were working at the St. Louis World's Fair. According to newspaper accounts of the day, the Greek contingent was made up of waiters, and South Africa was represented by several Zulus who were on show at the Fair.

In St. Louis, as in Paris, it was the so-called Olympic officials who failed miserably—an augury of things to come.

From the start of the modern Games the athletes, when left alone to test their skills against each other, were magnificent. Ray Ewry of the USA, a one-time invalid who had taken up athletics on his doctor's orders, won three gold medals at Paris (though the medals did not assume tangible form: see above), and successfully defended all three of his titles at St. Louis. He won the standing high jump for the third time in London in 1908. All told, Ewry garnered a total of ten Olympic gold medals—a record that still stands as the greatest number of gold medals ever awarded a single individual. Another plucky competitor was the Quebec strongman Étienne Desmarteau. A Montreal policeman by profession, Desmarteau was told he could not get time off to attend the Olympics. He thereupon resigned from the force and hitchhiked his way to St. Louis. Up against tough American competition, Desmarteau won the 56-pound weight throw with a colossal toss of 34 feet 4 inches. Singlehandedly he had broken the U.S. monopoly of this event, and in the process set a record that was to stand for another sixteen years.

Italy's Dorando Pietri was the tragic figure of the 1908 London Games. First into the White City Stadium at the conclusion of the marathon, he collapsed several times. A number of people came to his assistance, among them the well-known mystery writer Arthur Conan Doyle, and finally officials carried him across the finish line. Pietri had to be disqualified, but the man who did not win the marathon became the popular hero of the hour, and the day after the race, Queen Alexandra gave Pietri a gold cup in recognition of his courage. The American Johnny Hayes, who came in second, was awarded the gold medal, and promptly became the forgotten man of the fourth Olympics.

Stockholm

It was the Stockholm Games of 1912 that established the Olympics as an enduring institution, and placed it where it has remained ever since—at the very summit of sports, the peak where the world's best athletes gather to test speed against speed, strength against strength, courage against courage. More than one million people watched the Games, and the Swedes built a magnificent stadium for the occasion.

"Keep fit" programs had long been part of Swedish home and school activities, and the Swedes enthusiastically welcomed the opportunity to join the Olympic movement. They proved themselves, moreover, to be superb organizers, and Stockholm was a milestone in technical innovation. The photo-finish camera made its first appearance at any Olympic Games in Stockholm; so too did electronic timing devices for track events. It was also the first time a public address system had ever been used at the Games.

As usual, the Americans dominated in track events. But it was a small country, Finland, that produced the hero of the Games—Hannes Kolehmainen, who began the Finnish tradition of brilliance in middle- and long-distance running, a tradition maintained to the present day.

Kolehmainen, winner of three gold medals, ran his hardest race against Jean Bouin of France, who held the world record for running the greatest distance in an hour. Halfway through the 5,000-meter final, Bouin was ahead, but 20 meters from the finishing tape, Kolehmainen put on a fantastic spurt to win by 0.1 second in the Olympic record time of 14 minutes 36.6 seconds —a record that stood until 1924 when another Finn, Paavo Nurmi, narrowly beat it.

Another formidable competitor, a man who was to be associated with the Olympic movement until he died in 1968, was the great American swimmer Paoa ("Duke") Kahanamoku, from Hawaii. In Stockholm he broke the world record for the 100-meter freestyle event with a time of 62.4 seconds. A remarkably durable competitor, the "phenomenal Kanaka" (as the press called him) won the silver medal in 1924 for the 100-meter freestyle in 61.4 seconds, and it took Johnny Weismuller (later to be world-famous as Tarzan), setting a new Olympic record of 59 seconds, to beat him.

At the conclusion of the Games, the hospitable Swedes staged a mammoth sit-down supper in the stadium for the 4,000 athletes and team officials. A ten-course meal was served, and a men's choir of 2,500 provided an after-dinner concert. The festivities concluded with a fireworks display in the early hours of the dawn.

Almost every Olympiad has had its sad and tragic side; and Stockholm was no exception. One of the most popular figures at the Games was Jim Thorpe, a full-blooded American Indian, and the greatest athlete of his day. His extraordinary prowess manifested itself quite early. Once, as a schoolboy, he represented his school in a track-and-field meet. The opposing side went to the railroad station to greet the visiting team, which turned out to consist of Jim Thorpe and his coach. Thorpe, however, was all that was needed—he ran away with eight first prizes! Representing the United States in the Stockholm Games, Thorpe won both the Pentathlon and the Decathlon. King Gustav of Sweden, in presenting him with two gold medals, called him the world's greatest athlete.

Then, on February 6, 1913, the Swedish Olympic Committee received a coldly worded letter from the U.S. Olympic Committee that declared Jim Thorpe to have been a professional athlete. Strict concern for amateur purity left the Swedish Committee little choice but to recommend that the IOC remove Thorpe's name from the list of Olympic winners. Thorpe's disqualification created an international uproar, but it was upheld.

Years later, F. A. M. Webster, a British authority on Olympic matters, described the disqualification as a "spiteful charge, since [Thorpe's] only sin against the amateur code had been that of receiving a dollar or so for pitching in a baseball game when he was little more than a schoolboy." To this day, however, the case of Jim Thorpe has refused to be laid to rest. In 1975, sixty-two years after the tragedy, and twenty-two years after Thorpe's death, President Gerald Ford formally requested the International Olympic Committee to reconsider the matter.

51

There were some marvelous Olympic moments between the two World Wars—the debut, for one, of Paavo Nurmi at Antwerp in 1920. Before his Olympic career ended at Amsterdam in 1928, Nurmi was to collect an astonishing nine gold medals (including three in relay events) for track and field. "The Flying Finn"—always racing with a stopwatch clutched in his hand; breaking, and breaking again, old records—raised the intensity of competition to white heat.

Then there was the incandescent heroine of the Los Angeles Games of 1932, 17-year-old Mildred Didrikson —everyone called her "Babe"—who broke Olympic and world records in three events and yet wound up with only two gold medals. She established a world record of 143 feet 4 inches with her first throw of the javelin, and another by running over the 80-meter hurdles in 11.7 seconds. In the third instance, however, the high jump in which she shared a new world record of 5 feet 5 inches with her compatriot Jean Shiley, she was disqualified because she went over the bar head first, which was against the rules at the time.

"The Babe" excelled in almost every sport, but as Mrs. Zaharias she turned professional golfer and won all the major women's tournaments in the world. She succumbed to cancer at age 42, but not before being

voted the finest female athlete of the first half of the twentieth century.

There was also a magnificent young black athlete from Cleveland, Ohio—Jesse Owens. In 1935, at an athletic meet in Ann Arbor, Michigan, Owens set or equaled no less than six world records: 100 yards in 9.4 seconds; 200 meters and 220 yards straight-line, each in 20.3 seconds; the 200-meter hurdles and 220-yard hurdles, each in 22.6 seconds; and a 8.13-meter long jump.

At the Berlin Games in 1936, Jesse Owens went on to earn four gold medals, winning the 100-meter in 10.3 seconds, the 200-meter in 20.7 seconds, the broad jump with 26 feet 5¼ inches, and the 4 × 100-meter relay, which established a new world record time of 40 seconds.

The idealism with which Baron de Coubertin founded the Olympic movement was sorely tried in Berlin. Hitler envisaged the Olympics—the first ever held on German soil—as an opportunity to show off the Third Reich to the world, and along with it demonstrate Aryan racial "supremacy." A stadium seating 100,000 was built, and the swimming hall was large enough to hold 20,000. When the Nazi dictator opened the Games of the Eleventh Olympiad on August 1, 1936, cameras recorded every event from a dozen different angles. The stadium was ringed with large red and black banners bearing the swastika, and all Nazi party members were instructed to come in uniform.

Germany won 101 medals out of a total of 420 and, for the first time, the United States failed to emerge as the top nation in the Olympic Games. Yet Hitler's attempt to offer physical feats as evidence of racial superiority backfired: at Berlin, the star of Leni Riefenstahl's film *The Gods of the Stadium* turned out to be the black athlete Jesse Owens.

Berlin was to be the last Olympics before World War II. The Games resumed in 1948 in London—a city still recovering from its wartime experience as the Luftwaffe's favorite target. It rained incessantly throughout the Games, there was a food shortage, and not enough housing for the 3,714 men and 385 women athletes in attendance. The prevailing mood, nonetheless, was a happy one and, as so often happens in the Olympics, a crowd-pleasing athlete emerged to dominate the proceedings and provide yards and yards of great newspaper copy. Fanny Blankers-Koen of Holland at first seemed like an improbable heroine. Twelve years earlier she had competed in the Berlin Games, placing only sixth in the high jump. In 1948, she was the thirty-year-old mother of two children, and had been told she was too old for Olympic competition. As matters turned out, she became the first and only athlete ever to win four gold medals in the women's track-and-field events at a single Olympiad. She took the 100-meter in 11.9 seconds, the 200-meter with an Olympic record of 24.4 seconds, the 80-meter hurdles with another Olympic record of 11.2 seconds, and won her fourth gold with the Netherlands relay team in the 4 × 100-meter. The crowds idolized "Flying Fanny," as she was quickly dubbed by the world press, and it was generally agreed that she could also have won both the long jump and the high jump had she entered those events.

1952–1976: *Citius, Altius, Fortius*

Nothing is more instructive than to examine the record books of previous Olympic Games. What might have won an athlete a gold medal in the 1932 Los Angeles Games would scarcely qualify a competitor for a bronze today, and merely to qualify for the 110-meter hurdles in the 1976 Montreal Games one would need a better time than that required to win the gold medal at the first Games in 1896. Athletes today run 9 to 20 percent faster than in the past, they jump 27 percent higher and 40 percent farther. In 1896, for instance, Neumann of

Austria was first in the 400-meter freestyle swimming event with a time of 8:12.6, while the 3:58.18 world record of America's Rick DeMont is less than half that. In 1920, Bottino of Italy won an Olympic victory in the top weight-lifting class with 270 kilograms, but at Munich, Nikolov of the USSR took the gold with 525 kilograms, and his countryman, Alexeyev, has improved on that by pushing the world record up to 645 kilograms.

At the 1952 Helsinki Games, the greatest applause went to the athlete who carried the torch into the stadium—the phenomenal Finnish runner Paavo Nurmi, winner of nine gold and three silver medals in previous Olympics, and now a 55-year-old businessman who had trained especially to run the single track lap.

That year, the element of surprise that seems always to be present at the Olympics was provided by Joseph Barthel of tiny Luxembourg, who had marched almost alone behind his national flag at the opening ceremony. Without helpers or teammates, Barthel won the 1,500-meter, breasting the tape with a new Olympic record of 3:45.1. His victory gave Luxembourg its first, and still its only, gold medal in Olympic competition.

The stars of the Helsinki Games, however, were unquestionably Mr. and Mrs. Emil Zatopek of Czechoslovakia. Emil Zatopek was already 30 years old at the time, and he didn't appear to be enjoying himself

pounding around the track like a locomotive, head tilted to one side, and face contorted with grimaces, as he won the 5,000-meter, then the 10,000-meter, and finally the most grueling race of all, the marathon. His wife, Dana, also triumphed by winning the women's javelin event with a new Olympic record throw of 165 feet 7 inches.

A few years later during the Melbourne Games the Zatopeks were best man and matron of honor at the much-publicized "Iron Curtain love story wedding" of Olga Fikotova and Harold Connolly, the gold medal winners, respectively, for Czechoslovakia in the discus event and for the United States for the hammer throw.

Melbourne also provided, unfortunately, a stunning example of the kind of inept and prejudiced refereeing that frequently accompanies judgment events like boxing, wrestling, water polo, and equestrian contests. In the dressage championship, the Swedish judge placed the three Swedish competitors first, the German judge awarded the first three places to the three German entrants, and a Danish judge placed a Dane first and Swedes third and fifth. The judges from Belgium and Chile awarded a tie for first to a Swede and a Dane, and placed a French competitor third.

The 1960 Rome Games were notable for the introduction of television coverage on a world scale for the first time. It was estimated that, as a result, some 140,000,000 people watched the Games—or, put another way, 900 times the total population of Athens at the time of the first Olympic Games 2,500 years ago; the era of the Super-Olympics had begun. The day before the opening ceremonies, St. Peter's Square in Rome was filled with thousands of athletes of all races and religions, who received the blessing of Pope John XXIII. The Church has changed its opinion since A.D. 393, and no longer considers the Games to be pagan.

As in Melbourne, the Soviets finished first, taking 103 medals out of 461, ahead of the United States, which won only 71. But it was African athletes who were in the news at the Rome Games, with the most memorable performance in the marathon being achieved by a then completely unknown runner, Abebe Bikila of Ethiopia, a member of the Imperial Household Guard. He won the marathon running barefoot, and millions of viewers remember the gymnastics Bikila performed after crossing the finishing line in the world's best time of 2 hours 15 minutes 16.2 seconds.

In Tokyo in 1964, Bikila amplified his contribution to Olympic history by winning the marathon for the second time in a row. He was watched by a crowd of more than half a million people—an Olympic record in itself. Abebe entered the marathon for the third time in the Mexico City Games of 1968, but had to drop out because of a leg injury. However, his countryman Mamo Wolde took the gold medal, for Ethiopia's third successive victory in this event. Runners from Kenya, Tanzania, and Tunisia have also astounded the athletic world with their prowess in middle- and long-distance running—something to be watched out for in the Montreal Games.

One of the least noticed contestants in the Rome Olympics was the 18-year-old U.S. representative in the light-heavyweight boxing division. With something less than exemplary modesty he told everyone within earshot that he was going to win an Olympic gold medal, and that in the next year or so he would become the world's heavyweight champion. He delivered on both promises. His name: Cassius Clay, known today the world over as Muhammad Ali.

Tokyo 1964 marked another milestone in Olympic history—the first time the Games had been held in Asia. The Japanese staged the most extravagant and colorful of all celebrations to that time, spending more than half a billion dollars in the process. Japan used the occasion as well to show off its advanced tech-

nology: computers, electronic timing devices accurate to a thousandth part of a second, cameras of the most advanced design, received almost as much attention as the competitors.

The Tokyo Games were unquestionably a dazzling success. Critics, however, began to charge that the Olympics were getting too big, too commercial, and that the athletes were getting lost in the promotion and the ballyhoo surrounding the Games.

The choice of Mexico City for the 1968 Olympics was severely criticized in many quarters. With the city being 7,347 feet above sea level it was thought that those accustomed to high altitudes would have an unfair advantage over those not so accustomed. And as things turned out, there were in fact many distressing scenes of athletes who had collapsed in the course of an event being revived with oxygen in full view of a worldwide television audience. Yet, despite the furor over altitude, the performances in short- and middle-distance track and field were little short of phenomenal, and Bob Beamon's long jump of 8.90 meters, a sensational 29 feet 2½ inches, has gone down as one of the greatest physical feats in Olympic history, and a record not likely to be broken at the Montreal Games.

If Baron de Coubertin had been alive at the time of the Munich celebrations, he might well have wondered aloud what was happening to his brainchild. Into an 80,000-seat, acrylic glass-covered stadium, some 10,000 athletes representing 124 countries—three times the number which had attended the 1956 Melbourne Games—marched in the gaudy Parade of Nations. The

U.S. Olympic team alone counted more athletes from a single country than the total number from the thirteen nations represented at the 1896 Games. The overall expenditure of $750-million was more than three times what Mexico City had spent on the 1968 Games. It was to be the biggest and costliest Olympics in the history of the Games and the hope was that peace, harmony, and Bavarian *Gemütlichkeit* would prevail. A sign in the Olympic Village read: NO NATIONS, MANY CULTURES. As events unfolded, however, it was to be the saddest of all Olympics.

Almost 900,000,000 people viewed the proceedings, the largest audience in the annals of TV. What they saw, however, was no tribute to the Olympic spirit. It is certainly true that ever since the Games were revived in 1896, they have too often been marred by accusations of sloppy officiating, power politics, poor sportsmanship, and the unseemly and chauvinistic piling up of team points, and Munich may have been no worse in such respects than earlier Olympiads; but perhaps because so many people were watching, it seemed so. Television viewers watched with dismay as Pakistani fans mobbed the referees after Pakistan was upset in the field-hockey finals by West Germany. Then there was the water-polo match between Yugoslavia and the Soviet Union: angered by actions of the Cuban referee, the Yugoslavs spat on him and beat up his bewildered brother.

Another incident involved Rick DeMont, 16 a long-distance swimmer from San Rafael, California. DeMont won the 400-meter freestyle, beating out Australia's Brad Cooper—but was then disqualified because an illegal drug, ephedrine, had been found in his urine specimen. As an asthma victim, however, he had been taking the drug for years, and had noted this fact on his Olympic medical form. Despite an appeal from his coaches, the IOC barred DeMont from further competition and insisted that he return his gold medal. De-Mont thus became the second Olympian since Jim Thorpe in 1913 to be compelled to return a medal.

It was against this backdrop of poor sportsmanship and downright incompetence that the Arab terrorists struck. On September 5, in the second week of the Games, a group of Palestinian guerrillas from the "Black September" movement scaled the 6½-foot fence surrounding the Olympic Village and seized Israeli hostages. For 20 hours, world attention was focused on the three-story building at 31 Connollystrasse. In what is now conceded to have been a badly bungled security operation, eleven Israelis, one German, and five terrorists died violently. Avery Brundage, the 84-year-old president of the IOC, declared that "the Games must go on," and they did. Yet despite the effort at business as usual, the Twentieth Olympiad ended badly—one magazine labeled the Munich Games "one of the sorriest athletic spectacles in history."

The Summer Olympic Games of Modern Times

YEAR	CITY	COMPETING NATIONS	COMPETITORS
1896	Athens	13	311
1900	Paris	16	1,505
1904	St. Louis	7	1,609
1906	Athens (interim, without medals)	21	901
1908	London	22	2,666
1912	Stockholm	27	4,742
1916	Berlin (canceled because of World War I)	—	—
1920	Antwerp	26	2,741
1924	Paris	45	3,385
1928	Amsterdam	46	3,905
1932	Los Angeles	39	2,403
1936	Berlin	51	4,069

YEAR	CITY	COMPETING NATIONS	COMPETITORS
1940	canceled because of World War II	—	—
1944	canceled because of World War II	—	—
1948	London	59	6,005
1952	Helsinki	69	5,867
1956	Melbourne	73	5,050
1960	Rome	84	5,393
1964	Tokyo	94	7,500
1968	Mexico City	119	7,230
1972	Munich	124	10,000
1976	Montreal	132	10,000

OLYMPIC PROTOCOL AND ORGANIZATION

Since an Olympiad is (self-evidently) an athletic occasion first and foremost, those who have no direct connection with sport, even if they be presidents, kings, or emperors, must yield precedence at such an occasion to athletes and those concerned with the management of athletic activities.

At the top are the members and honorary members of the **International Olympic Committee (IOC)**, a group that still contains one grand duke, three princes, five generals, and a roomful of sheikhs, sultans, barons, and other nobility. They are outranked only by the head of state of the country in which the Games are being held. In the case of the Montreal Games, this is H.M. Queen Elizabeth.

Next come the members of the **Organizing Committee (COJO)**, the chairmen of the international federations for given sports, such as the Track and Field Association and the International Equestrian Association, and then the chairmen of the respective **National**

Olympic Committees, followed by ranking guests. Those responsible for ranking guests from abroad are, on this occasion, the embassies in Ottawa and the respective foreign consulates in Montreal. It should be pointed out, however, that Olympic attachés are an official instrument of Olympic protocol. They maintain contact between the National Olympic Committees of their respective countries and the Organizing Committee, for during the Games the Olympic attaché becomes an aide to his country's *chef de mission.*

Ministers, heads of governments, and even kings receive no formal invitations to the Olympic Games— there are no official personal invitations at all, but simply a general invitation to the youth of the world.

The most solemn event of the Games is the opening ceremony, which follows a minutely prescribed protocol, from the arrival of the head of state to the lighting of the Olympic flame and the swearing of the Olympic oath. The same is true of the closing ceremony and the medal-awarding ceremonies.

During the Montreal Games there will be any number of more or less ceremonious occasions. However, only five of them are recognized as official: the opening of the IOC session on Tuesday, July 13, at 10 A.M., the reception given by the President of the Organizing Committee for the members of the IOC, the reception given by the Prime Minister of Quebec, Robert Bourassa, the reception given by H.M. Queen Elizabeth and the reception given by the Mayor of Montreal.

INTERNATIONAL OLYMPIC COMMITTEE: EXECUTIVE BOARD

President: Lord Killanin (Ireland)
1st Vice President: Comte Jean de Beaumont (France)
2nd Vice President: Jonkheer Herman A. van Karnebeek (Netherlands)
3rd Vice President: Mr. Willi Daume (Federal Republic of Germany)

Members: Mr. Constantin Andrianov (USSR); Mr. Juan
   Antonio Samaranch (Spain); Prince Tsuneyoshi Takeda
   (Japan); Major Sylvio de Magalhaes Padilha (Brazil);
   Mr. Mohamed Mzali (Tunisia)
Headquarters: The Queen Elizabeth Hotel
Telephone: 861-3511

The International Olympic Committee, to whom the
Congress in Paris in 1894 entrusted the control and
development of the Modern Olympic Games, is a
permanent organization. The IOC is the final authority
on all questions concerning the Olympic Games and is
represented in 132 countries by national Olympic Committees.

For each Olympiad, the National Olympic Committee of the host country takes charge. The Canadian
Olympic Association formed a Games organizing committee with a four-year mandate granted by the Quebec provincial legislature in 1972. That committee, the
Comité Organisateur des Jeux Olympiques (COJO), is
charged with the preparation and administration of the
1976 Olympic Games. Its mandate ends with the conclusion of the Games.

COMITÉ ORGANISATEUR DES JEUX OLYMPIQUES (COJO)

President and Commissioner General: His Excellency C.O.
   Roger Rousseau
Executive Vice President: Michel Guay
Director General: Walter Sieber
Vice President, Revenue: Gerald Snyder
Secretary Treasurer: Howard Radford
Head of Press Services: Michel Labrosse

Headquarters: 155 Notre Dame East
Phone: 286-1976
Mail inquiries: Communications Department, COJO, P.O.
   Box 1976, Montreal, Canada H3C 3A6
Telex: 05-25805

So now, after almost six years of preparation and some $1-billion in expenditure, a flower-and-flag-bedecked Montreal is ready.

At precisely 4:30 p.m. on July 17, 1976, the Olympic torchbearer will enter Olympic Stadium. Shortly after the Olympic flame has been lit, H.M. Queen Elizabeth will officially initiate the proceedings with a fourteen-word statement:

"I declare open the Olympic Games celebrating the Twenty-first Olympiad of the modern era."

The Montreal Games will have begun.

Sir George Williams Campus Bookstore: 1455 Maisonneuve (879-2855).

McGill University Bookstore: In the McGill Student Union Building, left-hand side of McTavish Street, above Sherbrooke (392-4747).

Mansfield Bookmart: A friendly rival to McGill's Bookstore, with excellent range in history, sociology, the fine arts, and literature and literary criticism. A great place to browse with intelligent sales help. There's also an excellent secondhand department with some rare treasures for those interested in Canadiana and Arctic material. Book-search service available, plus wide choice of poetry and "little" magazines (845-1872). 2065 Mansfield, near Sherbrooke West.

W. H. Smith: British bookstore chain. Complete selection of hardcovers and paperbacks, newspapers and magazines. Main store at 1004 St. Catherine West (866-8771) and branches, Place Victoria (861-5433) and Fairview, Pointe Claire (695-5200).

French Bookstores

Librairie Flammarion Paris Ltd.: A branch of the Paris firm. Excellent in all categories, and especially art, cuisine, travel, and children's books. 1243 University (866-6381).

Librairie Hachette (Canada) Ltd.: The latest bestsellers from France, plus newspapers, magazines, guidebooks, and good selection of Quebec literature. 554 St. Catherine West (842-3857).

Centre Éducatif et Culturel: The most popular bookstore of its kind in the city. Tremendous stock. Good place to pick up books for those intent on studying the French language. 2075 Mansfield (845-5719).

Librairie Québécoise: One of the most extensive

selections of current Quebec writing, emphasis on politics. 1567 St-Denis (845-0911).

Librairie Encyclopédique: Caters to nearby University of Quebec. 1635 St-Denis (845-0911).

Ho Chi Minh: Chinese Communist publications, posters, and *Peking People's Daily*. 131 Prince Arthur East (843-6061).

L'Ezoterik: Mystical and metaphysical. Widest choice in Montreal on the subjects of hermetism, the occult, Eastern thought. A good selection of star charts and tarot cards. 1707 St-Denis.

Specialty Bookstores

Cheap Thrills: Buys and sells used books, comic books, records of every variety. 1433 Bishop (844-7604).

Androgyny's: Feminist and Gay literature, plus non-sexist children's books. 1225A Crescent Street (866-2131).

418 Books: Mysticism and the occult. 2040 Mackay (933-8774).

Universal Book and Stamp Mart: Used magazines of every description. Paperbacks of the most lurid variety. 1064 St. Lawrence (866-0928).

William Wolfe: Old and rare books, manuscripts maps, and prints. A delightful bookstore in the London tradition. 222 Hospital in Old Montreal (288-5732).

Isobel Mackenzie: Rare books, collector's items, maps, and prints. Phone for appointment. 4162 St. Catherine West (933-5375).

Bernard Amtmann: Whether you are seeking a First Folio of Shakespeare's works, or the unpublished papers of some Canadian railroad magnate, chances are Mr. Amtmann either has it in stock or can quickly satisfy your requirements. One of Canada's best-known book dealers and auctioneers. 1529 Sherbrooke West (935-2262).

Grant Woolmer: Canadiana and Arctica. 2027 Mansfield (844-4956).

Canadian Bible Society: Religious books. 1450 Union (844-3368).

Diocesan Book Room: Religion, theology, Anglican prayerbooks. 1446 Union (842-7606).

Information Canada: Government of Canada publications. 1381 St. Catherine West (849-3201).

Double Hook: Extensive selection of Canadian books. Cozy bookshop where you often find authors sipping tea with the customers. 4174 St. Catherine West, east of Greene (932-5093).

The Book Nook: Enormous selection of second-hand books. Great for browsing. 651 Notre-Dame West (854-2966).

Corbeil-Hooke Arts & Crafts: Best selection of "how-to" books in the city. 1218 Drummond (866-7867).

BOOK REPAIRS AND BINDING

L'Art de la Reliure: Restores, repairs, rebinds old books and creates modern ones to suit your taste. 841 St-Sulpice (Old Montreal) (844-1831).

Belanger Vianney: Binding of periodicals and books. If you want three years of your favorite magazine bound, this is the place to visit. 7980 Alfred Anjou (353-2420).

CAMERAS

See "Photography: Equipment."

CAMPING

See "Sports Equipment."

CARNIVAL NOVELTIES

Henry Gordon's Party Center: Party supplies, masks, funny hats, along with large selection of magic tricks and books on the subject. 5317 Queen Mary Road (484-2322).

Malabar Costumes: Clowns, cowboys, dragons, matadors, old-fashioned ball gowns, etc. 422 Notre-Dame West (845-8169).

Johnny Brown: One of the largest theatrical supply houses in Canada. Catalogue offers list of more than 300 items, from leotards to pasties. There are judo and jogging outfits, masks, and shoes for midgets. Fascinating place. 2019 Mansfield (844-3221).

Joseph Ponton: Reputedly the oldest theatrical costumer in Canada. Hundreds of costumes, hats, papier-maché heads, wigs, and armor. Costume rental from around $10. 451 St-Sulpice, Old Montreal (849-3238).

CARPETS—ANTIQUES

Gallery of Persian Carpets: Mohammed Ali Aleboyeh's establishment contains a treasure trove of paintings, miniatures, and rugs. Prices range from a few hundred dollars to a small fortune. Definitely the place for carpet collectors. 1622 Sherbrooke West (935-5742).

Hick's Oriental Rugs: Fine and antique Oriental and Persian rugs. 1370 St. Catherine West (861-7283).

Gregory's Oriental Rugs: New and antique Oriental rugs. Also cleaning and repairing. 4201 St. Catherine West (932-4277).

Ogilvy's Department Store: Fifth floor, well worth a look. Occasional sale bargains. St. Catherine West at Mountain.

China Resource Products: Direct from China, magnificent rugs and carpets in wide choice of patterns. 1230 St. Catherine West (861-4530).

CATERING SERVICE

Montreal has hundreds of pizza parlors and delicatessens that offer 24-hour free delivery. The service is usually restricted to the neighborhood, although a few will deliver city-wide. Among the best, **Di Lallo** (see phone book for locations) for the finest hamburgers in the city, and **St-Urbain Bar-B-Q** for grilled chicken. Below, catering services for complete meals.

Eaton's: The Blue Cake Counter is a Montreal institution, which will deliver everything from a summer's picnic for two or meals for an entire Olympics. Call Mrs. Morrison at 842-9331, extension 248, or visit the store at 677 St. Catherine West.

Berthe Dansereau: Enthusiastic family concern that caters three-star meals and grand buffets. Expensive, but worth it. 243 Dunbar. Telephone orders 735-6107.

Buffet-St-Hubert: Speedy, efficient, with the most competitive prices in town. Dinner for two or two thousand. 4444 Jarry St. East (374-1550).

Buffet Bourgogne: Banquets, office parties, picnics, weddings. 7217 St-Hubert (274-6583).

Pumpernik's: Chinese and American cuisine. 5131 Décarie (487-3220).

Perlman's Kosher Caterers: 6053 Park Avenue (273-2458).

CHINA AND GLASS

The big stores such as Eaton's, Simpson's, Ogilvy's, The Bay, and Dupuis Frères have large stocks of modern French, Italian, and English designs.

Hemsley's: Extremely popular with U.S. visitors. Wide choice among Royal Copenhagen, Ginori, Rosenthal, and English bone china, also Waterford and Lalique crystal. Shipping arranged. 660 St. Catherine West (866-3706).

Henry Birks & Sons: Canada's finest gift store, widest possible selection of fine china. 1240 Phillips Square (392-2511).

China Shop: Fine English and Continental china and porcelain. Established thirty years ago, the shop also specializes in the repair of almost any piece. 1425 Bishop Street (849-1201).

CLOTHES—FOR HER

See also "Shoes."

St. Catherine Street between Bishop and Peel is where you'll find budget-priced fashion and many a bargain. 2020 University is another good place to shop for the latest trends, especially geared to those under 30. In Alexis Nihon Plaza (Métro: Atwater), your choice runs from the middle of the fashion ladder to the somewhat mad and improbable. It's a fun place to shop, especially on a Saturday, when it is crowded with teenagers and moms shopping with their daughters. Many of the most fashionable boutiques are located along Sherbrooke Street West between Peel and Guy, and on the streets in that area running south to St. Catherine. Westmount Square (Métro: Atwater) is an object lesson in high chic—few bargains here.

Montreal is Canada's fashion capital, with more manufacturers, designers, buyers, and boutiques than anywhere else in the country. Here are a few Montreal labels to watch out for—and it's worth noting that if you're from the U.S. you will be saving about 25 percent over your hometown prices on these manufacturers' clothes: **Molyclaire** (designer: John Warden) loungewear; **Malanson** (designer: Gordon Griffin) wool suits, pants, capes; **French Maid** (designer: Michel Robichaud) loungewear, pajamas, nightdresses; **Bagatelle** (designers: Margaret Godfrey and Nicola Pelly) suits, dresses, skirts; **Montroy Coat** (designer: Leo Chevalier) fur-trimmed and plain wool coats, jackets, skirts, capes; **The Market** (designers: Allan Goldin and Toby Klein) dresses.

You should keep in mind certain differences.

A New York size 10, for example, is about the same as a Canadian 12; also, proportions are slightly different —U.S. sizing is longer in the waist and less full through the bustline.

Antique and Recycled Clothes

Most Montrealers love to express their individuality in their choice of clothing, and mixing something old with something new is part of the secret of this mania for self-expression. Broad-shouldered coats, shawls, Boy Scout shirts, feather boas, ecclesiastical robes, all find a new lease in dozens of shops that specialize in antique or recycled clothes. Here is a select list of the best shops:

Bygone Threads: Fashion models, photographers, and trend-setters crowd this store, with its astonishing assortment of bowling shirts, bangles, silk nighties, Hawaiian shirts, 1930's velvet, and stacks of shoes from the Alice Faye era. High kitsch rather than elegance. Trades—clothes for clothes—are welcomed. 1433 Bishop Street (no phone).

Found Objects: The top of the line for *haute couture* of the Twenties and Thirties. The owner, Alma White, shops Paris, London, and the upper reaches of Westmount for her stock (see "Antiques and Bric-a-brac," page 144).

Xanadu: Faded blue jeans and women's clothes 1900–1940. 120 Prince Arthur East (282-4285).

Sentimental Journey: Crocheted gloves, beaded Art Deco purses, velvet dresses can be found in The Bay (La Baie) Department Store, St. Catherine St.

Mucha: Not a polyester fabric in sight. Instead, racks of fine old velours, silks, crepes, and chiffons, some dating back to the turn of the century. Also bags, purses, and hats. Prince Arthur at Hôtel-de-Ville Street (no phone).

Boutiques

Le Château: Young fashions at moderate prices have long made Le Château a favorite with the under-25's. 1310 St. Catherine East (866-2481); 2020 University

(282-0094); Place Bonaventure (861-8637); Alexis Nihon Plaza (933-7074).

Lily Simon: Where the upper crust shops. Very elegant, beautifully tailored *prêt-à-porter* (ready to wear) from Paris, Milan, and Rome. If you can't get to Paris this season, Lily Simon is the next best shopping venue. Most convenient midtown location: Le Cartier, 1115 Sherbrooke West, corner Peel (843-3663). Also at 1 Westmount Square (Métro: Atwater) and 1326 Beaubien East.

Rive Gauche: One of the few RG stores not licensed by Yves St-Laurent (although it carries his clothes). Has outstanding reputation for being first with the latest fashions. Worth a look-in to see what's happening in the pop end of Paris-Montreal fashion. Rive Gauche is a beautifully designed store that includes both men's wear and a children's shop. There's a splendid restaurant (La Bergerie) in the basement. 1254 St. Catherine West (861-9871); also at 1 Westmount Square and Carrefour Laval.

John Warden: A touchstone of Montreal fashion. This top Montreal designer specializes in the sporty look. In great demand are his superbly tailored safari suits. Prices medium to expensive. Also available, a small selection of his modestly priced loungewear done for Molyclaire. At 1407 Bishop (844-7431).

Michel Robichaud: Friendly rival to Warden, Robichaud's boutique features the designer's own clothes— elegant evening dresses, pantsuits, and loungewear. 2195 Crescent (844-6116).

Clubissimo: Considered a fashion leader among boutiques, features the clothes of Sonia Rykiel, among other top designers. What you read about in the latest Paris *Vogue* is likely to be found here. 2130 Crescent (844-5555).

Elle: Good clothes for over-25's. Mostly French imports. 2065 Crescent (849-5973).

Laura Ashley: Fashionable Mother-Earth type clothes, prints, paisleys, ruffles and tiny buttons, in this neat, friendly upstairs boutique. This British designer's clothes with the 1910 look can be worn from age 17 to 45. 2110 Crescent (843-8115).

Corinne de France: Paris imports, some for the older woman. 2020 University, also 1320 Sherbrooke West (842-9484).

Eric-Yane: Over-17 and under-30 are in seventh heaven here. Great clothes at medium to expensive prices. Tops, blouses, pants, skirts, long dresses. Some of the most beautiful dresses are French-designed and made in Turkey and Romania. Almost everything here is imported from France. 2075 Crescent (843-7755).

Yves St-Laurent: On Holt Renfrew's second floor is a tiny boutique with very big prices. Simple white jeans at $100, a blouse can set you back $450, a linen hat $85. Occasional markdowns make this worth a brief stop. Next aisle over: the superbly tailored clothes of Missoni, $200–$500. Holt Renfrew, Sherbrooke West at Mountain.

Maternity Clothes

Lady Madonna: Franchised branch of well-known New York designer. Motto of store is "Bellies are beautiful," and the clothes have genuine style and flair. Prices are moderate, and sales help are especially pleasant. 2080 Crescent (844-2516).

Great Expectations: Maternity wear designed with style. Canadian, American, and European. 1610 Sherbrooke West, near Guy (933-4180).

Unusual Sizes

Most of the department stores have fashion stock for tall, small, and large sizes.

The Bay: Wide choice for women from 5 feet tall to 6 feet 5 inches. Shoes from size 3 to size 14. Tall women who can afford the prices should visit Givenchy's Nouvelle Boutique collection at this store. St. Catherine West at Phillips Square.

Salon Juliette: A taxi ride from midtown Montreal, but worth it if you're size 14 to 20, 40 to 48, 14½ to 30½. 5457 Queen Mary Road (Snowdon). Phone 484-3558.

Pennington's: Medium-priced fashions for the tall and larger woman. Branches in Place Ville-Marie, Alexis Nihon Plaza, and 7915 Les Galeries d'Anjou (866-6741).

CLOTHES—FOR HIM

See also the section "Antique and Recycled Clothes" under "Clothes—for Her" and "Shoes."

For good, traditional, ready-made clothes and accessories, it's hard to outclass the major stores: **Holt Renfrew,** Sherbrooke West at Mountain, expensive, conservative, correct. **Ogilvy's,** St. Catherine at Mountain, caters to the businessman—durable, sober suitings; also good for tweeds and weekend clothes. **Eaton's,** 677 St. Catherine West, **Simpson's,** 977 St. Catherine West, and **The Bay** at Phillips Square are for individuals who expect good value for money in shirts, sweaters, ties, socks, underwear, suits, and sports clothes. **Dupuis Frères,** 865 St. Catherine Street East at St-Hubert offers you a choice of both the best and the worst in men's readymade clothes. In many ways the most interesting of the big stores, with the lowest prices on French *couture* shirts, and plenty of markdowns.

Boutiques and Bespoke Tailors

Brisson & Brisson: The city's (and some say Canada's) most superlative men's store. Continental elegance at its peak. Superb tailoring that can show Savile Row a lesson or two. Custom Italian shoes, Swiss shirts, Italian rainbow-colored sweaters. For the man who wants the finest—and is prepared to pay for it. 1472 Sherbrooke West (937-7456).

Croque-Monsieur: Elegant casual wear and accessories from France and Italy. 2065 Crescent (849-7476).

Ted Lapidus: Don't visit this boutique if your waistline is more than 32. If it's less, then the clothes of Paris designer Ted Lapidus are hard to beat when it comes to elegance and dash. Especially good for leather and fur-trimmed clothes. 1240 Mountain (861-3977).

Rive Gauche: Yves St-Laurent, Cardin, Missoni, Hechter are some of the great international names carried by this meticulously elegant store. From suits to collar buttons, everything a man needs to get through four seasons. 1254 St. Catherine West, Carrefour Laval, and 1 Westmount Square.

COINS AND MEDALS

Guardian Trust: Gold and silver coins, ancient and medieval coins. Also mint commemorative medals, including all the Olympic series. Gold and silver bars. 618 St. James (842-8251).

Lipson and Sons: One of Montreal's most active dealers in coins and medals. Paper, gold, silver, and rare coins. Central Station beneath Queen Elizabeth Hotel (866-1212).

Quebec Eastern Numismatics: Specialist in U.S. coins, also large selection of Canadian and European coins. 2055 Peel (842-1446).

CRAFTS AND SKILLED ARTISANRY
Canadiana

Centrale d'Artisanat du Quebec: Head and shoulders above any other handicrafts shop in town. Supported as it is by the government of Quebec, the store is literally a show-window for the dazzling talents of Quebec craftworkers. Two floors to browse through, and prices that begin around $2 and go up to $150 for outstanding wood-carvings. There's pottery, rugs, tapestries, stained glass, copper enameling, quilts (at reasonable prices), dolls, clothes, and various examples of art from Quebec's Indians and Eskimos. 1450 St-Denis (849-9415); also at 2020 University.

The Canadian Guild of Crafts: A nonprofit national organization, essentially a retailing operation for Canadian craftsmen. You'll find items from British Columbia here, as well as outstanding examples of Eskimo and Indian art. There are hand-woven ties at $5, handmade jewelry, wall-hangings, place mats, and pottery. 2025 Peel (849-6091).

La Soudure: Macramé, pottery, copper enameling, mobiles, silkscreens, and *ceintures flèchées*—woven "arrow" belts, traditional garb of the *habitant*. Le Viaduc, Place Bonaventure.

De Bellefeuille: Expensive and good. Leatherwork, Eskimo carvings, woven goods, and a superb selection of Quebec handicrafts. Place Ville-Marie (861-4158) and Place Bonaventure (878-4567).

International

Centre-d'Artisanat International: As long as you're on Peel Street, after visiting The Canadian Guild of Crafts, do look in on this shop. A remarkable range of African, Haitian, European, and Quebec craftwork. 1452 Peel (844-2537).

CYCLES

Peel Cycle Centre: The most conveniently located store in the city for rentals. They're open seven days a week, and you can rent by the day ($5 for 3- and 5-speed bikes) or by the week ($17–$50 for a 10-speed bike). The store also sells bicycles, and has a wide range of cycling equipment on sale. Owners are very helpful to out-of-towners. 1398 Sherbrooke West (844-8606).

See also under "Individual Sports," page 283.

Baggio Cycle and Sport: Strictly for the racing fan or the keen bicycle nut. Bikes for sale from around $100 up to $1500. Stock includes Raleigh, Torpado, and Mercier Tour de France. 6975 St. Lawrence (south of Jean-Talon) (279-5655).

ABC Cycle: A long-established and well-known name among Montreal bikers. They have a large stock,

including C.C.M. Raleigh, Apollo, and Peugeot.
They're also in the repair business. 5584 Park, near
St-Viateur (276-1305).

McWhinnie's: Many West-Enders can remember
getting their first bike from this firm. After almost fifty
years in business, McWhinnie's knows everything there
is to know about the bike business. They stock Peugeot,
Torpado, Apollo, Dynamex, Raleigh, C.C.M., and many
other top makes. 5866 Sherbrooke West (481-3131).

DO-IT-YOURSELF

Pascal's: The Pascal man in the red jacket is almost
as familiar as the mailman to Montrealers. The largest
retail hardware chain in the world, Pascal's stocks everything needed to make, fix, or repair what you will. Main
store, 301 Craig Street West, branches everywhere (866-
5692).

DOMESTIC HELP

Les Aides Ménagères: Cooks, cleaning ladies, cou-
ples, housekeepers, practical and baby nurses. Also
baby-sitters. 936 St-Joseph East (527-8351).

MacCallum Domestic Placement: Cooks, cleaners,
nannies, companion-housekeepers, nurses. 4795 St.
Catherine West (932-0436).

Baby Sitters' Service Bureau: Experienced sitters.
4253 St. Catherine West (932-2191).

Proxy Parents: Part-time child care by experienced
people. 6506 Sherbrooke West (481-4058).

We Sit Better: One of Westmount's favorites. You
have to pay a small membership fee to join the service.
Reliable and efficient. Provides care for the elderly and

convalescent, part-time child care, and baby-sitting. 4920 Maisonneuve West (482-9090).

Women's Information Centre: Women's movement help. 3595 St-Urbain (842-4781).

Day-Care Centers

There is an acute shortage of *inexpensive* day-care centers in Montreal. What is available is overworked and underfinanced. There is no shortage of the more expensive type of nursery care.

University Settlement: Children between the ages of three and six. Payment according to means. 3553 St-Urbain (844-6458).

Auntie Taub's: French-English, nice playground, good food, bus service. Transportation available. 7177 Nancy, near Côte-des-Neiges (733-1128).

NDG Day Nursery and Kindergarten: Bilingual pre-school training. Meals and transportation. 3471 Girouard, near Sherbrooke West (488-7174).

Preparatory Child's Day Centre: From 6:30 a.m. to 6:30 p.m. Qualified graduate teachers, large house, playground, weekly excursions. Summer branch in Laurentians. 6755 Fielding (488-3912).

DRUGS

There is no drugstore open all night now in the city.

EAR-PIERCING

Berkeley Jewelers: Ears pierced for $7.50 ($2.50 credit when earrings are bought). 1239 St. Catherine West (849-6864).

Ruth Thomas Studio: More than twenty years' experience in the business. By appointment. Suite 403, Medico-Dental Building, 1396 St. Catherine West (861-2363).

FABRICS

Marshall's: Wide choice among corduroys, cottons, silks, and voiles on several floors, as well as buttons, threads, and complete line of sewing supplies. Excellent for patterns. 1195 St. Catherine West (844-2558).

FISHING TACKLE

See "Sports Equipment."

FLOWERS AND PLANTS

The most inexpensive places to buy either flowers or plants are the outdoor markets (Atwater and Jean-Talon, see page 170), between May and September. If you're in town and want to send a friend a plant, **The Flower Box** sells the kind of expensive greenery that architects use in their newest buildings. Very posh and quite costly. They have shops in Westmount Square (931-7266) and Place Bonaventure (866-3378). A most reliable florist who offers city-wide delivery and reasonable prices is **Pinkerton's**, 5127 Sherbrooke West (Westmount) (487-7330). For midtown shoppers, the **House of Flowers**, 1112 Sherbrooke (842-4444), is in the highest category.

FOOD

Four food chains dominate the Montreal market-place: Steinberg's, Dominion, Marché-Union, and the

A & P. As elsewhere, the shopping week begins with a trickle on a Monday, rises to floodtide proportions by the weekend. Prices tend to be marginally higher on Friday and Saturday, and most supermarket managers agree that the best bargains are to be found on Wednesday. Characteristic of Montreal are the hundreds of Ma-and-Pa grocery stores (*épiceries*), crowded from floor to ceiling with beer, cider, fresh vegetables and groceries. Long after the supermarket has closed, **Danny's** or **Dupont's** will remain open, and most offer a delivery service as well. Of course, you'll pay more for the convenience, but Montrealers don't seem to mind. When the need is for a clove of garlic at suppertime, or a bottle of "Rapide Blanc" cider at 10 p.m., a few pennies here or there don't seem to matter.

Center City

Eaton's Gourmet Shop: Argentine honey, Maille's Green Herbs Flavored Mustard, canned patés, teas of every possible variety, brandied nectarines, excellent cheese counter (especially good choice of English cheeses), and meats. Eaton's ground floor, corner St. Catherine and University (842-9331, ext. 361-2).

The Bay's La Gastronome: Not quite as extensive a selection as Eaton's, but good all the same, and with the convenience of a Quebec Liquor Store, for wines and spirits, in the same building. The Bay, St. Catherine and Phillips Square (844-1515, ext. 350).

The Cheese Shoppe: Montreal's longest-established cheese shop, directly across from The Bay. Port-soaked Stilton, Gruyère, Camembert, walnut-covered soft cheeses, Wensleydale, and, of course, Quebec's own famous Oka. Cheerful atmosphere, everyone samples first, buys after. They'll ship cheese anywhere, and if you live in Montreal, you can get home delivery. 611 Maisonneuve West (843-3555).

Dionne Fils: This cozy shop, with its turn-of-the-century interior and white-coated shop assistants, is Montreal's most exclusive grocery store. Milk, groceries, meats, greens, seafood, and a wide range of gourmet foods. Gift baskets are a specialty. 1221 St. Catherine West, near Ogilvy's (849-2431).

Buywell Food Market: Rivals Dionne Fils in product quality. Excellent meat counter, with fine selection of cold cuts. Imported foods and cheeses. 1319 St. Catherine (842-1501).

Chez Louis: As long as you're in the neighborhood, this is the place for the best pastry and croissants to be found hereabouts. 2140 Mountain.

St. Lawrence (St-Laurent) Blvd.

Waldman's Fish Company: The biggest and best. A supermarket of the seven seas. Everything from spiny lobster to live turtles. Chances are, no matter how odd, if it swims, Waldman's has it. 74 Roy East (842-4483).

St. Lawrence Fish: Second only to Waldman's. 1195 St. Lawrence (866-5384).

Schwartz's Montreal Hebrew Delicatessen: The best smoked meats in town. 3895 St. Lawrence (842-4813).

Sepp's: The place to go if you're in the market for a Black Forest ham, a Swedish pickled ham, pure beef pepperoni, Norwegian smoked salmon. 3769 St. Lawrence (844-1471).

Old Europe: A small, unassuming shop that manufactures its own sausages and smoked meats. It has a formidable reputation for its Polish *krakowska* sausage, veal wieners, and pork links. 3855 St. Lawrence (842-5773), with a branch in Alexis Nihon Plaza.

Slovenia Meat Market: Magnificent sausages and cooked meats. 3653 St. Lawrence (842-3558).

Zagreb European Meats: Yugoslav specialties, and more than twenty varieties of sausages and salamis. 3900 St. Lawrence (844-9282).

4 Frères (Brothers) Supermarket: Greek-run supermarket, crowded, cheerful, incredible variety of olive oils, olives (in barrels), feta cheese, and usual range of greens, meats, and groceries. 3701 St. Lawrence (844-1874).

St. Lawrence Bakery: Has well-deserved reputation for low prices and highest quality. European breads, rolls, baked on the premises. Attracts loyal customers from all parts of the city. 3830 St. Lawrence. Open until 11 p.m.

Fairmount Bagel Factory: Don't be surprised to find a lineup here for the tastiest bagels in the city. Made before your eyes in the old-fashioned way. This small hole-in-the-wall store gets more customers on a weekend than many a giant supermarket. 263 St-Viateur West.

La Casa del Formaggio: Italian pasta, excellent cheeses (ricotta, buttira, mozzarella, Parmesan— ground to order—and many more). Wide range of garlic and other Italian sausages, as well as fresh olives in various grades. 6592 St. Lawrence.

Street Markets

From spring to fall two outdoor markets are in full operation on Atwater Avenue and on Jean-Talon Street. There are also several large indoor markets that are worthy of note.

Atwater Market: (Métro: Atwater). At the end of Atwater Avenue. Practically the whole of Westmount and NDG (Notre-Dame-de-Grace) shops here all sum-

mer long. (In the spring, incidentally, this is *the* place to come for shrubs, plants, and flowers at very reasonable prices.) Vegetables, homemade jams, fresh-laid eggs, honey, maple syrup, cheese, poultry, and meat all seem more fresh. Prices are also a shade cheaper than in the supermarkets, and are subject to negotiation. Actually, it definitely pays to comparison-shop. A pound of juicy red tomatoes on one stall is not necessarily the same price on another farmer's stall. Inside there is a meat market, and underneath the canopy you'll find shops specializing in West Indian foodstuffs and spices, a really worthwhile cheese shop with some of the lowest prices anywhere for Brie, Oka, and Cheddar—as well as a poultry shop that runs occasional "specials" on damaged chickens! On a Saturday morning, it's one of the most colorful places in the city. Great fun for visitors. 7 a.m. to 5 p.m. daily, Friday until 9 p.m. Closed Sunday.

Jean-Talon Market: (Métro: Jean-Talon). Mozart Street, just below Jean-Talon. About twice the size of the Atwater Market, this is also known as the "Italian Market," located as it is in the heart of Montreal's

"Little Italy." Otherwise it has much the same vegetables and other foodstuffs as the Atwater. Best time to
visit is from Thursday to Saturday. 7 a.m. to 5 p.m.
daily, Friday until 9 p.m. Closed Sunday. Not to be
missed are the neighborhood stores that stock everything you might expect to find in Rome or Naples.

Marché-Central: (Métro: Crémazie). Just above
Metropolitan Boulevard on L'Acadie is Montreal's
wholesale fruit and vegetable market. This is where the
supermarkets buy their stuff. They're not keen to sell
you a dozen oranges here, but if you want a couple of
sackfuls, that's a different matter. 7 a.m. to 3 p.m. Monday through Friday.

St. Lawrence Market: Just above Dorchester at 1195
St. Lawrence (St-Laurent). When the old outdoor
market was demolished in 1963, a group of merchants
simply moved indoors to what is now a meat and fish
market. Not to be overlooked here is **Enkin's,** one of
the city's leading importers of spices and exotic foodstuffs. And fresh fish daily, and in great variety, is to
be found at the **St. Lawrence Fish Company.** 7 a.m.
to 6 p.m. Monday through Friday, and until 5 p.m. on
Saturday.

Health Food Stores

Vogel Health Foods: Long-established, reliable
health food chain.

1186 St-Denis	861-9944
4191 St. Catherine West	933-1255
4960 Queen Mary Road	739-6130
Côte St-Luc Shopping Centre	488-3048
Jacques-Cartier Shopping Centre	674-1119
Carrefour Laval Shopping Centre	687-1698
Plaza Régional de Châteauguay	691-5331

Sandra's: Natural vitamins, teas, foods, cosmetics free of chemicals. 2055 Bishop (843-5070).

Miriam's Herbs and Health Foods: A family store that offers hundreds of different herbs, herbal teas and other herbal preparations, as well as packaged goods. 3677 St. Lawrence (844-2729).

Health Mission Santé: Whole foods, herbs, vitamins, granola, wide choice of teas. 1138 Bernard West (272-9386).

Naturex: Complete line of natural foods, also organically grown fresh fruit and vegetables, and frozen organic meat. Vitamins, books, cosmetics. 1125 Mont Royal East, corner de la Roche (526-5513).

Pural: Farm products, eggs, bread, vegetables, cereals, organic horticultural supplies. Extensive book department. 7494 St-Hubert (274-7979).

GALLERIES: PAINTINGS AND SCULPTURE

Most picture galleries are grouped on or around Sherbrooke Street West. Of those listed below, all are within easy walking distance of each other, and nearly all of them are open six days a week. Walking east from Peel Street, we begin with:

Walter Klinkhoff Gallery: Nineteenth-century Canadian and European painters. Krieghoff. "Group of Seven," plus modern Canadian and French works. Open Monday to Friday 9:30 a.m. to 5:30 p.m.; Saturday until 5 p.m. 1200 Sherbrooke West (288-7306).

Royal Gallery: Canadian paintings. Monday to Wednesday 9 a.m. to 6 p.m.; Thursday and Friday 9 a.m. to 9 p.m.; Saturday 9 a.m. to 5 p.m. 1420 Sherbrooke West (845-4383).

Galerie Moos: Contemporary Canadian, French, American paintings, sculpture, lithographs. Monday to

Saturday 9:30 a.m. to 5:30 p.m. 1430 Sherbrooke West (842-2747).

Lippel Gallery: Eskimo art: sculpture, prints, drawings; also African tribal art. Tuesday to Saturday 11 a.m. to 5:30 p.m. 1434 Sherbrooke West (842-6399).

Dominion Gallery: One of Canada's largest private galleries, and the only one with both a Rodin and a Henry Moore sculpture in front of it. Nineteenth- and twentieth-century Canadian, American, and European art. An outstanding gallery in every detail. Monday to Friday 9 a.m. to 5:30 p.m.; Saturday until 5 p.m. 1438 Sherbrooke West (845-7471).

Waddington Gallery: Eskimo sculpture in soapstone, calcite, and whalebone from the western and central Arctic. Contemporary and classic French, English, Canadian artists and sculptors. Tuesday to Friday 9:30 a.m. to 5:30 p.m.; Saturday until 4 p.m. 1456 Sherbrooke West (844-5455).

Marlborough-Godard: Twentieth-century international paintings, drawings, sculpture. Some fine young Canadian painters, but biggest strength of this gallery is in its outstanding collection of graphics. Tuesday to Saturday 10 a.m. to 5:30 p.m. 1490 Sherbrooke West (931-5841).

A cluster of galleries that should not be overlooked by the serious collector is to be found in the Crescent–Bishop Street area. Here is a guide to some of the most interesting ones:

Gallery B: Contemporary drawings and prints. Vehicule art. Leading modern American and Canadian artists. Upstairs at 2175 Crescent. Tuesday to Saturday 11 a.m. to 6 p.m. (844-6950).

Galerie Gilles Corbeil: Contemporary Canadian

and European artists. Tuesday to Saturday 10 a.m. to 5:30 p.m. 2165 Crescent (844-7174).

Galerie de l'Esprit: Interesting and imaginative selection of contemporary Canadian painters. Tuesday to Saturday 10 a.m. to 5 p.m. 2122 Crescent (845-5745).

Continental Galleries: Fine Canadian painting and sculptures. "Group of Seven" and their contemporaries. Monday to Friday 9:30 a.m. to 5:30 p.m.; Saturday 9:30 a.m. to 1 p.m. 1450 Drummond (842-1072).

Art Attic: Canadian and international graphics framed and matted at reasonable prices. Picasso lithographs $30 and up. 2185 Crescent.

Galerie Libre: Contemporary Quebec and Canadian artists and sculptors. Monday to Friday 10:30 a.m. to 6 p.m.; Saturday 10:30 a.m. to 5 p.m. 2100 Crescent (288-6080).

Galerie 1640: Canadian, U.S., Japanese, South American lithographs and watercolors. Tuesday to Saturday 11 a.m. to 5 p.m. 2175 Crescent (284-3112).

Galerie Gilles Gherbrant: Quebec and Canadian contemporary painting. Tuesday to Saturday 1 p.m. to 5:30 p.m. 2130 Crescent (843-7535).

Galerie Jeanne Newman: Always a fine place to discover up-and-coming Montreal artists. Tuesday to Saturday 10 a.m. to 5:30 p.m. 1452 Bishop (288-3653).

Elsewhere in the city you will find:

Vehicule Art: An avant-garde artists' cooperative with a gallery, modern dance, and "happenings." Tuesday to Saturday noon to 5:30 p.m.; Sunday until 5 p.m. 61 St. Catherine West (844-9623).

Galerie Martal: Some of the finest works of young Quebec potters, painters, sculptors, and tapestry-makers can be discovered here. Monday to Saturday 10 a.m. to 5 p.m. 1110 Sherbrooke West (845-2630).

Gallery Optica: The only gallery in Montreal specializing in photographic art. Tuesday to Saturday 10 a.m. to 9 p.m. 453 St-François-Xavier (844-9142).

Powerhouse Gallery: Both the familiar and the offbeat will be found in this third-floor gallery with its view of old roofs and poplar trees. Tuesday to Friday noon to 5 p.m.; Saturday 10 a.m. to 5 p.m. 3738 St-Dominique (844-4101).

Galerie André-Georges: Quebec and Canadian painting. Daily from noon to 11 p.m. 224 St-Paul West (845-3996).

Galerie Kostiner-Silvers: Contemporary Quebec and Canadian paintings, tapestries, lithographs. Tuesday to Saturday 11 a.m. to 5 p.m. 1374 Sherbrooke West (845-9239).

EYEGLASSES

There are hundreds of perfectly capable opticians available. Consult Yellow Pages for one nearest you. Recommended for prompt service and very reasonable prices: Simpson's, 977 St. Catherine West.

HAIRDRESSERS—WOMEN

The Montreal telephone book lists more than twelve columns of hairdressers, but of the more than 500 names, only half a dozen are at the top of the profession. Among these are: **La Coupe**, 1115 Sherbrooke West (288-6131); **Biba**, at Rive Gauche, 1254 St. Catherine West (866-3674); **René de Deauville**, 2330 Lucerne (735-1663); **Charles of Westmount**, Westmount Square (931-7251); **Henri Coiffure**, 1465 Crescent (844-1179). The going rate varies, but you can reckon between $15 and $25 for a cut and set, including tip.

HAIRDRESSERS—MEN

Among the most reliable are: **Place Ville-Marie Barber** shop; **Les Barbiers Bonaventure**, Place Bonaventure; **Hair Styling for Men** (Le Cartier), 1115 Sherbrooke West; **Hair People**, 1235 Crescent; **Émile**, Château Champlain; **Salon Michel-Ange**, 1276 St. Catherine East. Appointments are not necessary. Expect to spend between $5 and $10 for a razor or scissor cut and shampoo (including tip).

HOBBY AND MODEL CONSTRUCTION

Trainatorium: Model railroad enthusiast's haven. All makes, all gauges. Ships, planes, cars. They also do repairs. 5026 Sherbrooke West (487-4881).

International Hobbies: Wide range of kits of every description. Model trains, planes, boats, cars. Hobbyworker's tools. Supplies. Radio control equipment. Expert staff. 1626 St. Catherine West (937-3904).

Tandy Leather: Leather-workers' mecca, a branch of the well-known New York firm. 1224 Drummond (866-5144).

JEWELERS AND SILVERSMITHS

Henry Birks & Sons: Fine old Canadian firm. Long-established, reliable. Also stocks wide selection of gifts of every variety. 1240 Phillips Square (392-2511).

Gabriel Lucas: Partly owned by the Bronfman interests, and thus a fragment of a huge multinational empire. Highest reputation for superb quality jewels in magnificent settings. Imaginative gifts that cost plenty. 1 Westmount Square (937-0792) and 1476 Sherbrooke West (761-3421).

Hemsley's: Montreal's oldest diamond house. 660 St. Catherine West (866-3706).

Walter Schluep: One of Canada's finest artists. In the Cellini tradition, his modern pieces are collector's items. Phone for appointment. 1482 St. Catherine West (933-4495).

Hans Gehrig: Highly individual, one-of-a-kind pieces. Big, beautiful rings and semi-precious stones set in gold and silver. 1115 Sherbrooke West (843-5307).

KITCHEN EQUIPMENT

Helen Gougeon's Belle Cuisine: Quite the best of its kind in the city. Almost everything that a gourmet cook needs for his or her kitchen, from Sabatier knives to butcher blocks. There are magnificent tureens and paté crocks from France, and some excellent kitchen antiquities. 1200 Bishop (861-6751).

Leon Jung: Everything for the Chinese chef: woks, bamboo steamers, plus all the groceries. 999 Clark near Lagauchetière (861-9747).

Pol Martin's Kitchen Counter: Well-known Montreal chef offers choice selection of unique cookware. Great browsing. 2196 Crescent (844-3416).

LIQUORS AND SPIRITS

See page 57.

LOCKSMITHS

Bon-Ami: 24-hour service, Mr. Engel is on call for home, office, or automobiles. Phone 731-8116; at night, 739-3866.

National Locksmiths: 24-hour service. Home, office,

automobile locks. Phone 273-9396.

Able Locksmiths: City-wide day and night service (739-9300).

MAPS

Cartex: City wall maps of Montreal, plus handy pocket street guides. 1450 Marie Victoria (653-7831).

Government of Canada: Topographical, survey, and ordnance maps of every province. Information Canada Bookstore, 640 St. Catherine West (283-7877).

MUSIC

A & A Records: One of the largest stores of its kind in Canada. Pop, rock, classical. 1621 St. Catherine West (937-9579).

Dutchy's Record Cave: Considered to be the most potent influence on music in the city, Dutchy's supplies more than half of all the music played by discotheques and pop radio stations hereabouts. No carpets, just wall-to-wall music. 1238 Crescent (861-4303).

MUSICAL INSTRUMENTS

A walk along Craig Street West will bring you to a number of shops that sell new and secondhand musical instruments. One of the best-stocked is **Steve's Music Store**, 51 Craig West (878-2216). Another, well worth a look, is **Jack's**, 77 Craig West (861-6529).

NEWS DEALERS

Metropolitan News, 1248 Peel, below St. Catherine and near Dominion Square, is open 8 a.m. to midnight every day of the year. It stocks about fifty different Canadian dailies, plus the dailies from Chicago, Los Angeles, Paris, London, New York, and many other world cities (866-9227). **International News,** 2187 St. Catherine West (937-0474), has a wide selection of out-of-town newspapers, plus a wide choice of international magazines and literary quarterlies. **Wolfe's News Depot,** 1257 Guy (935-7044), is also a good bet.

All of the major hotels carry *The New York Times* and the *Wall Street Journal.* Especially well stocked with out-of-town newspapers is the Sheraton–Mount Royal. Finally, for English periodicals and newspapers, **W. H. Smith & Sons,** 1004 St. Catherine West.

PHOTOGRAPHY
Equipment

Montreal prices tend to be lower than Europe's, but, unfortunately, higher than New York's. One reason is stiff import duties; another, a tendency to "fair-trade," meaning fair trade for the dealer, a tough deal for you the customer. All the same, if you have your eye on a Nikon or a Hasselblad, most salespersons (except in the big department stores) are willing to negotiate. The big five camera stores in Montreal are: **Centre Professional de la Photographie,** 6324 Sherbrooke East, in the city's East End (255-6171); they stock just about every known make of camera. **L. R. Viala,** 1280 Maisonneuve East, also in the East End, near Amherst (526-2535). **NDG Photo Supply,** 1197 Phillips Square (facing The Bay, 866-8761), also 5488 Sherbrooke West (489-8401); good range of equipment, knowledgeable staff; they rent, repair, and allow one-month trial with exchange if you're not satisfied. **Simon's Cameras,** 11 Craig West, near Clark (861-5401); wide selection of both new and secondhand equipment. **Mitchell Photo Supply,** 1015 Dominion Square (866-4032); one of the most conveniently located stores for the midtown visitor; well respected, long established, with helpful sales staff; they also do printing, developing. **Montreal Photo Centre** has five locations—1101 St. Catherine West, Place Ville-Marie, Place Bonaventure, 2020 University, and (for camera repairs as well) 1481 St. Catherine West.

Worth noting are the names of several specialist dealers. Hasselblad owners will find rentals, sales, and service available at **Photo-Kina Technic,** 595 Maisonneuve West (849-9386); Rollei users should also visit this store. In addition, all the major department stores have photographic departments, the best among them being **Eaton's,** 677 St. Catherine West.

Printing and Enlarging

Most drugstores take film and they generally return prints in about a week. For faster service, try any of the camera stores listed above. A chain operation that we have used with entirely satisfactory results for both color and black-and-white is **Direct Film,** which has branches in almost every corner of the city. For the one nearest you, call 374-4200. At **Maxi Photo,** 4284 de la Roche (526-3263), they're experts in super-sized blow-ups and photo murals.

Repairs

Camerasound Repair: cameras, flash equipment, exposure meters. 1255 Phillips Square (861-0804).

The Camera Clinic: 620 Cathcart (861-4444).

Camera Technic: 140 Crémazie West (388-8334).

E.F. Camera Craft: Leica, Nikon, Linhof, Hassel-blad, Compur specialists. 4265 St. Catherine West (935-2348).

SAUNAS AND STEAM BATHS

You can obtain both kinds of heat in Montreal, dry and steam. For those who prefer the dry Finnish method, there are **Finnish Massage,** 1117 St. Catherine West (844-1439), and **Sonastek** (men only), 173 St. Catherine East (845-1738). **Sauna Neptune** (men only), 456 La Gauchetière (871-9522), is open 24 hours a day, offers both Turkish and sauna baths, whirlpool, gymnasium, swimming pool, and massage room. One of the best-known Turkish baths—old-fashioned, very cheery steamy atmosphere—is to be found at the **Colonial Turkish Baths,** 3963 Colonial (285-0132). They offer a Ladies Day each Tuesday from 1 p.m. to 10 p.m.

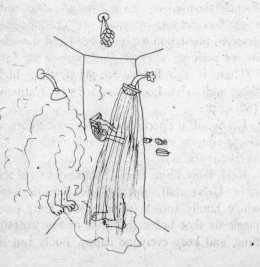

SECRETARIAL SERVICES

Anne Leach Reg'd.: Résumés, manuscripts, theses, executive typing, duplicating and bookkeeping service. 1117 St. Catherine West (288-3795).

The Business Centre: Private offices available. Typing, telephone answering, Telex, and photocopying. 2121 Trans-Canada Highway, near Airport (684-6944).

Your Secretary: One of the largest operations of its kind in Montreal. Bilingual secretarial service. Telephone answering, typing, translation, copying, simultaneous translation. 3422 Durocher (849-6466, 849-2897).

Tape Recording Center: Tape recordings for conferences. 5239 Park (276-7477).

SHOES

Betty's for Ladies: *Le dernier cri* in Italian and French shoemaking. Expect to pay $60 and up for shoes, $90 and upwards for boots. This store has a well-deserved reputation for being head and shoulders above its competition. 1237 St. Catherine West (288-8013).

There is also **Betty's for Men,** same high-quality shoes and styles. Located at 1018 St. Catherine West (861-4058).

Dr. Scholl's: Specialists in foot care. Shoes, supports, clogs, exercise sandals, foot aids. 1801 St. Catherine West (935-6629).

Real Tony Shoe Shop: Westmount's most lovable store. Great staff, especially on Saturdays when the whole family comes for a tryout. Tony manages to juggle six shoe boxes and three or four customers at a time, and keep everyone happy. Boots and shoes for entire family. They also repair while you wait. 1346 Greene (935-2993).

Bally: Exclusive shoes for men and women. Several outlets: Place Bonaventure, 767 St. Catherine West, 1 Westmount Square (931-4622).

Bata Shoes: Large stock of men's and women's shoes at reasonable prices. 1021 St. Catherine West, Place Bonaventure, Alexis Nihon Plaza (933-1224).

Earth Shoes: One product only; the negative heel shoe designed by Anne Kalsø of Copenhagen. If you can get used to them, they're supposed to improve your posture. 1427 Stanley (842-5885).

Roots: Naturally contoured shoes. 2065 Bishop (843-5995).

SHOESHINE

It is, alas, almost impossible to find a shoeshine stand in this city. One of the few places left is in the Queen Elizabeth Hotel, Lower Level.

SPORTS EQUIPMENT

Arlington Sports: One of the biggest outfitters in the city. Always worth checking for bargains in skis and ski equipment (a very competitive business in Montreal). Also archery, track and field, fencing, most other sports. Camping equipment, and wide range of shoes and clothing. Outlets at:

1410 Stanley (midtown) 288-0181
7201 Les Galeries d'Anjou 353-9000
West Island Mall 683-8400

The head office is at 845 Plymouth, Town of Mount Royal (731-3546).

The Mountain Hut: Considered by many to be *the* sports store. Friendly, chatty, informal atmosphere. Knowledgeable staff. Message board. Every possible type of outdoor equipment in stock. Especially strong in ski and mountain-climbing gear, but good in almost every other department as well. 1324A Sherbrooke West (842-2851).

Murray and Company: Long-established; extremely knowledgeable staff. Excellent choice of sporting goods. Hockey players' mecca. 1440 McGill College (842-9401).

Peel Cycle Centre: Getaway gear of every variety. Essentially for the nonprofessional outdoorsman. Bicycles, canoes, backpacks, hiking boots, cross-country skis, snowshoes. Bicycle and ski rentals. 1398 Sherbrooke West, corner Bishop (844-8606).

Siren Ski Shop: Very friendly, very knowledgeable shop that is particularly good for cross-country skiing enthusiasts. Mrs. Siren, a Finn, knows everything worth knowing about skiing, and is usually on hand to give expert advice. Downhill, touring, racing skis, plus repairs and rentals. 6131 Sherbrooke West (482-2734).

STAMPS

AHV Stamps: Stamps and catalogues. Large selection, from new issues to classics. 2015 Drumond (845-2853).

F. G. Atkinson: British Colonial and Commonwealth stamps from Queen Victoria to Queen Elizabeth. Albums and supplies. 3300 Cavendish (486-4906).

Harnat Stamp Company: Auctioneers and dealers. Canada and B.N.A. Specialist in covers. 2615 Van Horne (733-2684).

J. Reisz: Stamps of the world. 4629 Park (843-7213).

TATTOOING

International Tattooing Studio: Sir Winston Churchill's mother had one, and so did Janis Joplin. If you would like to join the club, the skin-deep art is still practiced in Montreal. 1011 St. Lawrence (St-Laurent), below Dorchester Boulevard (866-6070).

TELEPHONE ANSWERING SERVICE

TAS: Long-established, reliable, 24-hour service. 640 Cathcart (866-6921).

TELEVISION—RENTALS

A most competitive business in this city. It will be well worth your while to comparison-shop for the best possible deal. Here is a brief listing of some of the most reliable firms:

Granada TV: One of the largest in the city. Prompt service, satisfaction guaranteed. No deposit required, and no service or maintenance. 7413 St-Hubert (274-7765).

Colorvision: Like Granada, this is an international company. Special rates for senior citizens. 1502 St. Catherine West (935-6563).

Inter-City TV: 24-hour delivery. No deposit. Free delivery. 4988 Pide la Savanne (342-4545).

TOBACCO

As befits a city that prides itself on its enjoyment of the finer things of life, cigar-smokers and serious pipe enthusiasts are well provided for. All of the major hotels possess excellent tobacco shops, the best among them being located in the Queen Elizabeth. Here you will find all the great cigars of Cuba and Brazil, perfectly kept in humidors. Easily the finest cigar emporium in the city is

Dunhill Humidor: 977 St. Catherine West. On the ground floor of Simpson's. Upmann, Ramon Allones, Montecristo, Hoya de Monterey are among the best-known names. They can be bought singly or by the box. Cuban cigars are expensive, of course. Expect to pay from 75 cents up to $5.00 for a Churchill-sized beauty. Remember that Cuban cigars are not allowed into the United States (although this situation may change).

Henri Poupart Ltd.: 1331 St. Catherine West (near Crescent). Another fine shop. Although there is an ample selection of cigars, cigarette- and pipe-smokers make up the bulk of the trade. The choice among cigarettes is truly astonishing. Whether you are from Helsinki or Bangkok, chances are good that your favorite brand will be available. As for pipe tobaccos, there are literally hundreds to choose among. Every great British and European name is stocked, as well as a wide assortment of American tobaccos. The walls are lined with pipes, ranging from modestly priced corncobs to elegant Charetons that cost upwards of $150.

Dan's Tobacco Shop: 2025 Union. The pipeman's Nirvana. Dan Spiegel, the owner, has spent a lifetime not only selling (and smoking) pipes, but also studying their history.

Finally, no discussion of tobacco merchants would be complete without reference to the thriving

L. Robichaud: 435 Craig West. Heavy smokers, as

distinct from *aficionados*, are attracted here by the low prices. The store does a land office business in mail orders, selling this way to more than 3,000 regular customers. If you're looking for a 20-cent cigar with some Cuban content, this is the only place in town to find it. All the same, don't expect it to compare with a $2 Ramon Allones.

TOYS AND GAMES

Dominion Play World: A tremendous selection of almost every kind of toy for every age group. Place Bonaventure (861-5161).

Toy World: For your run-of-the-mill type of mass-produced toys. Place Ville-Marie (866-1992).

The Toy Box: Don't go here for the standard items (they'll cost more). Do go here for the unusual, the imported goodies from England and Scandinavia. Good selection of educational toys. 1 Westmount Square (931-4545).

Ogilvy's: The basement of this department store is the place to take the kids (and there's a handy cafeteria right next to the toys). Standard children's toys, to be sure, but the prices are right, and they don't mind the youngsters trying everything out. Corner of St. Catherine and Mountain (842-7711).

Holt Renfrew: For rich uncles or aunts who want something well made and one-of-a-kind, try the fifth floor. Of course, it will be expensive, but will probably last forever. Sherbrooke Street, corner Mountain (842-5111).

La Boutique Gabriel Filion: Probably Montreal's best toy shop. Sturdy and imaginative toys from all over the world. Also children's books and some furniture. Down a flight of stairs at 1378 Sherbrooke West (843-8421).

Eating and Drinking

Menu

LA CUISINE EST
UN ART DIFFICILE;
SACHEZ ATTENDRE
— Curnonsky

Half the fun of being in Montreal, of course, is going to the restaurants. There are more than 5,000, and at least 500 of them are in the well-worth-a-visit category. It is hardly an exaggeration to say that you can eat almost as well here as you can in Paris, and little wonder—that's where many of Montreal's best-known chefs learned their profession.

Although there are countless Italian, Greek, Polish, Hungarian, Russian, and other ethnic eating places in this city, it is (needless to say) *le restaurant français* that dominates the gastronomic scene. If you are nostalgic for the good little bistro where you could dine on a rosy *gigot* of lamb with *haricots*, or frog's legs Provençal, Montreal is the place to go, this side of the Atlantic. As a matter of fact, we hear that today Parisians are succumbing to *le quick-lunch*—which, if true, may account for the considerable influx of French chefs, rôtisseurs, sauciers, and pastry cooks into Quebec in recent years. Certainly Montrealers have not followed suit: this remains a city where leisurely dining is the rule rather than the exception, and where business is transacted "between the pear and the cheese." Shortly after the Angelus is played at noon on Notre-Dame's clanging bells, business comes to a fitful halt and does not really pick up speed again until after 3 p.m., when the last stragglers reappear in their offices.

A particularly attractive aspect of Montreal dining is the hospitality with which guests are treated. Every restaurant mentioned in this book is worth at least three stars for its good manners (even if not in all other respects), and you will find that there is little or none of that you-can't-drink-red-wine-with-fish snobbery, so irritating elsewhere. It is presumed that you know what you are ordering, and if you have any questions, your waiter is glad to offer advice. Menus, you will find, are almost always printed in both French and English, and English is universally spoken and understood.

THE CUISINE

Montreal is a fabulous place to sample the first three of the four branches of French cookery, as defined by Curnonsky, the great gastronome and writer: *la haute cuisine, la cuisine bourgeoise,* and *la cuisine régionale.* (His fourth category, *la cuisine improvisée,* need not concern us.) The list of restaurants that you will find on pages 200–29 has been carefully chosen to provide the widest possible choice among the three.

Once you have grasped Curnonsky's neat definition, it will readily be understood that although, say, La Marée, Chez Pierre, and Les Filles du Roy are all French restaurants, their respective menus invite you to quite different gastronomic experiences. **La Marée's** Pierre Garcin offers *la haute cuisine,* that is to say, food that is elaborately prepared, and enriched by the art of the saucier. I've had some memorable meals in La Marée—particularly noteworthy is M. Garcin's *turbot à la Parisienne,* a snowy white fish braised in a white wine sauce and decorated with tiny morsels of lobster, mushrooms, truffles, and *quenelles* so light they dissolve on the tongue.

At **Chez Pierre,** on the other hand, you must not expect to find such great, traditional set-pieces. The snowy white tablecloths complement well-prepared middle-class French cookery; it's the kind of food that goes nicely with a glass of unpretentious table wine, and represents *la cuisine bourgeoise* at its finest.

At **Les Filles du Roy**, you find *la cuisine régionale*, home-style *québécois* cooking served by waiters and waitresses in traditional costumes. In a cheerful rustic atmosphere the guests dine on such typical Quebec fare as *ragoût de boulettes* (meatball stew), *tourtière* (meat pie), and duck cooked in maple syrup.

The restaurants that *I* enjoy the most in Montreal are on what the French call *le circuit bourgeois*; they are modest in price, and one is often agreeably surprised by the chef's specialty of the day. Among such places are Le Chalutier, Le Mazot, Chez Pierre, Le Colibri, and the Auberge St-Tropez, and in them you will rub shoulders with "real Montrealers" who come to enjoy, not so much the ambiance, as the plain, well-prepared meals that indicate a real cook is in the kitchen. In such establishments you will not find *scampis à l'absinthe* on the menu; what you *will* discover are such hearty dishes as *langue de boeuf aux champignons* (beef tongue in mushroom sauce), *cotelettes de porc au cidre* (pork chops braised in cider), *coq au vin* (chicken stewed in a wine sauce), and *bourride*, the garlicky fish soup of Provence. At lunch, such a meal, accompanied by a *carafon* of wine, will usually cost less than $6.

Montrealers follow the French habit of dining, preferring the hors d'oeuvres to be eaten as a stimulus to the palate, and accompanied by an aperitif such as kir (white wine and cassis), rather than a hard liquor that dulls the taste buds. Typically, you will find *tomates tranchées* (thinly sliced tomatoes in oil and vinegar with a little chopped parsley sprinkled over them), *crudités* (olives, radishes, and celery sticks dressed with oil, lemon, and seasoning), *artichauts vinaigrette* (artichokes with a vinegary dressing), a slice of pâté, or *champignons à la grècque* (mushrooms stewed in olive oil, with lemon and Mediterranean seasonings).

Your choice of entrees in any Montreal restaurant will be more extensive than in any other Canadian city. Nevertheless, even the finest restaurants tend to be lazy, and most menus feature a cluster of "old reliables" such as *canard à l'orange* (duck in orange sauce), *poulet rôti* (roast chicken), and *boeuf bourguignon* (beef stew in red wine). My recommendation is, don't be so easily satisfied. Before ordering, ask your waiter a question or two: what is the specialty of the house? the *spécial du jour*? In any good restaurant, he will be more than pleased to help you make your choice.

To complete a fine meal, you should order cheese *followed* by dessert, as in France. Such a pause provides a rest for the palate and for the stomach. Oka is Quebec's great cheese. It is made by the Trappist fathers in Oka, Quebec, and will remind you of France's Port Salut, soft and creamy with a distinctive taste.

Almost every French restaurant in town serves *crême caramel*—custard baked in caramel—and there is usually a house pastry. If you want a soufflé for dessert, decide on this and order it when you first sit down—it takes considerable time to prepare.

PRICES, HOURS, RESERVATIONS

Dining out—as opposed to eating out—is not cheap. In Montreal, a couple can expect to pay anywhere from $20 at a bone minimum to $50 and up at one of the top restaurants. A particular point to note is the wide availability of a *prix fixe* lunch: at noontime you can visit the finest dining establishments in Montreal and find the bill coming to less than half the cost of a meal after dark. The smaller menu usually includes hors d'oeuvres, entree, one vegetable, dessert or cheese, and

coffee. Visitors interested in economizing might wish
to consider making lunch the main meal of the day,
thus taking the opportunity to sample the great restaurants at that hour, and making a more modest choice
for the evening meal.

Most restaurants are open for lunch between the
hours of 12 noon and 3 p.m., and for dinner from 6
p.m. to midnight or 1 a.m. Everyone seems to choose
8 p.m. for their dinner reservations, so you will be
doing yourself a favor if you dine before or after the
rush hour; keep in mind also that some restaurants have
two dinner "sittings," one early, one late. Reservations
are important in Montreal, they are scrupulously hon-
ored, and the scruples should be reciprocal. Should you
change your mind at the last moment, do call the
restaurant.

Wine is expensive in most restaurants (a sore point
with Montrealers) and the selection is not as wide as
you would find in, say, London or New York. During
the lunch hour most establishments sell wine *en carafe*,
but the *carafons* disappear at twilight, limiting your
choice to the *carte du vin*.

DRINK

You can drink in four kinds of places in Montreal:
taverns, brasseries, bars, and pubs.

Taverns and Brasseries

Taverns are an antiquated throwback to the days
when women weren't supposed to drink in public at all.
By law, a woman cannot enter a tavern, and the tavern-
keeper can (and might) throw out a woman who tries.

Each year there are fewer and fewer taverns around. Most of them either have or are about to convert to (co-ed) brasseries. Among the few of these bulwarks of male chauvinism remaining, easily the best is **Magnan's**, on the corner of St. Patrick and Charlevoix in Point St. Charles. Yves Magnan, one of the owners, is a city councilor, and his mother (who can't enter the tavern proper) works the kitchen at the rear, serving up some of the best short-order cooking in Montreal at rock-bottom prices. **Rymark's**, 1201 Peel, is another popular spot, famed for its pig's knuckle blue plate special; and at least three generations of college students have done time in the **Mansfield**, on the street of the same name, above Maisonneuve. "The Mans" (rhymes with "dance") is one of McGill University's landmarks.

A brasserie is a tavern that has been liberated by women, and there are around fifty of them now in Montreal, with the number increasing yearly. Easily the best one in town is **Le Gobelet**, 8405 St-Laurent (Métro: Jarry), which offers excellent Quebec-style cooking in surroundings that emphasize Quebec's past. In summer, the rooftop terrace is open. **Brasserie des Fortifications**, 262 St-Paul East in Old Montreal, serves solid and simple fare in a pleasant setting. One of the cheapest places to dine in Montreal is the **Brasserie Bonaventure**, 735 Mansfield. Along with the draft beer, you can get a nicely done rib steak here for under $3.

Licensing hours for brasseries and taverns are from 8 a.m. to midnight, Monday through Saturday. Closed Sunday, legal holidays, and election days.

Pubs and Bars

Taverns and bars have always been part of the Montreal scene, but it's the pubs nowadays that are the boom industry in the realm of public drinking—a reflection of the growing prosperity of Quebec and a changing life-style. Middle-class in the extreme, they cater to the after-5 office crowd. No tavern habitué would be seen dead in a pub (and, indeed, many pubs station bouncers at the door to make sure "tavern types" keep out). The greatest concentration of pubs occurs on or within a stone's throw of Crescent Street. By 11 p.m. most evenings it is difficult to squeeze into the trendier places. Nearly all pubs, with few exceptions, open around 2 p.m., and close around 3 a.m., Sundays included.

Most pubs do sell liquor, of course, but it is beer that is consumed in quantity. Among the more popular Montreal beers are Molson's, Labatt's "50" (ask for a "cinquante"), Laurentide, and Brador—the last-named reputed to be the strongest beer brewed in Quebec, and sold only in bottles. You can also find such foreign beers as Carlsberg (brewed locally under license), Tuborg, Heineken's, Löwenbrau, Guinness, Watney's, and McEwan's Strong Ale.

As elsewhere, it is the customers that both reflect and embody the essential character of the pub. The **Sir Winston Churchill**, on Crescent Street above St. Catherine, with its multiple bars and oak paneling, is always packed. Actors, stockbrokers, newspapermen, sophisticates and would-be sophisticates congregate here. Singles predominate, as this is a good place to meet people. **Thursday's**, a couple of doors down from the Sir Winston, is where you find singles galore, in a very mod chrome-and-leather setting with a background of hard rock music. The young crowd, mainly undergraduates from McGill and Concordia University, gather at the **John Bull Pub**, 120 Maisonneuve West; the **St. James Pub**, Drummond above Maisonneuve, which has another branch on University above Dorchester; **Tiffany's**, Crescent above Maisonneuve; and the **Bistro**, Mountain above Maisonneuve.

The **Rainbow Bar & Grill** (1430 Stanley) is an entertainment bar and restaurant that features live music Monday, Tuesday, and Wednesday, and free movies on the weekend. The management runs a "Happy Hour" (two beers for the price of one) from 5 to 6 p.m. daily. **The Hunter's Horn,** Peel above Dorchester, is a cheery Irish pub which attracts a gregarious late-twenties–early-thirties type crowd. Mahogany bar and fine collection of Irish political pamphlets. Reporters from the *Gazette* frequent **Mother Martin's**, 980 St-Antoine. Beyond the bar is a large restaurant that serves corned beef and cabbage and similar hearty fare, and there is always live entertainment, English music hall songs and Irish ballads. Painters, poets, and would be revolutionaries are at home in the **Hotel Nelson** bar, Place Jacques-Cartier in Old Montreal. Live folk and rock music are the background. The **Iroquois** across the street is equally lively; the jargon of the motorcycle fraternity provides the background talk. TV and radio types from the Maison du Radio-Canada across the street favor the bar at **Le Script,** Dorchester and Wolfe. You can sit at the small bar, or at one of the tables that line the wall beneath the TV set.

Fashion models, dress designers, and photographers prefer the elegant, intimate green surroundings of **Le Vert Galant**, Crescent above St. Catherine, or (especially during the day) **Thursday's**, already mentioned. The upwardly mobile gather nightly at the **Ritz-Carlton,**

Sherbrooke at Mountain. Ambiance and decor un-hurried, quiet and pleasant. Advertising and PR types crowd **Oliver's**, Crescent below Maisonneuve, and **Cafe Martin's** well-upholstered downstairs bar, Mountain below Sherbrooke. Top Business People entertain out-of-towners in the bar at **Alti-théque 737**, Dorchester at University, with its magnificent sunset view of the city.

Among the better-known Gay male spots are the **Rocambole**, 1426 Stanley; the **Limelight**, Stanley above Dorchester; **Bud's**, 1250 Stanley; and the **Apollo**, 5116 Park Avenue. Transvestites, and people who like to look at transvestites, head for **Le Saguenay**, St-Laurent below Dorchester. Hockey players, sports writers, and almost everyone who's anyone in the world of sports rub elbows at **Butch Bouchard's**, 881 Maisonneuve East, or the **Bar-B-Barn**, 1201 Guy.

Whether you're alone or with friends, one of the pleasantest places in town is **L'Escapade**, on the 36th floor of the Château Champlain. It's also a great spot to watch a sunset. The upholstered bar is a cheerful elbow-to-elbow place for conversation, and the tables by the huge windows look out on a glittering view of the city.

Out-of-towners in search of fun usually find it at **La Sexe Machine**, Crescent below Maisonneuve, which features topless waiters as well as topless waitresses. **Le Carrefour**, Place Ville-Marie, known to its regulars as "The Swamp," is popular among the young business crowd who work in P.V.M. Freddie Langan, bachelor and well-known man-about-town, claims more male-female contacts are made here than in any other spot in Montreal. According to Langan, the expression used by both sexes is, "Let's go alligator-hunting at The Swamp."

The Pescatore Bar at **Le Tour Eiffel**, Stanley below Maisonneuve, has a unique atmosphere. Patronized by

middle-aged swingers, divorcees, and some of the most interesting characters in Montreal.

The best *kir* (white-wine-and-cassis aperitif) in town is mixed in the tiny downstairs bar of **Le St-Amable**, Rue St-Amable in Old Montreal. Decor is Quebec pine and brocade. The best Irish or Spanish coffee is served in the sawdust-strewn **Barnsider** on Guy below Sherbrooke. Ian MacDonald, a *Gazette* columnist who has extensively field-researched the subject, declares emphatically that the best martini is poured in the **Golden Hind** bar in the Queen Elizabeth Hotel. The best "French '75" (champagne and gin) is blended at the **Sir Winston Churchill Pub**.

If I had to choose the six best drinking spots in Montreal—necessarily excluding several that others would almost certainly include—they would be: L'Escapade in the Château Champlain; the Sir Winston Churchill Pub, Crescent Street; the Rainbow Bar & Grill, Stanley Street; The Hunter's Horn, Peel Street; the Maritime Bar in the Ritz-Carlton; and the downstairs bar in Thursday's, Crescent Street.

RESTAURANTS

I have used a rating system of four stars to none to express my overall judgment of each of the establishments described below. All such ratings, needless to say, involve a substantial element of subjectivity; in any given instance, it is almost inevitable that one person will see, say, three stars in the culinary heavens where another can espy only one. Nevertheless, the effort seemed worthwhile for the sake of whatever guidance it may offer the reader.

Elegant and Expensive

****CHEZ BARDET · 591 *Henri Bourassa Blvd.*

381-1777. Closed Sunday. Reservations advisable. Credit cards: AE, DC, and Chx

Everything about Bardet's is superb—easily the city's finest restaurant. Dishes are typical of the French *haute cuisine* repertoire, and they are done with extraordinary finesse. For hors d'oeuvres, try *les escargots à la mode de Saulieu;* for an entree, a beautiful steak *à la Cler-*

mont, smothered with a *duxelles* of finely chopped mushrooms, bound with cream, or salmon when it is in season, grilled over fennel twigs and served with shallot butter. I particularly like the *carré d'agneau,* a rack of lamb served with puffed potatoes and *haricots* (reserve this dish ahead of time). For dessert, the splendid *soufflé au Gran Marnier* is sufficient for four, and the *meringue Chantilly* is equally magnificent. Only the host at the table will receive a menu with the prices listed. Although dinner for two will cost around $50–$60 with wine, there is a generous *table d'hôte* that includes a half-bottle of wine, for under $20 per person. Incidentally, don't take a taxi to Bardet's—it'll cost a fortune. Use the No. 2 line Métro; the restaurant is next door to the Henri Bourassa station (last stop).

***LE ST-AMABLE ·
199 Rue St-Amable, at Place Jacques-Cartier
866-3471.   Open every day.   Reservations advisable.
Credit cards: AE, CB, DC, Chx

Situated in the heart of Old Montreal; the narrow alley entrance is a reminder of bygone days. Inside, the scene is early Canadiana, with pine furniture and soft lights. The food is classic *grande cuisine,* and you must have patience, because it does take time. Chef Garcin is justly proud of his *caille à la mode landaise* (roast quail stuffed with *foie gras,* served with a mouth-watering grape sauce) and his pheasant for two. Outstanding also are the seafood crêpes and the *soufflé Armorique* made of sole, lobster, and truffle mousse. The long, narrow room can seem crowded, but the service is polished and courteous, and the wine list adequate.

Dinner for two, with wine, $50–$60. A simplified *à la carte* and *table d'hôte* luncheon can be had at about one-third the dinner price.

***CHEZ LA MÈRE MICHEL ·

1209 Guy St., betw. St. Catherine and Dorchester

934-0473. Closed Sundays. Reservations advisable.
Credit cards: AE, DC

Not the most expensive of the deluxe restaurants, but
certainly the pleasantest, if you care for ambiance, polite
and efficient service, and well-prepared food. The
owners, the Delbuguets (she is "la mére Michel"), have
put their souls and hearts into their establishment, and
their menu is like no other in the city. It is hard to
choose between their *filet de sole normandine* (which
is *really* sole and not whiting) and their lobster soufflé
and their *lapin Archiduc* (rabbit in a white wine sauce
—and a great favorite of mine). For dessert, the house
specialty is a *mille-feuille*, extremely thin layers of puff
pastry alternated with fresh strawberries. The wine list
is excellent.

Dinner for two, with wine, $35–$40.

***LE FADEAU ·

423 St-Claude St., betw. Notre-Dame and St-Paul

878-3959. Open every day. Reservations advisable.
Credit cards: AE, CB, DC, Chx

I keep coming back here with out-of-town guests. Located in Old Montreal, this is one of the most beautiful
and comfortable dining rooms in the city, with its
white walls, tapestry-upholstered chairs, candlelit tables.
The service is faultless; the menu aspires to the dignity
of *grande cuisine* (for instance, there is a lobster gratin
named after the famous French chef Fernand Point).
Here the chef is especially talented with game and
poultry (crisp duckling cooked with apples and prunes
in a slivovitz sauce; roast quail; pheasant *à la* Souvaroff).

Meat dishes include a rack of lamb for two, served pink in the French style with all nine *bouquetière* vegetables (tomato, celery, spinach, green beans, white asparagus tips, rissolé potatoes, carrots, artichoke hearts, and cauliflower). The wine list is one of the best in Montreal, with many good ones available in half-bottles. Menu fairly expensive.

Dinner for two, with wine, about $50.

***HÉLÈNE DE CHAMPLAIN · *St. Helen's Island*

873-2373. Open every day. Reservations advisable.
Credit cards: AE, DC, CB, Chx

A delightful restaurant, owned and operated by the city of Montreal—a showcase of Quebec *gastronomie*. Located in the middle of the St. Lawrence River, with breathtaking views from the windows (after dining, you can stroll around the tiny island), it is only 10–15 minutes away from midtown by taxi or subway. The menu is exceptionally good, with numerous regional dishes available (ask about the specialty of the day), ranging from Brome Lake duckling to lobster from the Madeleines. A remarkable choice of wines, offered at the most reasonable prices to be found in Montreal. And you dine in baronial splendor in surroundings reminiscent of an old French hunting lodge. Lunch daily between 12 noon and 2 p.m.; in the evening there are two dinner sittings, at 6 and 8 p.m., and you must be punctual.

Dinner for two, with wine, $35–$45.

***LE VERT GALANT · 1423 *Crescent St.*

844-4155. Open every day. Reservations advisable.
Credit cards: AE, CB, DC, Chx

Très chic, this may be the most romantic restaurant in Montreal. The waiters seem to glide through the candlelight, and the immaculately set tables, arranged in a series of well-upholstered nooks and crannies, are perfect for deep and private talk. Chef Jean Lebrun, one of Montreal's finest culinary artists, gives you a choice range from *soufflé de homard Nantua* to stuffed turbot poached in champagne. For four or more, he will create a special dinner (48 hours' notice required). After dinner, there is a disco-club for those who want to keep the evening going.

Dinner for two, with wine, around $40–$50.

LES HALLES · *1450 Crescent St.*

844-2328.   Closed Sunday.   Reservations advisable.
Credit cards: AE, CB, DC, MC, Chx

Enormously popular with the "in" crowd of divorcees, businessmen, PR types, and so forth, this is certainly a most attractively decorated spot—fashioned after a restaurant of this type in the wholesale market of Paris. The cashier sits in a birdcage, wine bottles are in racks along the downstairs wall, there are Parisian street signs everywhere, and the waiters bustle about in black jackets, white vests, and long white aprons. The food, although well prepared, is not imaginative: snails, omelettes, soups, and casseroles and grilled steaks. And the chairs are hard and uncomfortably close to your neighbors'.

Dinner for two, with wine, $35–$40.

GIBBY'S · 298 *Place d'Youville (Old Montreal)*

844-8495. Open every day. Reservations desirable.
Credit cards: AE, CB, DC, MC, Chx

A cheerful, cozy place to dine, Gibby's occupies the ground floor of a meticulously restored 200-year-old building. The room is splendid, with its wide, polished pine floors, exposed beams, and stone walls, and the seating arrangements—Windsor chairs and well-spaced tables—are comfortable. The menu is not exciting, limited as it is to such familiar favorites as filet mignon, shrimps *provençale*, Dover sole, scampi, chicken-in-the-basket, and various cuts of steak; but everything is carefully prepared. The service is pleasant, with occasional lapses. Wine can be purchased by the bottle or by the measured carafe.

Dinner for two, with wine, $35–$45.

GUINGUETTE LES TROIS · 273 *St-Paul East*

866-5311. Open every day. Reservations desirable.
Credit cards: AE, CB, DC, MC, Chx

If you are visiting Old Montreal and wish to enjoy lunch in pleasant surroundings, Guinguette les Trois can be recommended. It occupies a 200-year-old building at the foot of Place Jacques-Cartier. The main dining room, with its beamed ceiling and pine floors, is extremely attractive. Service is attentive and the bill of fare adequate, and at noon moderate in price; but at night it is a different matter—far more elaborate, with entrees ranging in price from $7 to $15. In addition, the restaurant is somewhat stuffy at night, making the small dining rooms seem overcrowded—and all the tableside *flambées* don't help. Also, the excellent house wine by the carafe is unavailable at night and the wine list is expensive.

Dinner for two, with wine, $40–$50.

** LE MAS DES OLIVIERS · 1216 *Bishop St.*

861-6733.   Closed Sunday.   Reservations advisable.
Credit cards: DC, CB, Chx

This is a delightful and invariably crowded restaurant
with an excellent kitchen. The cuisine has a strong
Provençal flavor, and dishes such as sea bass flambéed
over fennel twigs and snails are very well prepared here.
Charming decor and polished service.

Dinner for two, with wine, $35–$45.

*** RITZ-CARLTON (LE CAFÉ DE PARIS AND MARITIME BAR) · 1226–28 *Sherbrooke St. West*

842-4212.   Open every day.   Reservations desirable.
Credit cards: AE, CB, DC, MC, Chx

The incomparable Chef Pierre Demers has made the
dining rooms here without question amongst the finest
in Montreal—or anywhere else, for that matter. Two
places to dine well in the Ritz (downstairs is a more
ordinary restaurant) are Le Café de Paris and the
Maritime Bar, each with its particular following. Le
Café de Paris is off the main entrance, and you dine in
high-ceilinged splendor on *filet de sole à la Ritz, scampi
à l'absinthe,* and, of course, Chef Demers's *crêpes aux
crabes*—fish and crustaceans being his specialty, although there is also a fine choice of meat and poultry
dishes. Monday to Wednesday there is a pianist; Thursday to Saturday a trio provides music for dinner dancing. The Maritime Bar has a marine decor, and is
always crowded. Try the lobster bisque which tastes as
though an entire lobster has been reduced for one
bisque. Everything on the menu is beautifully prepared,
but you should ask the waiter for the specialty of the
day. Following the English custom, the Maritime Bar
also offers late-night snacks at a reasonable price.

Dinner for two, with wine, $50 and up.

*** QUEEN ELIZABETH (BEAVER CLUB) ·
900 Dorchester Blvd. West

861-3511. Open every day. Reservations desirable.
Credit cards: AE, CB, DC, Chx

If you are looking for the most Canadian place in town—not French Canadian, but turn-of-the-century-railroad Canadian—this is the place. Dining here is like being aboard one of those great transcontinental trains that once flashed across the face of North America. The service is prompt and attentive. Should you need a pad to scribble on, it is by your side. The martinis arrive in goblets, and at the end of the meal the check (likely to be high) arrives in a discreet brown folder. The good Canadian fare is magnificently prepared—Malpèque oysters, among the best available anywhere, roast ribs of beef, rack of lamb *provençale*, and fish from Canadian waters, such as Winnipeg goldeye, Arctic char, and Gaspé salmon. The dessert cart is rolled up to the table to tempt you.

Dinner for two, with wine, $45 and up.

Moderate to Expensive

**½LA BERGERIE · 1254 St. Catherine St. West

861-9871. Open every day. Reservations desirable.
Credit cards: AE, MC, DC, CB

I like this restaurant, with its excellent kitchen and attentive management. The owner, Serge Jeunet, who already has two successful dining places (Auberge St-Tropez and Le Mas des Oliviers) in the neighborhood, may have gone a little too far in his concern for "atmosphere": La Bergerie (The Sheepfold), situated in the basement of the chrome-and-glass Rive Gauche building, is a stage-designed reproduction of an old Quebec farmhouse. But the food is extremely good. Outstanding among the hors d'oeuvres are the stuffed and creamed *artichauts bergère* and the mushroom caps filled with marrow and covered with sauce bordelaise (*champignons farcis bordelaise*); among entree specialties, a bean dish (*cassoulet montagnard*), rabbit in sorrel (*lapin à l'oseille*), duck with green peppercorns (*canard au poivre vert*), and excellent lamb encrusted with garlic (*épaule d'agneau*). There are steaks and fish too, plus a plentiful assortment of desserts. Service can be slow, but everything else is superior.

Dinner for two, with wine, $25–$35.

**CHEZ PAUZÉ ·
1657 St. Catherine St. West near Guy Street

932-6118. Closed Monday. Reservations advisable.
Credit cards: AE, CB, DC, MC, Chx

Montreal's oldest seafood restaurant (not a single meat dish on the menu) is extremely popular and good. Food is prepared in the simplest manner possible and served with efficiency and dispatch. The nautical decor sets off several large and comfortable dining rooms, and everyone seems to be in good humor. Apart from the more familiar shellfish, visitors might wish to try the distinctive-flavored Winnipeg goldeye, Arctic char, and (in season) Malpèque oysters.

Dinner for two, with wine, $25–$35.

**½LE COLIBRI · *1485 Mansfield near Sherbrooke*
844-0618.   Closed Sunday.   No reservations.
Credit cards: Chx

This small restaurant of only a dozen tables is one of the best in Montreal. The kitchen is about the size of a hatcheck room, and the total complement of staff is the chef, his wife at the cash register, and a friend of theirs who acts as the waiter. The food is wholeheartedly French, and both it and the wine are reasonably priced.

Dinner for two, with wine, $20–$25.

**CHEZ DELMO · *211–15 Notre-Dame St. West*
849-4061.   Closed Sunday.   Reservations desirable.
Credit cards: AE, CB, DC, Chx

A popular lunchtime rendezvous for businessmen from the nearby financial district, Delmo's offers seafood in plain, down-to-earth surroundings that will remind New Yorkers of Schrafft's. There are two immensely long mahogany bars for counter service on either side of a long and narrow tiled room, and a small dining room at the rear with tables and chairs. Food ranges from good to excellent. The lobster bisque, the poached salmon with hollandaise sauce are both outstanding. Other specialties include a rich Dover sole Walewska, and shrimps Nantua. Service is speedy and efficient, although at lunchtime you may have to wait up to half an hour for a table if you don't have a reservation. The wine list is most reasonably priced.

Dinner for two, with wine, $25–$35.

**½LE CHALUTIER · 395 *Le Moyne St. off McGill*

845-1607
Closed Sunday, Monday night, Saturday noon.
Credit cards: AE, MC, CB, Chx

This is a small, utterly unpretentious, reasonably priced restaurant which specializes in seafood (*chalut* means "trawl-net") and has a truly excellent chef. His special hors d'oeuvre is *la crêpe au four maison*, a paper-thin crêpe stuffed with minced chicken, mushrooms, and onions, creamed and gratined. The *coquille St-Jacques*, with its ample portions of scallops and mushrooms, serves as an entree, and there is a shrimp *coquille*, as well as pepper steak and lobster. Ask for the chef's special of the day. Wines are modestly priced.

Dinner for two, with wine, around $20.

**AUBERGE ST-TROPEZ · 1208 *Crescent St.*

861-3197.   Open every day.   Reservations advisable.
Credit cards: DC, CB, Chx

Run by the same manager as Le Mas des Oliviers, a man with quite an eye for a romantic backdrop; here the setting suggests an old Humphrey Bogart movie—say, *Tangiers*—what with the beaded curtains and stuccoed walls. The cuisine is again Provençal. Fish soup (occasionally a bouillabaisse), *coq au vin provençale*, frog's legs, and rabbit sautéed in white wine are among the regular items.

Dinner for two, with wine, around $30.

***LA PICHOLETTE · 1731 *St-Denis St.*

843-8502. Closed Monday. Reservations advisable.
Credit cards: AE, MC, Chx

What Crescent Street is to English-speaking Montrealers, St-Denis is to the French. Surrounded by bistros and bookstores, La Picholette stands in a class by itself. The owners, Mme. Ginette Van den Berg and M. Jean-Pierre Panchaud, are from the Swiss Romande (a *picholette* is a type of small carafe used in that region), and are as attentive to detail as hawks. The menu is ambitious and agreeable, as is the friendly service. Hors d'oeuvres especially recommended include the *champignons farcis provençale* (stuffed mushrooms Provençal style) and the *escargots à la crème étau cognac du chef* (snails in a rich cognac sauce); entree specialties are *lapin sauté chasseur* (rabbit sautéed in a wine sauce) and *canard aux pêches* (duck garnished with peaches).

Dinner for two, with wine, $25–$35.

**½CHEZ PIERRE ·
1263 *Labelle St. near St. Catherine*

843-5227. Open every day. Reservations advisable.
Credit cards: AE, DC, Chx

Although the management has changed in recent years, this is one of Montreal's oldest established dining spots, the kind of place where Maman and Papa bring Oncle Antoine for dinner. Hors d'oeuvres include an excellent *pâté de maison*, *moules marinières* (mussels in their own juice and garlic), and *crêpes pannequet "Abel,"* filled with mushrooms and served with a cheese sauce. You have a choice of more than a dozen main courses, ranging from *caille au riz sauvage* (quail and wild rice) to pepper steak, or the house specialties—a steak *grand veneur* (with a wine sauce) and *canard à la Diane* (a half-duck which has been marinated, then baked slowly and flambéed at the table with Calvados).

Dinner for two, with wine, $25–$35.

*½ DUPONT & SMITH · 1454 Peel St.

288-5106. Open every day. Reservations not necessary.
Credit cards: AE, DC, CB, MC, Chx

This is one of the best and most reasonably priced places in the city if you enjoy roast beef cut from the joint. Should you want other dishes, then reconsider: Dupont & Smith has been known to take as long as 30 minutes to prepare a simple dish of chicken. For a hamburger and a beer, there is a small room to the right as you enter, which is open to the street in summer months. I recommend the ground-floor grill room, which is decorated with a fine mural that sets off the tapestried chairs and snowy white tablecloths, and where the chef stands in one corner, behind an enormous side of deliciously pink roast beef. Service is fair in the grill room, but for speedier attention during the busy lunch hour, go upstairs and eat in the bar.

Lunch for two, with drinks, $15–$20; dinner, about double the price.

** LE PAVILLON DE L'ATLANTIQUE · 1454A Peel St.

849-1368. Open every day. Reservations desirable.
Credit cards: AE, DC, CB, Chx

Next door to Dupont & Smith, the Atlantic Pavilion is a beautifully run fish restaurant. The oyster stews, mussels, shellfish, and smoked Gaspé salmon are excellent. There is a wide choice among Canadian lake and ocean fish, and there is nearly always a special lobster dinner available. Service is brisk and cheerful, seating arrangements are comfortable, and the wine list is adequate. Lots of nautical atmosphere, and you can sit in captain's chairs or booths. Families are made most welcome.

Dinner for two, with wine, $20–$30.

**½CLUB DES MOUSTACHES ·
2070 Mountain St.

842-3481. Closed Sunday. Reservations not required.
Credit cards: AE, DC, CB, Chx

To reach the Club you enter the ground-floor bar (beneath the blue awning) and push your way through its colorful clientele of students and artists, past the bathrooms and down a couple of steps—and there before you is a virtual copy of a Parisian Left Bank bistro, the creation of Louis Tavan, one of Montreal's most imaginative restaurateurs. His menu includes such Parisian favorites as *tripes à la mode de Caen*, calf brains in butter, kidneys Madère, *boeuf bourguignon*, and, one day a week, couscous. (The *spécialité du jour* is always written on a slate.) You can order wine by the carafe or by the bottle. The mirrored and muraled walls, the cheerful waiters, who scribble your order on the paper-covered marble table, all contribute to a truly cheerful ambiance. This is one bistro where you can try out your French with perfect equanimity.

Dinner for two, with wine, $15–$20.

**LE PARIS · *1812 St. Catherine St. near Guy*

937-4898. Open every day. Reservations advisable.
Credit card: Chx

This little restaurant seems to have been around forever, and obviously caters to regulars who make up 95 percent of its satisfied clientele. The inspiration here is good, well-prepared food, from a menu that rarely changes—don't expect adventure. Pepper steak, roast chicken, frog's legs, *sole amandine* are the kind of dishes you will find. Wine can be bought by the glass or by the bottle. Tables are too close together for comfort,

and particularly crowded on weekends; but service is
quick, and the atmosphere cozy and friendly.

Dinner for two, with wine, $20–$25.

** CHEZ FANNY · 1279 *St-Hubert St.*

842-3481. Closed Sunday. Reservations desirable.
Credit cards: AE, DC, MC, Chx

Another of restaurateur Louis Tavan's inspirations—
a re-creation of a Provençal village complete with cobbled street and *pétanque* court, and, in the evenings, a
strolling accordionist. Perhaps more important is that
Chez Fanny offers the best South-of-France menus in
town, from *bourride* (garlic-flavored fish soup) to rabbit
provençale. Service can be slow at times, but there's no
question about the cheerful atmosphere.

Dinner for two, with wine, $20–$25.

TWENTY SPECIALTY RESTAURANTS
Moderate to Expensive
Canadian

*** LE FESTIN DU GOUVERNEUR ·
St. Helen's Island
866-1267

Two sittings nightly, except Monday,
    at 6:30 and 9:45 p.m.
Tickets at any Ticket Reservation Service outlet,
    phone 878-3811
No credit cards.

A most unusual entertainment-with-food—a reenact-
ment of a 1691 feast. Go preferably with family or
friends and assemble with other guests, first in an ante-
chamber for a glass of spiced wine. There one of you

will be selected "governor" for the evening and escorted
to the head table. Once inside the former powder room
of the Old Fort, you are seated at candlelit tables, and
the feast begins: *tourtière*, vegetable soup, Cornish hen
and baby corn, sugar pie, tea, and fresh fruit, all served
without benefit of salt and pepper, tablecloths, napkins,
or forks, just as it would have been served in 1691. An
opera singer is host, and a singing cast with remarkably
good musical accompaniment helps out at table, re-
filling your wine glass as soon as it is empty. The evening ends with the enactment of a well-staged plot, and
it is all great fun. Highly recommended.

Tickets $14.95 per person.

LES FILLES DU ROY · 415 *St-Paul St. East*

849-6556.　Reservations desirable.　Open every day.
Credit cards: AE, DC, NC, CB

Named after the "king's daughters"—the 1,000 young
and old Frenchwomen who came to New France with
dowries from King Louis XIV to become the wives of
settlers—the restaurant reflects the style of the period:
stone walls, exposed beams, waitresses in eighteenth-
century costume. And the dishes, similarly, are all from
the cookbooks of early French Canada: to begin, *croû-
tons à l'ail* (squares of hot bread spiced with garlic),
fèves au lard à la canadienne (a small dish of pork and
beans); then, traditional main dishes like *tourtière* (a
ground-meat pie), *ragoût de boulettes* (meat balls, pork
hocks served in a spicy sauce), *cipaille* (a variation of
the *tourtière*, with a filling of various meats and/or
game and onion); and for dessert, you can choose sugar
pie, maple syrup with thick cream, or bread soaked in
maple syrup served with cream. Good hearty fare.

Dinner for two, with wine, $25–$30.

American

**½ BARNSIDER STEAK HOUSE · 2250 *Guy St.*

935-8454. Open every day. No reservations accepted.
Credit cards: AE, Chx

If you enjoy noise, jollity, and good steaks, this is the place. But remember, no reservations, and if you go on Friday or Saturday, get there before 8 p.m. or be prepared to wait a good hour. The American owners have not spared the showmanship: the interior has the look of a well-weathered barn, and youthful waiters offer friendly, if distracted, service as they rush around the sawdust-strewn floors, trays piled high with dishes. The meat is top quality, grilled over charcoal. There is a generous salad bar with no limit on the helpings, which are included in the price of the entree, and wine is obtainable by the carafe and is adequate. Children are welcome, and so is anyone with a birthday to celebrate (the management provides a cake and singing waiters).

Dinner for two, with wine, $30–$40.

*** THE FIVE STARS · *Peel and Sherbrooke*

845-1234. Open every day. Reservations desirable.
Credit cards: AE, CB, DC, and Chx

Elegant surroundings, perfect service, and the best prime ribs in town. The steaks also approach perfection, and the menu also offers a wide choice of other dishes. Wine list is extensive. Located in the Constellation Hotel.

Dinner for two, with wine, $45 and up.

** JOE'S STEAK HOUSE · 1459 *Metcalfe St.*

842-4638. Open every day. Reservations not accepted.
Credit cards: AE, DC, CB, Chx

A big, cheerful, noisy establishment with plenty of Western flavor. Try Joe's "special prime-rib" steak.

Dinner for two, with wine, $25–$35.

Delicatessen

** SCHWARTZ'S · *3895 St-Laurent Blvd.*

Open every day.

Along with Mayor Drapeau, Schwartz's is an enduring Montreal institution; it's a grubby, run-down-looking place that attracts both the cabbies and those of *bon ton.* The kitchen—or should we say, stove—is along one wall and contributes to the atmosphere. The pastrami sandwiches, known locally as "smoked meat," are terrific. So, too, is the rib steak, which arrives accompanied by a bite-sized portion of fried liver. The waiters, who appear to have taken their basic training at Minsky's Burlesque, are born raconteurs and enjoy chatting with the customers. A particularly good spot if you are hungry late at night, or wish to soak up some of the local atmosphere. Prices are extremely reasonable. No liquor served. No credit either.

*½ BEN'S · *990 Maisonneuve Blvd. West*

844-1000.   Open 22 hours every day.

Just the place to take the football team at 4 a.m. in the morning. Ben's offers shelter from the storm, a place to sit and schmooze over a sandwich, and Ben's special mixed-fruit punch (30 cents a glass). A double smoked-meat sandwich plate that includes 7 ounces of pastrami, French fries, cole slaw, and a pickle costs $2.60. The cheapest sandwich on the menu is peanut butter (45 cents) and the most expensive dish is their rib steak at $4.25. No liquor served. No credit.

Greek

**½SYMPOSIUM · 5334 *Park Ave.*

274-9547.   Open every day.   Reservations desirable.
Credit cards: AE, DC, MC, CB, Chx

If you enjoy the music and the food of Greece, you'll
love young Sara and Stelios Panayotakopoulos's pleasant
restaurant, where the interior resembles a whitewashed
monastery, with books piled on ceiling-high shelves and
the waiters costumed in white monk's garb. Sara greets
you at the door, and Stelios helps out with the spirited
Greek dancing which begins at 9 p.m. and continues
beyond 3 a.m., with everyone joining in. The hors
d'oeuvres include octopus in oil, bite-sized spinach-and-
cheese pies, stuffed vine leaves, and garlic-spiced yogurt
and cucumbers; main courses: moussaka, numerous

lamb dishes, a choice of fish, and there is the usual
assortment of sweet Greek pastries. The Greek wines
start at $8 a bottle. Service is pleasant and warm, with
some homey inefficiencies. Note: you don't tip—a 10
percent service charge is added to the bill.

Dinner for two, with wine, around $30.

*** PSARA TAVERNA · *5334 Park Ave.*

Open every day.
Credit cards: AE, DC, MC, CB, Chx

This Piraeus-style seafood tavern is on the floor below the Symposium and is owned by the same management. The food is plain but excellent, and it's a great place to bring the family. The menu is written on a slate near the kitchen: the house serves first a five-item plate of traditional Greek hors d'oeuvres, accompanied by fresh-baked bread. All the fish and seafood is brought to your table in a large basket to choose from, and is sold by the pound at prevailing rates; fish averages $2.50 a pound, as does fried squid. A large fish is usually enough for two people to share. A bottle of retsina is $5.50, a bottle of red Boutari $6.

Dinner for two, with wine, $15–$20.

* PANTHEON · *1437 St-Laurent Blvd.*

Open every day.
Credit cards: DC.

Although there is a printed menu, this is a typical look-and-choose-from-the-counter Greek restaurant. No atmosphere at all—the kind of place that obviously has a good neighborhood business and is not out to impress you with its decor. You can eat cheaply and well on their good *avgolemono* (a soup of egg, lemon, and chicken broth), Greek salad with oregano-sprinkled feta cheese and plump black olives, their excellent *spanakopita* (spinach-and-cheese pie), a well-prepared moussaka, as well as various lamb dishes; fish is sold by the pound and served broiled. Greek wines are available at moderate prices.

Dinner for two, with wine, about $15.

Italian

*** OSTERIA DEI PANZONI · 1194 *Mountain St.*

866-8119. Open every day. Reservations advisable.
No credit cards

The best Italian restaurant in Montreal, with perhaps
the worst decor. Cement walls and ceramic tiled floors
make conversation *à deux* extremely difficult. The food,
however, more than compensates. The *fettucine Alfredo* is magnificent, and the soups, which include
stracciatella alla romana (a clear broth with egg), are
noteworthy. The *canneloni* is outstanding, a specialty of
the house, as is the scampi. There is an excellent choice
among fish and veal dishes, one especially recommended
being *bocconcini alla romana*, a veal dish prepared with
a savory mushroom sauce. The service is first-rate, and
the waiters are both attentive and helpful.

Dinner for two, with wine, around $30.

*** OSTERIA DEL CACCIATORE ·
1247 *Dorchester West*

861-8791. Open every day. Reservations desirable.
Credit cards: MC, Chx

Outstanding for its delicate North Italian cuisine. The
inspired chef/owner is Angelo Mirra, who once worked
for the Italian Line, and most recently at Dei Panzoni. Since Chef Mirra does all the cooking himself, service can be slow; but the waiting is definitely
worthwhile. Especially recommended are the veal
dishes. Try his *portofoglio del cacciatore*—thin scallops
of veal rolled with layers of prosciutto and cheese,
served in a red wine and cream sauce that has been garnished with shallots. Another mouth-waterer is *ravioli
Caterina dei Medici* (Mirra makes his own pasta)—

bite-sized jackets of pasta filled with a mixture of minced chicken breast, ricotta cheese, spiced with nutmeg and served with a creamy sauce.

Dinner for two, with wine, $30–$40.

** LA RUSTICA · 1175 *Union Ave. near Phillips Sq.*

861-8078. Closed Sunday. Reservations desirable.
Credit cards: AE, DC, CB, Chx

This Italian country-style restaurant is rapidly moving up in gourmet circles. The present chef really knows how to cook, and if you enjoy pasta don't miss his *fettucine "rustica"*—noodles, mushrooms, small peas, and prosciutto. The veal dishes are well prepared, as are the seafood dishes. The decor is charming, from the tiled ceiling to the red-painted tables and chairs. The wine list represents the choicest wines of Italy.

Dinner for two, with wine, $20–$30.

** LA FENICE · 6877 *St-Hubert St.*

271-0105. Open every day. Reservations advisable.
Credit cards: AE, DC, Chx

Don't let a three-dollar cab ride from the city center to a working-class district, nor the steep flight of stairs leading to the dining area, deter you. This is a chef's restaurant, and every dish reveals loving care. The service matches the kitchen's artistry. There are two or three small rooms and it is like dining with your Italian in-laws, so intimate is the atmosphere. The menu lists pasta, seafood, and meat dishes. Especially to be commended is the *fettucine du chef*. If you have a favorite dish, it is worth phoning ahead. The owner/chef imports his own wines.

Dinner for two, with wine, $25–$35.

** PAESANO · 5192 *Côte-des-Neiges*

731-8221. Open every day. Reservations desirable.
Credit cards: AE, DC, CB, Chx

On weekends it seems as though all Montreal has brought the family to dinner at the family Paesano's Italian *palazzo*. The decor is Hollywood-Italian: marble statuary staring blankly from behind fronded palms, bronze doors from some long-demolished cathedral dominating a dining room already aglow with illuminated stained-glass windows. Service is prompt and efficient. The menu includes the usual pasta dishes and also features a wide choice of pizzas. A lot of fun whether you are a family, or a group of twenty, or dining alone.

Dinner, from $2.50 to $10 per person, depending on your choice.

*½ CHEZ VITO · 5412 *Côte-des-Neiges*

735-3623. Open every day. Reservations desirable.
Credit cards: AE, MC, CB, Chx

Paesano's rival down the street. The menu is not quite as long as Paesano's, but is more varied. If Craig Claiborne is correct that an Italian restaurant should be judged by its veal, then Chez Vito gets very high marks. Prices are reasonable, about the same as Paesano's.

THE OLD SPAGHETTI WAREHOUSE · 29 *St-Paul St., Old Montreal*

Open every day.
Credit cards: AE, DC, MC, Chx

One of the few places in Old Montreal where you can eat on the cheap. The food is adequate, although the spaghetti on the occasions we have sampled it has been overcooked and the sauces taste as though they came out of cans rather than the chef's cooking pot. Garlic bread is simply rolls served at the table with a pot of garlic butter. Nevertheless, a meal can be eaten here for from $1.85 (spaghetti with tomato sauce) to $4.25 for veal *à la* Valentino. A good place to go with the family or a large group, since the decor is splendid and the atmosphere cheery. There are dozens of hanging lamps, palm trees, plants, and a grandfather clock which chimes at odd moments. Upstairs is the preferred place. Try for a window table and watch the street action below. Open until 2 a.m.

Argentine

* EL GAUCHO · *2150 Mountain St.*

  842-3485. Open every day.
  Reservations desirable.
  Credit cards: AE, DC, CB, MC, Chx

A restaurant that combines decorative flair and a menu that is brief but satisfying. The meat roasts on vertical spits above an open fire. The tiled floor, black oak chairs and tables, *serapes* and whips, and the gaucho-garbed waiters remind you more of late movies on TV than of Buenos Aires. All the same, the food is excellent, and the service equally good. Quite the best item on the menu is the grilled lamb. Not expensive either.

  Dinner for two, with wine, about $20.

Irish

* THE HUNTER'S HORN · *1214 Peel St.*

  861-8022. Closed Sunday. Reservations desirable.
  Credit cards: AE, DC, CB, Chx

A cheerful Irish pub which serves such plain and hearty dishes as corned beef and cabbage, Irish lamb stew (especially recommended), fish and chips, and a variety of steaks. At times the patrons at the bar are somewhat overcome with memories of the "Old Sod" and the singing reaches formidable sonic highs; this can be delightful or a bit overwhelming, depending on your mood. The restaurant's decor is late-nineteenth-century Dublin. Service is excellent.

Dinner for two, with ale, about $20.

Indian

** CURRY HOUSE · 1978 *Maisonneuve West*

932-0241.   Open every day.
Credit cards: AE, DC, CB, Chx

If you like pungent, spicy Indian food this is perhaps the best of Montreal's half-dozen Indian/Pakistani restaurants. There are about a dozen different curry dishes, and they can be ordered hot, meaning extra fiery, medium, or mild.

Dinner for two, $15–$20.

Japanese

**½ KYOTO · 2055 *Mansfield*

849-8061.   Open every day.   Reservations desirable.
Credit cards: AE, CB, Chx

An interesting Japanese steak house with excellent food that is prepared and cooked in front of you. Each table seats eight persons and features a built-in grill. The menu includes soup, salad, a shrimp dish, steak, dessert, and Japanese tea. Scampi or chicken can be had instead of steak.

Dinner for two with wine or sake, around $30.

Vegetarian

CUCKOO · 2055 *Bishop*
O-PTI-ZOIZO · 27 *Ontario West*
LA BONNE TABLE (*which also serves non-vegetarian meals*) · 1145 *de Bullion and Dorchester*

Vietnamese

*½VAN LANG · 1434 *Bleury near Maisonneuve*

844-5786. Open every day.
Credit cards: AE, MC, Chx

For an inexpensive lunch or dinner, and a pleasant introduction to a cuisine unfamiliar to most Westerners, the Van Lang is to be recommended. Vietnamese cuisine is close in style to the cooking of China and Japan. Among recommended dishes are the *poisson à la marmite à la mode du sud*—South-Vietnamese-style fish in a marmite sauce—and *chao gío*—egg rolls filled with a delicious mixture of crabmeat, black mushrooms, and transparent noodles. Complete dinners for two from $6.

Russian

**TROIKA · 2171 *Crescent*

849-9333. Open every day. Reservations necessary.
Credit cards: AE, CB, DC, MC, Chx

Specialties of the house include such familiars as beef Stroganoff, chicken Kiev, and blinis (thin pancakes), served in a romantic candlelight atmosphere helped along by balalaika music provided by strolling musicians. Dinner for two, with wine, between $40–$50, although for half the price you can enjoy a supper of *zakuski* (appetizers) washed down with ice-cold vodka drunk Russian-style in one gulp.

Portuguese

*½ SOLMAR · 3699 St-Laurent Blvd.

844-7748.   Open every day.   Reservations desirable.
Credit cards: DC, MC, CB, Chx

A great favorite with the local Portuguese population.
Here amid the smoke and wine you can hear the mourn-
ful *fado* sung by both entertainers and guests. For open-
ers, try mussels Portuguese style, clams in white wine
sauce, or fried squid. As for entrees, the pork and
clams is a good typical Portuguese dish, and *bacalhau*,
codfish prepared in a white sauce, is a special taste.

Dinner for two, with wine, around $15.

Swiss

**½ LE MAZOT · 1668 St-Denis St.

844-7171.   Closed Sunday in summer.
Reservations desirable.
Credit cards: AE, DC, CB

One of the nicest restaurants in Montreal. Tremendous
value, excellent service. Very Swiss, with rustic Alpine
interior, waitresses in dirndl skirts, and a wall-length
mural of the Alps. Food is good to excellent, and includes such Swiss specialties as *raclette valaisanne*,
bundnerfleisch (the dried beef of the Grisons), and
sausage salad. There is always a *table d'hôte* available.

Complete meals from $2.50 per person.

TEN INEXPENSIVE RESTAURANTS

** MAZURKA · 64 Prince Arthur East

Open every day

Just off St-Louis Square, this Polish restaurant is a local landmark for the hungry. Pepper steak, veal marengo, wienerschnitzel, or *pirogys*—the food is lovingly prepared. Complete meals cost from $1.50 to $5, and service is excellent. Anyone who is Polish gets a special welcome here, but you don't have to be to enjoy the amazingly low prices and excellent home cooking.

**PAM-PAM RESTAURANT · 1425 *Stanley Street*

Open every day

Long established Montreal hangout. This warm, cozy restaurant is home-away-from-home for those who like to linger over their food. And whether it is pastries (amongst the best in town) or Pam-Pam's Middle European-style food—goulash, boiled beef and horse-radish, paprika veal—the price is right.

Complete meals from $3.00 and up.

*½STASH'S CAFE-BAZAAR ·

261 St-Sulpice St., by Notre-Dame Church

Open every day

A nice place to take the entire family. Cheerful, bright atmosphere. Stanislaw Pruszynski serves the nearest thing to a home-cooked meal in the city. On the menu are a choice of soups, chili, boiled dumplings, potato pancakes, and goulash in paprika sauce. A three-course meal begins around $3. For non-smokers only.

* CARMEN · 2063 *Stanley St.*

Open every day

A coffeehouse that serves Hungarian and Middle European food. The service is friendly, the portions plentiful. À *la carte* dishes from $1.65 and up. Favored by a young crowd which enjoys the ambiance—and the seventeen different kinds of coffee available.

WELCOME CAFE · *corner Clark and Lagauchetière*
Open every day

Most inexpensive choice here is rice and gravy for 35 cents. Chinatown's cheapest restaurant. Green wooden benches and plastic covered tables. Don't bother to hang up your coat.

**LUNG FUNG · *81 Lagauchetière*
Open every day

One of Chinatown's best restaurants. Ignore the plastic decor, and steep stairs. Though the menu may seem a bit top-heavy with the standard varieties of chow mein and chop suey, it's the numerous other *à la carte* dishes that give Lung Fung its true distinction. Try No. 125, *war tip ming ha*—shrimps that have been flattened out and are served on tiny rafts of fried bread accompanied with cherry sauce. Delicious also is the fried beef in black bean sauce. Alcoholic beverages available.

*CRÊPERIE BRÉTONNE (TYBRIEZ) ·
933 Rachel St. East
Closed Sunday and Monday

Popular with students. The chief dishes are onion soup (considered by some connoisseurs the best in town) and coquille St-Jacques, and the large, thin Brittany-style crêpes that come with a variety of fillings. The latter range in price from 80 cents to $2. Worth trying here also is the Quebec cider.

**LE BATELEUR ·
Prince Arthur near St-Louis Square

Graham Greene's Quiet American would feel at home in this Vietnamese restaurant. The atmosphere is one of intrigue and mystery: joss sticks, macramé hangings, subdued lighting. You'll be delighted at both the mood of the place and the very reasonable prices. Everything is as neat and as clean as a ship's galley in the open kitchen off the tiny dining room. Dishes range in price from $1.25 for *rouleau impériale*—crisply fried egg rolls stuffed with noodles and shrimps—to $4 for Vietnamese-style chicken, dipped in egg batter and deep-fried. No liquor license, but guests-are invited to bring their own wine.

Dinner for two, around $12.

** TEAN HONG · *Lagauchetière near Clark*

Open every day

Probably the outstanding Cantonese cooking in the city. The menu runs to several hundred dishes, but there is a small list of daily specials for those not familiar with Chinese cuisine. Dishes I like here include snails in garlic sauce, *chow har kew* (shrimp in black bean sauce), and steamed sea bass with ginger sauce.

Dinner for two, $8 to $10. Also recommended: their $1.49 lunch special, which includes dessert and a pot of tea.

**RESTAURANT UBALDO · 6562 St-Lawrence Blvd.

Closed Sunday

A small neighborhood haunt in the heart of the Italian section. Decor is strictly 20th-century plastic, but the cooking is terrific—and so are the prices. Most dishes around $3.00, and wines, mainly Italian, all less than $7.00. Try the *calamari* (squid deep-fried in a light batter and sprinkled with lemon juice), Veal Scallops Marsala, or the *cannelloni alla Rossini*.

Dinner for two, $10–$12.

Montreal After Dark

One of the most beguiling aspects of Montreal after dark is the sheer *variety* of available entertainment. We should stress, though, that this is no Sin City: by and large, what you find here is (to coin a phrase) good, clean fun. There are few massage parlors (at least not along the steamy lines of those found in Toronto and Bangkok), no gambling casinos, and the red-light district disappeared years ago.

Nightclubs are not particularly fashionable (although Montreal boasts a Copacabana, a Stork Club, and an El Morocco). By contrast, discotheques and supper clubs are enormously popular, and cater to every taste from the chic to the Gay. Thursdays and Fridays are the really big nights in the discotheques (Saturdays are reserved for going out with the woman or man you met at the disco the night before). **Dominique's**, the **Baldaquin**, and **Don Juan's** are the top of the heap.

The poshest supper clubs are the Hotel Bonaventure's **Le Portage**, the Château Champlain's **Le Caf'Conc'**, and the Queen Elizabeth's **Salle Bonaventure**—all three very expensive.

Bars do a tremendous trade in this city, the best night of the week being Thursday, for reasons known only to Montrealers (see "Drink," page 194). **Rockhead's Paradise**, and **Norm Silver's Mustache**, all clubs that feature music, are for customers who want to be in that number when the saints go marching in.

Montreal's coffeehouse scene has all but vanished. Of those that remain, the **Yellow Door** and **Cafe Golem** are perhaps the best known, attracting a student crowd who come to listen to both rock and folk music.

The great glory of Montreal is, of course, the terrace-cafes and bistros, hundreds of them, with the liveliest to be found in Place Jacques-Cartier and along St-Denis Street.

A *note on local habits*: It is quite usual for women to go to bars and discotheques in pairs, but a single, unescorted woman is not infrequently frowned upon. Some hotels actually refuse to serve a woman alone, although such refusal is, strictly speaking, against the law. A bit of advice for men—wear a coat and tie when going to a discotheque. The doorman often decides whether or not you get in by the uniform you wear.

DINING AND DANCING

SALLE BONAVENTURE ·
Queen Elizabeth Hotel, 900 Dorchester West
This supper club is classy rather than brassy. Excellent *à la carte* menu. The entertainment—top-name singers and performers—is usually a notch above that found elsewhere. Between shows, there is dancing that mixes traditional with the mildly mod. Cover charge. Price range: expensive. Nightly from 9 p.m. Reservations 861-3511. AE, CB, DC, Chx.

LE CAF'CONC' ·
Hotel Château Champlain, Place du Canada
Traditional nightclub entertainment in a somewhat showy setting. Chorus line *à la* "Folies Bergères" is the big number. Dancing. Satisfactory food. Cover charge. Price range: expensive. Nightly from 8:30 p.m. Reservations 878-1688. AE, CB, DC, Chx.

L'ESCAPADE · *Hotel Château Champlain,*
Place du Canada
Midnight-blue dining and dancing in a penthouse. Easily the most spectacular of Montreal's rooftop rest-

aurants. A good-time kind of place which seems to appeal to all ages. There's no show, only dancing that alternates between traditional and mod. Food is good to excellent. Dinner 5:30 p.m. to midnight. Dancing 9 p.m. to 2 a.m. Price range: moderate to expensive. Cover charge. Reservations 878-1688. AE, CB, Chx, DC.

LE PORTAGE
Hotel Bonaventure, Place Bonaventure

Food is fine, so is the dancing, but the entertainment often disappoints. Cover charge. Nightly from 8 p.m. Price range: expensive. Reservations 878-2331. AE, CB, DC, Chx.

THE FIVE STARS ·
Constellation Hotel, Peel and Sherbrooke

Roast beef and popovers are the dinner specialty, and the room is beautiful. The dancing is strictly to work off the calories. No cover. Reservations 845-1234. Price range: moderate to expensive. AE, CB, DC, Chx.

ALTI-THÈQUE 737 ·
Place Ville-Marie, University and Dorchester

That's the height above sea level, not street level. Nevertheless, it's high enough to offer some of the most

splendid views of the city. The place is always crowded.
Food is essentially a buffet, plus a few specialties.
There's dancing, and the groups who provide the music
have names like "The Explosion"—fair warning. Nightly
from 9 p.m. Price range: moderate. Cover charge. Reservations 861-3511. AE, CB, DC, Chx.

LA RESERVE · *Windsor Hotel, 1170 Peel Street*

In the Windsor Hotel, La Reserve offers a candlelit
Mediterranean ambiance for dress-up dining and dancing. The music is on the safe side—waltzes, tangos, foxtrots. The food is fair-to-good. Price range: moderate
to expensive. Nightly from 8 p.m. Reservations 866-9611. AE, CB, DC, Chx.

RUBY FOO'S · *7815 Décarie Boulevard*

A big, splashy, expense-account Chinese restaurant that
can seat 1,100 people, making this the city's largest
restaurant. You dine among jade statuettes and hanging
lanterns, or else in Edwardian splendor in the Chambord Room, with its gaslight globes. Dancing is comfortably traditional. Noisy, cheerful atmosphere, about
a 10-minute cab ride from midtown. Price range: expensive. Reservations 731-7701. AE, CB, DC, Chx.

MOSTLY MUSIC

ROCKHEAD'S PARADISE · *1252 St-Antoine*

The patrons, black and white, jam the stairs shoulder
to shoulder simply to get into Rockhead's. Once inside,
the ladies are pinned with a carnation, courtesy of the
owner, Mr. Rufus Nathanael Rockhead. The best
time to go is about 10 p.m. There are three shows
nightly, Tuesday–Sunday. The best seats are in the
horseshoe bar on the mezzanine, and what you hear is

ear-splitting soul music. There is a dance floor that's packed between the acts. The food is good, and you can drink everything from beer to champagne. Reservations: day, 861-3243; night, 861-2161.

BLUE ANGEL CAFE · *Drummond Street, between St. Catherine and Dorchester*

You'll find country singers and pickers here, and the spot is generally regarded as the domain of homesick Maritimers (people, that is, from the Maritime Provinces to the east). The most interesting night of the week is Monday, when the stage show takes a night off and country music fans take over. Anyone who can pick and strum with any skill gets aboard, and the patrons sit back and enjoy it all.

NORM SILVER'S MUSTACHE · *1433 Closse Street*

The house has a policy of booking Canadian rock groups, and the crowd is mostly college students, who get a bit rowdy at times. Dancing between shows. There is a cover charge on weekends. Near the Forum.

BOÎTE À CHANSON · *410 St-Vincent*

From June to September you can't do better than visit this barnlike room to listen to Quebec folk music. It's elbow to elbow inside, and everyone seems to have a good time. In Old Montreal (just off Place Jacques-Cartier).

LE PATRIOTE · 1474 *St. Catherine East*

The shrine of *québécois* pop-culture in Montreal. Practically every great name on the French-Canadian musical scene has appeared here. Decor is overblown rural Quebec, and the clientele take their pop seriously. Tuesday–Friday at 9 p.m. Saturday and Sunday at 8 p.m. Reservations 523-1131.

DISCOTHEQUES

CHEZ ACHILLE · 1558 *St-Denis*

The St-Denis crowd—i.e., mainly French-speaking and young. Terrific place for the under-25's who enjoy crowds, smoke, and ear-splitting rock. It's all part of the booming "St-Denis Strip," the French alternative to the largely Anglo Crescent Street scene. Dress informal, leave your tie and jacket at home. Reservations 844-4615.

LE BALDAQUIN · 424 *St-François-Xavier*

Well established and fashionable. Clientele are the kind of folks who carry credit cards. Anyone over 25 will feel comfortable here. Off the crowded dance floor, with its king-sized canopy, there are velveteen love seats for relaxing. A dress-up discotheque: jackets and ties are *de rigueur*. In Old Montreal. Reservations 849-4249.

CLUB 21 · *Constellation Hotel, Peel and Sherbrooke*

On the roof of the Constellation Hotel, the windows soar two stories, offering a splendid night view of the city. Claude Phillipe's orchestra takes turns with jukebox rock. Clientele is well heeled, well dressed, and over 25. Reservations 845-1231.

DOMINIQUE'S · 1455 *Stanley*

Everyone knows Dominique's, one of the most popular spots in town after dark. It seems to attract a cross-section of ages and types, no particular group predominating. There's a singles bar on a dais overlooking the postage-stamp dance floor. Various rock groups alternate with recorded music. Doorman is fairly strict in matters of dress: jackets and ties. Reservations 845-0033 (although most people just take their chances).

DON JUAN'S · 2022A *Stanley*

One of the city's best-known meet-markets. A get-together joint for the under-thirties. Convivial, colorful, crowded. Dress is casual and reservations really don't matter. Phone 844-1345.

MARQUIS DE SADE · 36 *St-Paul East*

Montrealers who regularly tour the disco-circuit invariably include a call at this Old Montreal spot. With its stone walls, two dance floors, and several bars, it can be fun. Clientele over 25 and "on the town." Reservations 866-4081.

LA SEXE MACHINE · 1469 *Crescent Street*

If your idea of a discotheque is Mod Porno decor, and a huge bar area where the waiters and waitresses wear nothing more concealing than a G-string, then you'll be at home here. Conventioneers and tourist groups adore the place. Any age can get passed through the multi-breasted front door.

VALENTINO'S · *Queen's Hotel, 700 Peel Street*

A converted hotel ballroom, of regulation vastness, all chandeliers and high-beamed ceilings. There's certainly room enough to dance, and you'll be surrounded by some of the most weird and wonderful sunset-to-sunrise people you'll ever find. Weekends are the best.

Come as-you-think-you'd-like-to-be. Dress is anything from blue jeans to glitter rock. Reservations 866-2531.

SPECIAL PLACES
FOR SPECIAL PEOPLE

THE LIMELIGHT ·
Stanley Street between St. Catherine and Dorchester
The freakiest disco in town. Fashion people love it, mostly for the atmosphere created by all those people, both Gay and Straight, who live to dress. The name of the game at the Limelight is who-can-outdo-who. Platform shoes, bumps and grinds, sequinned denims, feather boas, sun-bleached curls. Best time to arrive is around 11 p.m. and things don't really slow down until 4 a.m. You line up on Stanley Street to pay an entrance fee of $1 weekdays, $3 on weekends.

VALENTIN'S · *291 Mount Royal West*
Where else can a gentleman send another gentleman a bottle of champagne without anyone raising an eyebrow? Women like the place, hip Straights are not frozen out, and the chic Gay adore it. There's a supper

club with two shows nightly, and action that goes on until dawn. Upstairs is a flashy disco for patrons who want to practice their bumps and grinds. Price range: moderate to expensive. Reservations 849-1371.

COFFEEHOUSES

YELLOW DOOR CAFE · 3625 *Aylmer*
McGill student hangout. They serve the cheapest lunches in town, provide a message board, and at night Montreal singers like Penny Lang and Bruce Murdoch are on hand for those who want to try out the local folk scene.

GOLEM COFFEE HOUSE · 3460 *Stanley*
Friendly little place, where you can read your *Mass Psychology of Fascism* alone or, on Thursdays, Saturdays, and Sundays, listen to live folk music after 9 p.m.

WHERE YOU CAN JOIN IN THE FUN

ST. JAMES PUB · *Drummond at Maisonneuve*
For an inexpensive night on the town, it's hard to beat the value offered here. There are dancing and entertainment nightly. Tuesday is Amateur Night, and drinks for the ladies go for half-price during the talent contest, which runs from 7 to 10 p.m. There is always a "Brew and Stew" special for $1.99.

COCK 'N' BULL PUB · 1946 *St. Catherine West*
A genuine British-run pub, where the bar is awash in sudsy ale and noisy with the twang of Cockney voices. Wednesday and Sunday there's Dixieland music, around 11 p.m. every other night there is a talent show

with a $5 prize, but really big and riotous amateur night comes on Monday. Lovers of English beer will find Whitbread's, Bass, and McEwan's Pale Ale on tap here.

THE HUNTER'S HORN · 1214 *Peel Street*

There is an Irish country pub with a Parlour upstairs. There, after a few rounds of Guinness, you can easily imagine yourself in Killarney, particularly when the customers join the band in rounds of "Danny Boy" and "Galway Bay." (See also page 223.) Nightly 7:30 p.m. to 2 a.m., on Sunday to 1 a.m.

SYMPOSIUM · 5534 *Park*

Sara and Stelios, the owners of this Athenian restaurant, don't mind if you come for a meal or merely a glass of *ouzo* with your Greek coffee. What's more, they adore company, and so does the band. It's hard to keep from joining in the dancing, and even if you don't know how, all you need do is join the line and follow your partner's steps. On weekdays till around 3 a.m. On weekends till dawn. Reservations 274-9547.

Entertainment

There's plenty to see and hear in Montreal, and whether your taste runs to the music of Charles Aznavour or of Beethoven, the plays of Shakespeare or of Quebec's own Michel Tremblay in *joual*, there is plenty to choose among. A recent calendar of one month's events listed opening nights for four plays in English, nine in French (including Eugene O'Neill's *Long voyage vers la nuit*), thirty-eight concerts and opera performances, two ballets, fourteen movies, and forty-one lectures. To obtain the latest information, check the local newspapers, or pick up a free copy of the city's calendar of events from your hotel. Montreal's helpful Visitors Bureau (872-3561) will also be glad to assist you, and in the summer you can also get the calendar of events and other help at the "log cabin" tourist office in Dominion Square.

THEATRE

There are a dozen-odd theatres in Montreal, and about twice that number of acting companies. There is no theatrical district as such; the playhouses are scattered all over the city. Since theatre here is subsidized by all three levels of government—federal, provincial and municipal—playgoing is a relatively easy thing to do, even on a modest budget: ticket prices range from $2.50 to about $10 top.

A great many theatres are closed in summer, but there is no hard-and-fast rule as to which ones. Almost every theatre in Montreal closes one day a week, usually Monday, so most have performances Sunday night. Evening performances begin at 8 or 8:30 p.m. and usually end between 10:30 and 11. Theatre programs are almost always free. Matinees are at 2 or 2:30 p.m. Dress is a matter of personal choice, but playgoers tend to dress down in Montreal.

French Theatre

THÉÂTRE DU NOUVEAU MONDE ·
  84 St. Catherine West
  861-0563

Under the direction of Jean-Louis Roux, the TNM is famous for sumptuous productions and a repertoire that embraces both the classical French theatre and modern theatre from Alfred Jarry to Tennessee Williams.

THÉÂTRE PORT-ROYAL ·
  Place des Arts at St. Catherine and Jeanne-Mance
  842-2112

One of the three halls at P.D.A., this 800-seat theatre is currently the home of **La Compagnie Jean Duceppe**. The repertoire includes the best from England and the United States. You may find Harold Pinter's *Le Gardien*, for example, or Tennessee Williams's *Un Tramway nommé désir*. Jean Duceppe has a well-deserved reputation for flawless productions. Also in its repertoire is *Charbonneau et le Chef*, a play about corruption in Quebec that—like *The Drunkard*—audiences never tire of seeing.

THÉÂTRE DE QUAT'SOUS · *100 Pine Ave. East*
  845-7277

Closed July and August and most Mondays. All tickets $3.75, students $2.75. Tuesday, students and senior citizens $1.75. Located in the student quarter, in the general vicinity of McGill and the University of Quebec, the Quat'Sous attracts young audiences to its performances of new and innovative Quebec and French plays.

THÉÂTRE D'AUJOURD'HUI · 1297 *Papineau*

523-1211

Closed July and August and most Mondays. Quebec playwrights presented by a strong company. Your French must be up to it, of course.

THÉÂTRE DU RIDEAU VERT · 4664 *St-Denis*

845-0267

Closed June, July, August, and September, and most Mondays. Quebec and French plays, performed by a distinguished company.

ÉCOLE NATIONALE DE THÉÂTRE DU CANADA, NATIONAL THEATRE SCHOOL ·
1182 St-Laurent Blvd.

842-7954

Closed June, July, August, September. Performances given in French and English in two different halls of the Monument National Theatre. Spirited but uneven productions are the rule here.

THÉÂTRE MAISONNEUVE ·
Place des Arts at St. Catherine and Jeanne-Mance

842-2141

Open all year round. The second largest of P.D.A.'s theaters, this 1,300-seat hall rents its four walls to various theatrical groups in between concerts and other events. A big, elegant setting for some of the best (and worst) productions staged. You're likely to find a work by the excellent playwright Michel Tremblay here.

English Theatre

At the time of Expo '67, one writer summed up Montreal's English-speaking theatre in a word: "scant." Today there are more theatrical groups than theatres to house them, but here is a brief rundown on what kind of thing is where:

CENTAUR THEATRE ·
  453 *St-François-Xavier, Old Montreal*
  288-1229

Open all year round. Closed Monday. Matinees Wednesday and Saturday. Ticket prices: Centaur I—$4, students, $2.25; Centaur II—$5, students, $2.75.

Housed in the old Stock Exchange Building, the Centaur is the "little miracle" on St-François-Xavier Street, filled to capacity night after night, presenting some of the best theatre to be seen anywhere in Canada. Thanks to artistic director Maurice Podbrey, the Centaur has built a reputation for exciting productions. There are actually two theatres: the recently opened, 450-seat Centaur II and the smaller Centaur I. Centaur II is for major productions, Centaur I is a studio theatre for new works and experimental productions by outside groups.

SAIDYE BRONFMAN CENTRE ·
  5170 *Côte-St. Catherine Road*
  739-2301
  Tickets $2.50 and $3.50, students $1.00 and $1.50.
  Closed Friday.

A gift to Montreal from the city's wealthiest family, the Bronfmans. The Centre is strongly community-oriented, and there are several young acting ensembles that perform here—best to check the local papers.

You're likely to find plenty of surprises at the SBC, ranging from Brecht's *Galileo* to the latest hit from Tel Aviv.

REVUE THEATRE · *1858 Maisonneuve Blvd. West*

937-2733

Tickets $3.50 and $4.40, students $2.50 and $3.50.
Closed Monday.

Arleigh Peterson, a one-man phenomenon, owns, operates, directs, and chooses the repertoire. You can find him taking reservations at the theatre at 9 a.m., and you'll find him closing up at midnight after counting the receipts. It's one of the few theatres in town that pays any attention to black playwrights.

It is impossible to categorize the Revue Theatre. You may find a dumb musical, or a brilliant production of Tennessee William's *Small Craft Warnings*. Convenient downtown location.

DOUGLASS BURNS CLARKE THEATRE ·
1455 Maisonneuve West

879-4341

Closed from June 1 to about November 5, and varying nights in the week. Tickets $1, students and senior citizens 50 cents. Student and amateur productions staged in the theatrical facility of Concordia University.

LA POUDRIÈRE · *St. Helen's Island*

526-0821

Tickets $3.50 and $5, students $2.
Open all year round. Closed Mondays.

A beautiful theatre in a magnificent setting. Easily reached by Métro (St. Helen's Island stop), it is at its best in summer, when you can stroll around the island before or after the performance. It is during the summer months that English productions are performed, mainly light stuff. During the winter, international productions in French and German are staged.

COMEDY AND VARIETY

Some people say that the M and the L in MONTREAL stand for music and laughter, and it's hard to disagree. The greater share of this entertainment is found nowadays in the city's bars, pubs, and *boîtes*. A full listing will be found beginning on page 232, in the previous chapter. What follow are the spots to go for the Big Spectacle.

FORUM · *St. Catherine St. and Atwater*

Métro: Atwater. 932-6131

Everyone from Mick Jagger to Ol' Blue Eyes to the Harlem Globetrotters has played the Forum. It's the home of the Montreal Canadiens, and between games the management rearranges the floor plan to happily seat 16,000 fans avid to watch their favorite stars.

PLACE DES ARTS ·

St. Catherine St. and Jeanne-Mance

Métro: Place des Arts. 842-2112

Montreal theatre and concert life is centered around the magnificent Place des Arts (see page 84 for more details). Owned and operated by the city, it is subsidized by both city and province at the rate of around $1.5 million annually, which makes low box-office prices possible. P.D.A. is where you are likely to find, appearing during the same week, the Royal Winnipeg Ballet, comedian George Carlin, and the Rajko Hungarian Gypsy Orchestra. Check newspaper listings.

THÉÂTRE DES VARIÉTÉS · *4530 Papineau*

526-2527

Closed Sundays. Two shows Saturday at 7 and 11 p.m.,
the rest of the week at 8 p.m. Admission $3 and $5.
The only really good old-fashioned music hall in town.
An evening here is always enjoyable, and even if you
can't speak a word of French, the farce is so broad, the
singing so carefree, it doesn't much matter. Actor-
director-producer Gilles Latulippe, who also owns the
place, often writes his own musicals. They're full of
double-entendres and local humor with plenty of broad
winks. Great fun, not to be missed.

LE PATRIOTE · *1474 St. Catherine St. East*

523-1131. Admission $3.50 and $4.50. 8 p.m.

If you don't like politics with your entertainment,
scratch Le Patriote off your list. But as a favorite haunt
of Quebec nationalists, it's a great place to go if you're
in the mood for protest songs. The nice thing about Le
Patriote is that you can always find the singer's record in
a music store later, and so take home a souvenir of
Quebec.

CONCERTS

As with the theatre, so with serious music and ballet—
concert-going is an inexpensive proposition in Montreal,
and only occasionally will you have to pay over $5 for
a decent seat. Church organ recitals—a noteworthy
aspect of the local musical scene—are either free or at
a quite nominal cost. Furthermore, as the *Gazette*'s
music critic Jacob Siskind points out, it is perfectly possible to attend five free musical events a week during
the season. To help you make your choice, consult the

weekend editions of the newspapers, or obtain a free copy of the city's *Calendar of Events* (see page 280).

PLACE DES ARTS ·
St. Catherine St. at Jeanne-Mance
Métro: Place des Arts. 842-2112

The great concert hall (one of three) in the Salle Wilfrid-Pelletier can accommodate 3,000 people in the utmost comfort. Not a column anywhere to block the view. This hall hosts anything from rock to classical music, including all performances of the Montreal Symphony Orchestra. Seats generally $4 to $8, a little higher for the opera and the ballet. Get there by Métro, taxi, or on foot by way of St. Catherine Street.

SALLE CLAUDE CHAMPAGNE ·
Vincent d' Indy School of Music, 220 Vincent d'Indy
739-8211

Concerts, chamber music, recitals. Also used by the Société de musique contemporaine du Quebec, which offers music of this century. Concerts here are either free or inexpensive.

REDPATH HALL ·
  McGill University, Sherbrooke West near McTavish
  392-4501

Concerts and recitals. Public regularly invited to listen
to members of the McGill Faculty of Music, or senior
students, in recital.

MAURICE POLLACK CONCERT HALL ·
  McGill University, 555 Sherbrooke West
  392-4311

Officially opened in 1975, this small hall has been ac-
claimed for its superb acoustics.

LA POUDRIÈRE · *St. Helen's Island*
  Métro: St Helen's Island. 526-0821

Principally a theatre, but used from time to time for
mini-operas and concerts.

ST. JOSEPH'S ORATORY ·
  3800 Queen Mary Road
  733-8211

Free concert every Sunday afternoon at 3:15. Church-
music pilgrims from the world over are attracted here by
one of North America's most magnificent mechanical-
action pipe organs. Bach's Passacaglia and Fugue in
C Minor is a regular part of the repertoire.

  Many other churches are similarly known for their
concerts of liturgical music. Among them: Notre-Dame
Church (Old Montreal), United Church of St. Andrew's (Westmount), St. Mathias (Westmount), and
Sanctuaire Marie-Reine-des-Coeurs.

CINEMA

First-run English-language movies are to be found
mainly in the midtown area. There are a couple of

dozen such first-run houses, all told; among the most comfortable (and most expensive) are **Cinema Place Ville-Marie**, Place Ville-Marie (866-2644), **Place du Canada**, Hotel Château Champlain (861-4595), **Atwater I**, Alexis Nihon Plaza (935-4246), and **Westmount Square Cinema**, Westmount Square (931-2477). Along St. Catherine Street are a number of more old-fashioned movie palaces, which feature first-run films in an atmosphere of popcorn and gilded plaster. Most satisfying interiors are in the **Palace**, 698 St. Catherine West (866-6991), and **Loew's**, 954 St. Catherine West (866-5851). For all movies, check the daily papers.

Montreal also has a considerable number of porno houses. Skin-flicks are big business here, in fact, and the city fathers, prudish in the extreme on other matters, appear to close their eyes. Among the better known: **Eros**, 59 St. Catherine East (288-5513), **Eve**, 1229 St. Lawrence Boulevard (861-3151), **Le Beaver**, 5117 Park Avenue (844-8671), and **Guy**, Guy and Maisonneuve (931-2912).

Among the best places to see French-language films are: **Cinema V**, 5550 Sherbrooke West (486-7395), **Elysée**, 35 Milton Avenue, just off St. Lawrence Boulevard (842-6053), **Parisien**, 480 St. Catherine West (861-2697), and **Alouette**, 318 St. Catherine West (866-2807).

Repertory cinemas abound in Montreal. Catering as they do to movie freaks, their price of admission is seldom higher than $1, and many houses have midnight matinees. Among the more noteworthy is the **Piccadilly** (English), 5025 Sherbrooke West (486-2811), which regularly schedules comedy festivals; the complete *oeuvre* of Woody Allen is an example of the kind of fare you will find here. The **Outremont** (French/English), 1248 Bernard West (277-4145), is a moviegoer's delight, with a carefully planned program that offers the best international cinema for a bargain 99-cent admission.

Cinema Participation (French/English), 550 Sherbrooke West (283-4753), is run by Canada's National Film Board and shows both new and old NFB films. Showings Tuesday evening at 8 p.m. Admission is free. Film buffs should also check out **Le Cinemathèque Québécoise** (French/English), Bibliothèque Nationale, 1700 St-Denis (844-8734): Canadian films, particularly those made in Quebec, as well as films from Africa, Eastern Europe, and France. Admission is usually under $1.

Among university film showings, one of the best programs is that offered at **Concordia University's Campus** (French/English), 1455 Maisonneuve (879-4349). It parallels New York's Museum of Modern Art in the range of its retrospective series. Thursday to Sunday at 7 and 9 p.m. Students 50 cents, others 75 cents. The film series at Concordia's **Loyola Campus** are equally outstanding. Chosen by one of Canada's leading film critics, Marc Gervais, they are built around such subjects as The Gangster, Orson Welles, The Horror Film, and so forth. Every Wednesday at 7:30 and 8:45 p.m., in the F. C. Smith Auditorium, 7141 Sherbrooke West (482-0320).

You can eat, drink, and get your movies free at **The Annex**, 1445 Bishop, a cinema restaurant frequented mainly by students. Try to get there before 7 p.m. Another good spot is the **Rainbow Bar & Grill**, 1430 Stanley, which schedules films from time to time as part of its entertainment.

TELEVISION

Turn on a TV set in Montreal, and you're not likely to think you're home. In comes Radio Quebec, the educational channel of the Quebec government, and a

program called *"Au Coeur des Mots"* ("The Heart of Words"). Shift to the French-language channel of the Canadian Broadcasting Corporation, and there is Mlle. Louise Forestier singing "Le Réel du Matin"; switch again to Telemetrepole, the local outlet for TVA (the major French-language private network), and you might see the popular French-Canadian country-and-Western show *Ranch à Willie*. In brief, the TV set is a marvelously quick way to discover what makes Quebec different from the rest of North America. And, of course, you can find the English-language channels of both the Canadian Broadcasting Corporation and CTV, Canada's major private network.

Because of Mount Royal, which puts a good deal of Montreal into electronic shadow, cable TV is commonplace. Almost all the major hotels are on cable, and that means a TV viewer has a choice of a dozen TV stations: five in Montreal, plus Ottawa, Sherbrooke, Burlington, Vermont (CBS), Plattsburgh, New York (NBC), and Poland Spring, Maine (ABC), plus Vermont Educational TV.

The *Montreal Star*, *Gazette*, and *La Presse* all publish

TV/listings on Saturday for the week ahead, and there is a regional edition of *TV Guide*. One point to remember is that, since most sets were not made with cable TV in mind, the numbers on your dial do not always match the designated channel numbers. In most hotel rooms, however, there is a card which indicates where given TV stations are to be found on the cable.

RADIO

AM: Among the best: the CBM (940) English-language and CBF (690) French-language outlets of the publicly owned Canadian Broadcasting Corporation—both offer commercial-free classical music, jazz, live concerts, drama, documentaries, news, and talk programs. CJAD (800) is a mellow, community-oriented station that mixes pop music and information programs in about equal proportions; CFCF (600) has a lunch-pail approach, heavy on sports, crusades, and breezy talk shows; CKGM (980) programs the rock 'n' roll Top 40; CFMB (1410) is a multilingual station broadcasting in many languages, among them Arabic, Greek, Polish, and Portuguese; CJMS (1280) offers the French-language Top 40 and high-powered rock.

FM: Try the CBM (95.1) English-language and CBF (100.7) French-language outlets of the Canadian Broadcasting Corporation for high-quality, commercial-free programming; CKVL (96.9), a French-language community-oriented station, with live shows plus music; CHOM (97.7), once Montreal's "underground" voice, nowadays mainstream rock; CFQR (92.5), middle-of-the-road music, plus some chatter; CFGL (105.7) French-language pop-rock and talk.

Quebec City

If you possibly can, when you are planning your trip to Montreal, make time to visit Quebec City, the capital of Canada's largest province, and easily the most beautiful of all Canadian cities. Less than three hours' ride from Montreal by car or bus, or little more than thirty minutes' flying time, brings you to North America's only walled city, a natural fortress that dominates the first narrows of the St. Lawrence River.

If Montreal is the heart of French Canada, Quebec City—in the eyes of many French Canadians—is its soul, *La Vieille Capitale*. There are almost 440,000 people living here. Most speak French, and only French, a fact that perhaps more than any other gives Quebec City its other-side-of-the-Atlantic quality. Only half of the population actually lives in the city proper, the other half being spread out in the twenty-two municipalities that make up the Quebec Urban Community. The average Quebecer is white-collar and middle-class, and approximately 10 percent of the population are government civil servants.

The city is magnificently situated on an eight-mile-long plateau of solid rock which varies in width from a few hundred yards to three miles at its widest point. With its Citadel and strong points dominating the river, it inspired Charles Dickens to call it "the Gibraltar of America." Its lowest point, the CPR tunnel that goes *under* the Plains of Abraham and emerges at Wolfe's Cove, is at sea level. The city's highest point is "Edifice G," a starkly modern government office tower which is 715 feet high.

Try to find a hotel in Upper Town, which is the Quebec City of the postcards, the one most people visualize. Within easy walking distance lie most of the good hotels, restaurants, and shops. The map on page 260 will give you a clear idea of where everything is located. The Quebec Urban Community's Tourism and Convention Centre, 60 Rue d'Auteuil (522-4071), also gives away free a good map of the central area. Highly recommended as well is their free booklet, in both French and English, *Walking Tour of Old Quebec*.

Climate has had much to do with the development of the city's special charm. Seized in winter's rigorous grip for six months out of every year, Quebecers refuse to be hurried. Perhaps because so much of their lives is spent indoors, they have developed the gift of *hospitalité* to an extraordinary degree. This is a genuinely friendly place, the kind of town where everyone seems to know everyone else. You'll quickly discover that the taxi driver is related to the woman who runs the recommended restaurant, and she, in turn, is an old friend of the man who licenses bicycles, and he's related to "someone in government," just in case you need something straightened out.

In spite of an upbeat economy, and a great deal of new construction and federal spending, chiefly in the newer areas, Old Quebec—the ancient walled city— still retains a certain provincial air. Some hotels and pensions still lock their doors by 11 p.m. If you plan to stay out later than that, the room clerk will give you the key to the front door.

As a tourist attraction, Old Quebec is without peer. I don't know any town quite so downright picturesque. A visitor can be excused for thinking it was all created by Walt Disney. "*Non,*" a local resident will tell you, "*c'est M'sieur Disney qui nous a imité.*" ("It's Mr. Disney who copied us.")

Merely to call it picturesque, however, does not do

it justice. Gray and green from May to September, gray and white the rest of the time, this is indeed a hauntingly beautiful city; and it has the capacity to awaken a sense of history in all of us. As you stroll around Place d'Armes or Place Royale, you are treading historic ground with every footstep—everywhere there are reminders that Cartier, Brébeuf, Champlain, Frontenac, Laval, Talon, Jolliet, Wolfe, and Montcalm have all gone before you. Gaze down at the old town from the vantage point of the Citadel or Dufferin Terrace, and call to mind these words of Charles Dickens:

The motley crowd of gables, roofs and chimney tops, in the old hilly town immediately at hand; the beautiful St. Lawrence sparkling and flashing in the sunlight, and the tiny ships from below the Rock from which you gaze, whose distant rigging looks like spiders' webs against the light . . . forms one of the brightest and most enchanting pictures the eyes can rest upon.

And this enchantment it still holds today.

WHERE TO STAY

Until quite recently, Quebec City suffered from an acute shortage of hotel rooms which made itself felt most strongly in the summer and during the Winter Carnival. In the last 18 months, however, the number of rooms has jumped dramatically, by some 2,000. Even so, it's best to reserve rooms in advance. If you haven't done so, check with the Quebec Urban Community Tourism and Convention Centre at 60 Rue d'Auteuil (522-4071). The office is open Monday to Friday from 9 a.m. to 8 p.m., and during the summer months every day from 9 a.m. to 10 p.m. Tell them what you wish to pay, and they will do their best to find you suitable accommodations.

If you go to any of the first-class hotels in Quebec City, expect to pay $25 to $45 per day for a single room, $35 to $55 for a double (Château Frontenac, Quebec Hilton, Loew's-Le Concorde, L'Auberge des Gouveneurs, Holiday Inn, Quality Inn). Dropping in price ($20–$30), you will also be content at the Victoria, Voyageur Laurentien, Clarendon, Château Laurier, Old Homestead, Louis Jolliet, and Motel Royal. A particularly good bargain in this group is the Clarendon, an old-fashioned English-style establishment.

In the next price category down are the Manoir Ste-Geneviève, Manoir d'Auteuil, Maison de Logement la Mansarde, and Cap Diamant House. Dropping still further in price (to from $2 to $6 a night), but still clean and comfortable, are Au Bon Gite, Manoir Hébert, Au Pigeon Voyageur, and the Brochu.

Le Centre International de Séjour du Québec at 69 d'Auteuil (694-0755) is a youth hostel and charges $2 a night for members, $2.50 (if space available) for nonmembers. It also has a kitchen and a cafeteria which serve 50-cent meals.

SIGHTSEEING

The best way to see Quebec City is on foot—there never was a town so perfectly made for strolling. Mind you, there is no such thing as a level street here: the lay of the land is rather akin to a roller-coaster, and there'll be plenty of huffing and puffing as you climb some very steep and narrow streets and lanes. Of course, you don't have to walk up from Lower Town—there's an elevator at the foot of Dufferin Terrace that will carry you back to the Upper Town for 25 cents.

The next best choice is to hire a horse-drawn *calèche* in Place d'Armes and go clip-clopping around the principal sights. Yet another good bet is to take one of the several mini-bus tours that are available. For the quick once-over, these open-top buses are awfully good value, and you get a bilingual history lesson thrown in with the ride. Both Gray Line and Maple Leaf, the principal sightseeing specialists, offer an out-of-town trip to the famous religious shrine of Ste-Anne-de-Beaupré; especially to be recommended is the evening tour, which includes a drive to Montmorency Falls, a

1 Jardin des Gouverneurs
2 Wolfe-Montcalm Monument
3 Château Frontenac
4 U.S. Consulate
5 Place d'Armes
6 Anglican Cathedral of the Holy Trinity
7 Ursuline Convent
8 Basilica of Notre-Dame
9 Quebec Seminary
10 Notre-Dame-des-Victoires Church
11 Chevalier House
12 Louis-Jolliet House and Cable Elevator
13 St-Louis Gate
14 Post Office
15 Tourism and Convention Centre, Q.U.C.

P Parking areas

visit to one of the oldest farmhouses in the area (and a sampling of home-baked bread), and of course the miraculous shrine itself—in time for the evening candle-light procession. Here are a few useful addresses:

Gray Line Sightseeing Tours: Place d'Armes
   Reservations: 688-9633
Maple Leaf Sightseeing Tours: Place d'Armes (opposite
   Château Frontenac). Reservations: 692-2435
Visite Touristique du Québec: 2631 Place Beauséjour,
   Ste-Foy. 651-0340. Starting point is your hotel.
La Compagnie d'Excursions Maritimes de Québec:
   Cruising on the St. Lawrence, upstream to Cap
   Rouge; downstream to Montmorency Falls. Also
   moonlight cruises. 10 Dalhousie Street. 692-1159.
Red Carpet Flights: 15-minute flights over the city and
   the Île d'Orléans (Island of Orleans). Phone 872-
   1200 for details.

A Walk Through Quebec's History

Begin the tour from the west end of Dufferin Terrace, near the monument to the founder of Quebec, Samuel de Champlain. From the famous boardwalk you have a clear view, from a height of 200 feet, of the city of Levis on the opposite shore, of the Island of Orleans to the east, and the expansive St. Lawrence River.

Jacques Cartier, the seafarer from St-Malo in Brittany, searching for a direct water route to India and Cathay, explored the St. Lawrence from the Gaspé to Montreal (then the Indian village of Hochelaga), mapped the coastline, and claimed Canada in the name of the King of France—a quite theoretical claim at the time, all the interior being still in Indian hands.

In 1608, Samuel de Champlain (memorialized in the names of a thousand motels, bridges, restaurants, and automobile agencies throughout Canada) founded Quebec, building his fort, or "Abitation," on the site of the present Notre-Dame-des-Victoires Church, which will be found in Place Royale, just below the terrace. It was Champlain, an organizer without peer, who created Lower Town for trade and commerce, Upper Town for administration.

New France was founded as a business proposition. The Company of One Hundred Associates, a group of private entrepreneurs whose charter with King Henry IV gave them all rights to the territory, remains a fascinating example of contract law. Essentially, all the territory stretching from Labrador to Florida was theirs and their heirs', forever. They were delegated the royal power to grant titles and estates. Special note was taken in the charter of the Indians, whose conversion under the supervision of Jesuit missionaries (no French Protestants were allowed into the colony) was a prime objective. The Iroquois, Hurons, and Algonquins were pronounced human beings, possessed of souls and capable of being converted. When you visit the Quebec Museum in Battlefields Park, be sure to take special note of the marvelous Victorian painting by Suzor-Cote entitled *Jacques Cartier Arrives at Stadacona* (now Quebec City), which neatly sums up the mythic aspects of the occasion: Cartier is surrounded by groveling Indians who appear dumfounded at the sight of the splendidly attired Europeans.

Walk through the "Latin Quarter" in Old Quebec's Upper Town. Of special interest are the **Hôtel Dieu Hospital**, the **Ursuline Convent**, the **Cardinal's Palace** and **Seminary,** and the **Basilica of Notre-Dame,** all built between 1638 and 1678. By the eighteenth century, Quebec was a thriving center of missionary activity in North America; the town began to grow around the heavily buttressed walls of the convents and monasteries. As in Montreal, the Catholic Church was given enormous grants of land—more than 2,000,000 acres. Of this, 891,845 acres went to the Jesuits, 693,324 acres to the Bishop and Seminary of Quebec, and 250,191 acres to the Sulpician Order, seigneurs of the Island of Montreal. Three and a half centuries later, the Church is still one of the largest landowners in the province.

Proceed to **Place Royale** in Lower Town. From Place d'Armes you walk down the winding Côte de la Montagne to Notre-Dame Street, one of the oldest streets in Quebec. Place Royale is directly ahead. The churches, monasteries, and convents of Upper Town represent one strand in the Quebec story; here, in the streets around this, the city's oldest square, is the other strand. For Quebec was a city settled by traders and merchants—in sharp contrast to New England, where the English colonists tilled the land and farmed the fields, the French settlers were chiefly concerned with Indian trading. Seek out the **Chevalier House,** the house of **Joseph Charest,** and the **Maison Beaudoin.** The style of life in these homes was patterned after European society, and the ladies who inhabited them brought jewels and elegant dresses to the frontier. They gave lavish entertainments, drank good wine, and enjoyed theatre—Corneille's *Le Cid,* performed in Quebec in 1646, was the first theatre seen in Canada.

Fur trading and the salvation of human souls, then, may be said to have been the leading industries of early Quebec. One major obstacle to the colony's ex-

264 · smith's montreal

pansion and development was constant war with England, an on-again, off-again affair. The result was population that remained small and that confined its concerns largely to trade and the improvement of fortifications.

The year 1759 marked a cardinal turning point: Quebec City was besieged by the British. After weeks of bombardment which reduced much of both Lower and Upper Town to ruins, the British general James Wolfe launched his attack. Moving under cover of darkness, he led his men up the sloping cliff at L'Anse au Foulon (Wolfe's Cove). By the morning of September 13, he had 5,000 soldiers in place at the top of the 180-foot-high cliff. The British line, formed a few yards east of where Wolfe's monument now stands, extended across the Plains beyond Grande-Allée. The French line of battle was drawn up near the present site of the Citadel, and extended across Grande-Allée, in the vicinity of what is now Claire Fontaine Street. Scarcely twenty minutes elapsed between the start of the battle and the collapse of the French lines. Both Wolfe and the French general, Montcalm, were killed. Five days later, the British took over Quebec City, effectively ending French power (but not French influence) in Canada.

A few years afterward, the British colonies to the south of Canada began a rebellion against the mother country. The American insurgents thought they would find allies for their cause among the newly conquered French Canadians. It was a plan that no doubt looked good on paper, but the British—anticipating trouble among the predominantly Protestant American colonists —had only recently, in 1774, passed the Quebec Act, guaranteeing Quebecers the right to preserve their language, laws, and religion. As matters turned out, the French refused to come over to the American side.

George Washington approved the invasion of Canada, and in 1775 two American expeditionary forces were sent to Quebec. The first, under General Richard Montgomery, came up via the Hudson Valley and Lake Champlain. The second, commanded by Colonel Benedict Arnold, came up via the Kennebec through Maine, then overland and down the Chaudière to Quebec City. Montreal fell to Montgomery in November 1775, and he proceeded down the St. Lawrence to Quebec City.

Côte de la Montagne (Mountain Hill), Champlain Street, Sous-le-Cap (the narrowest street in North America) were some of the places where the battle raged most fiercely. Montgomery's attack, made during a fierce snowstorm at dawn of New Year's Eve, 1776, was a total failure. Cannon fire cut down Montgomery himself and a dozen others outside the walls. Arnold was repulsed not far from Sous-le-Cap, and withdrew. Quebec, the gray city on the rock, was never to be attacked again.

The British Army garrisoned Quebec City for almost a hundred years, and when you walk to the Citadel and stand on its ramparts, you can imagine what this colossal fort cost British taxpayers. It was never needed to defend Quebec, and today stands as a monument to the English Regime, as do the walls, the great stone gates to Upper Town, and many of the buildings in Artillery Park.

As the century progressed, shipbuilding became a major industry. Between 1797 and 1897 Quebec shipyards launched more than 2,500 ships, and the Port of Quebec became the most important in Canada, shipping prodigious quantities of wheat and lumber to

Europe. For most of the nineteenth century, Quebec was the greatest timber port the world has ever seen.

The rest of the story is one of great political and social changes. No one who knew Quebec City at the end of World War II would easily recognize it today. Although everything within the walls of the Old City remains intact, everything beyond has changed, and changed dramatically. The city's population has long since burst its ancient stone seams, spreading across the river to Levis, north to Charlesbourg, east to Montmorency, westward to Ste-Foy. Grande-Allée is worth driving along just to see what happens to a central urban thoroughfare that has been submerged in a decade of expansion and growth. Around a revived historical core, the city is on the move—and on the make. The port is the most vivid example of Quebec City's new look. The fastest-growing port in the country, it is already in direct competition with Halifax and St. John's and by the time you read this, may well have surpassed its archrival, Montreal.

And yet, for all its attention to the present, Quebec City remains fascinated by its French past, a sentiment best expressed in the provincial motto that is inscribed in flowers in the garden on Place d'Armes: *Je me souviens* (I remember). The past is a cherished subject in Quebec—and so too is the future. Quebec City has arrived at a period of second growth.

Principal Sights

PLACE ROYALE · The historic heart of Quebec City, located at the foot of Cap Diamant, close to the St. Lawrence River. It was here that Champlain built the "Abitation," the first fortification in Quebec. From Upper Town, either walk down the Côte de la Montagne or take the Dufferin Terrace elevator in front of the Château Frontenac; and you enter an enchanted area of enormous historic interest. In recent years the Quebec government, with a little help from Ottawa, has poured almost $20-million into the meticulous restoration of Place Royale; today, with all the nineteenth- and twentieth-century buildings removed, it looks much as it did two centuries ago—the greatest concentration of seventeenth- and eighteenth-century buildings in North America.

Among the chief points of interest: **Notre-Dame-des Victoires,** one of the oldest stone churches in North America (1688); the **Beaudoin House,** on the spot where the founder of Detroit, Antoine de la Mothe Cadillac, once lived; the magnificent house of **Jean-Baptiste Chevalier,** now perfectly restored (don't miss the collection of Quebec furniture inside), the **Charest House,** with its eighteenth-century walls and ceilings and an English cannonball of 1759 embedded in the masonry. The merchant tradition of the area has been revived with the arrival of numerous arts-and-crafts shops. A fine way to complete your visit to Place Royale is to take a ferry ride across the river to Levis. You'll find the ferryboat at the end of Notre-Dame Street. From the deck you'll get the perfect view of the city of Quebec.

THE CITADEL · The British spent $35 million—an enormous sum in 1803—building this star-shaped fortress with its four bastions, secret passages, musty dungeons, and heaven knows what else. Young children adore it, and if you have them in tow, be sure to arrive before 10 a.m. so you can watch the colorful ceremony of the Changing of the Guard. The well-loved "Vandoos," the Royal 22nd Regiment, and their mascot, a billy-goat named Baptiste, perform the elaborate foot-stamping ritual with disciplined perfection. There is a museum with all kinds of early military hardware, including some captured American cannon. A walk along the top of the immensely thick walls offers a magnificent view of the city. From the rear of the fort you can walk down 300 or so wooden steps to the Lower Town. The Citadel is located just off St-Louis Street, and is open daily. There is a small admission fee.

BATTLEFIELDS PARK · Superb urban park overlooking the St. Lawrence; famous as the field of battle—the Plains of Abraham—where British arms defeated the forces of France in 1759, thus ending French power in North America after some forty years of struggle. Historians continue to argue over the details, but few dispute that it was a tremendous feat for the British general, Wolfe, to march an army up the steep sides of the cliff under cover of darkness, thus surprising Montcalm's superior French force. Walk across the Plains of Abraham and down to Wolfe's Cove, where the army landed in small boats. Both Wolfe and Montcalm were mortally wounded in the 20-minute battle. Montcalm was carried dying to the city, and was buried near the walls of the Ursuline Convent. Wolfe was carried to the rock where his monument now stands in Battlefields Park. It was at Wolfe's Cove, also, that

Benedict Arnold landed a force in 1775 as part of the unsuccessful American campaign in Canada (see page 265).

There are entrances to the park all along Grande-Allée. It is recommended that you enter near Bourlamaque and pay a short visit to the Quebec Museum, which features the arts and crafts of the province.

CHÂTEAU FRONTENAC · This splendid fairy-tale castle, with its great expanse of green-coppered roof, its dormer windows, spires, and portcullis, is Canada's best-known hotel. It was built at the turn of the century by the Canadian Pacific Railroad, for its customers. It is the most dramatically sited hotel in Quebec—perched high above Dufferin Terrace, with unparalleled views of the St. Lawrence. The hotel has sheltered scores of the great and highly placed, among them King George V, Marshal Foch, King George VI and Queen Elizabeth, the King and Queen of Thailand, Juliana of the Netherlands, Franklin D. Roosevelt, and Winston Churchill.

JARDIN DES GOUVERNEURS · Just below the Château Frontenac. Here, in a quiet green setting, stands a monument to two opposing generals, Montcalm and Wolfe. The Latin inscription reads:

MORTEM · VIRTUS · COMMUNEM · FAMAM · HISTORIA · MONUMENTUM · POSTERITAS · DEDIT

Valor gave them a common death, history a common fame, posterity a common monument.

PLACE D'ARMES · Two of Upper Town's principal streets, Ste-Anne and St-Louis, more or less begin in the "Place of Arms." Called Grande Place during the French Regime, it is one of the liveliest squares in the city, and a starting point for the exploration of Upper Town.

THE BREAKNECK STAIRS · These connect Lower Town to Upper. After visiting Place Royale, proceed along Champlain Boulevard, and turn right at the new Department of Transport building along Petit-Champlain Street. You are now at the base of the cliff. At the end of Petit-Champlain is Sous-le-Fort, a street that got its name from its position directly under the old St-Louis fort that once dominated the cliffs. The steps lead up Mountain Hill, and offer the visitor a formidable, appetite-whetting climb.

PARLIAMENT BUILDING · The home of the Quebec National Assembly, it stands on an elevation near the walls of the Old City, on Grande-Allée, just beyond the Porte St-Louis (Gate). The structure is in Renaissance style, and was erected in 1886. The National Assembly is in session from 9 a.m. to 4:30 p.m. Monday to Friday. The debates, which are in French, and often lively, usually take place in the afternoons and evenings. There are guided tours every half-hour when Parliament is not in session. Ask at the Information Desk, in the main lobby, or phone 643-2725.

In front of the building is a rich assortment of Victorian and other statuary. The frock-coated gentleman on the plinth, pointing in the general direction of the city, is Honoré Mercier, premier of the province at the end of the last century. The bronze statues which surround the circular fountain facing the main entrance are the work of Philippe Hébert, and constitute a tribute to the aboriginal tribes of Canada.

URSULINE CONVENT · For more than three centuries the Sisters of St. Ursula have lived and worked here. The nuns, many of them from wealthy families, originally came from France to do missionary work among the Indians. In the process they founded the first private school for girls in North America. There is a small but fascinating museum where you can see (among other things) the original *huche*, or oven, in which the bread was made in those early days. Then there is the Wheelwright silver: Esther Wheelwright, as a child, was captured by the Abenaki Indians. The Sisters discovered who she was and educated her, and she became an Ursuline nun. Her people sent up, from what was then faraway New England, a miniature of her mother and a spoon and fork of the family silver. Also here is the skull of General Montcalm, whose body was laid to rest in a British shell hole by the Chapel walls. On Donnaconna Street, just off St-Louis. Before leaving, visit No. 6 Donnaconna Street—one of the narrowest houses in North America.

Churches

BASILICA OF NOTRE-DAME · Often described as an architectural gem, this seventeenth-century church resembles a wedding cake inside, all white and gold, so that it glows even on the darkest of winter days. It was built in 1650 and served as the cathedral of a diocese that then extended from Canada to Mexico. The Basilica is located across from City Hall, at the corner of Buade and de la Fabrique.

NOTRE-DAME-DES-VICTOIRES · (See also page 267.) Grateful for several victories over the British, the settlers of New France dedicated this lovely church to the Blessed Virgin, giving it the name of "Our Lady of Victories." It was completed in 1688. During Wolfe's siege of 1759, the little church was almost flattened by the British guns across the river in Levis. Over 150 houses were destroyed by the bombardment, but the church somehow survived, though it then had to be largely rebuilt. The main altar is formed in the shape of an old fort. The church is the focal point of Place Royale in the Lower Town.

ANGLICAN CATHEDRAL OF THE HOLY TRINITY · Completed in 1804, this was the first cathedral of the Church of England ever built outside the British Isles. It was constructed at the personal expense of King George III, and cost him £18,000. It is the only church in North America that has a Royal Pew emblazoned with the King's arms. An altarcloth of gold and crimson velvet is from hangings in Westminster Abbey at the time of George III's coronation, and the Duke of Richmond, once Governor of Canada, lies buried beneath the chancel. The interior is rather like several church plans in one. There is a domed space, a nave and aisles, and galleries that run the length of the church. The dozens of electric lightbulbs around the top of each column create an odd effect on the viewer.

Other Points of Interest

RUE DU TRÉSOR · More Left Bank than Paris's Left Bank is this tiny, medieval-looking street just off Place d'Armes. It is almost certainly the most photographed street in town, crowded as it is with painters and artists selling their creations. A good deal of the "art," unfortunately, is repro—the copying machine provides the basic drawing, and a touch of color is added. But for $5 what do you expect? It's all good fun, and well worth a visit.

QUEBEC MUSEUM · Located in Battlefields Park, the museum contains much that will delight history buffs. Among many objects and paintings that relate to early Quebec, the most precious is the original instrument of Quebec's surrender in 1759. There is also a good collection of wooden statues and altarpieces from Quebec churches.

LAVAL UNIVERSITY · Two miles west of the Plains of Abraham is the new campus of Laval University. The oldest French-language university in America, it grew out of the old Quebec Seminary, founded in 1663. The 500-acre main campus accommodates some 30,000 students in two dozen buildings—none of them of any particular distinction, and not worth the drive if you're interested only in sightseeing. But note: the university sponsors plenty of worthwhile cultural events. For information, phone 656-2571.

MUSÉE DU FORT · "See Guns Flash! See Cannons Smoke!" says the handout given visitors at the door of this museum. Well worth a visit, particularly if you have young children. Inside there is an enormous scale-model reproduction of the city of Quebec as it was 200 years ago. The six sieges of Quebec are reenacted before your eyes, complete with sound effects and music. Opposite the Château Frontenac at 10 Ste-Anne. Popular admission prices. Children under six free.

ARTILLERY PARK · For more than 250 years, armies were stationed here—French, then British, and lastly Canadian. Its chief role within the city's fortifications was to defend the city against attacks coming from the St. Charles River. Currently the park is being restored, at a cost of some $16-million. Its information center will be found at the corner of St. John's and d'Auteuil streets.

QUEBEC SEMINARY · After visiting the Basilica of Notre-Dame, look out for an iron gate to the left of the

Basilica which is the entrance to the Seminary. Walk through the portal of the Seminary into the courtyard, where you will see a fine group of seventeenth-century buildings. There is a sundial above the door dating back to 1773. It was here that American officers were held in 1776 after being taken prisoner during Montgomery and Arnold's attack on Quebec.

RESTAURANTS

For authentic Quebec cuisine, it's hard to beat **Aux Anciens Canadiens**, located in the beautifully restored Maison Jacquet on Rue St-Louis. In a candlelit setting, you'll dine off *cretons* (a meat spread made out of pork), *fèves au lard* (baked beans), yellow pea soup, *tourtière* (meat pie), *tarte à la ferlouche* (molasses pie), or custard with maple syrup. Also recommended is **The Baker's Inn**, 8790 Rue Royale.

Among the city's most renowned French restaurants are **La Traite du Roy**, Rue Notre-Dame, in Place Royale—and there's dancing at the discotheque. **Le Bonaparte** on Grande-Allé and **Le Continental** on Rue St-Louis are in the same category. All are richly appointed in decor and expensive, and all point with pride to their prize gastronomic specialties. Museumlike in its ancient setting is **L'Ancêtre** on Rue Couillard, where the house *spécialité* is *escalopes de veau* in white wine sauce. Superb wine list. On the same street is **La Chaumière**, a Belgian-French restaurant; its specialty, *la pièce de boeuf gastronome*, grilled with mustard and a hint of garlic, has made this one of the best-known restaurants in Quebec. Also very good, and somewhat less expensive, is **Chez Rabelais** on Petit-Champlain in Lower Town.

If you like Italian food, try **Chez Guido** on Ste-Anne. It's expensive but sumptuous.

Quebec City has a number of very good brasseries, where lunch with a draft beer costs between $2 and $5. **Les Gaulois**, across the street from City Hall, is full of Quebec characters and offers a special experience. If you're looking to try Quebec cider, think of **Brasserie Cidrerie d'Youville** on St-Jean: the cider is excellent, and the food cheap. On St-Louis is the **Passe-Muraille**, which serves fresh oysters on the half-shell in season, and one of the pleasantest outdoor terraces will be found at **La Nouvelle-France** on Rue du Trésor.

NIGHT LIFE

The tempo of Quebec City night life is still, by and large, small-townish. Quebecers are not cosmopolites—just ordinary Canadians, many of them government workers, whose lives have been certified as orthodox by the Provincial Government.

Well-heeled visitors will discover that all the major hotels offer dinner, dancing, and entertainment. For a drink and a bit of music, it's hard to surpass the Château Frontenac. Your neighbors are likely to be politicians and lobbyists, with a sprinkling of figures from the business world.

It is widely believed that more serious political moves are made in the Château's bars than on the floor of the National Assembly. The new Quebec Hilton also attracts some of this activity, and, in addition, has the glass-walled **Le Toit du Québec** (The Roof of Quebec) for dinner dancing. Easily the best-known discotheque is **La Traite du Roy** in Lower Town. Another popular spot is **Le Boulet** (The Cannonball), where nude-party

scenes are flashed on the wall every few seconds just to get you into the appropriate mood. **La Renaissance** has the reputation of attracting the best-looking girls—and therefore the guys—in Quebec. It's perfectly *au fait* for women to go alone to discotheques, and they do. After the clubs and bars close, and the rest of the town is sleeping, those left standing usually head for the **Châlet Suisse**, just across from the Château Frontenac. Once known as the Aquarium, the name was changed after the fish succumbed to the late-night crowd and the pungent aroma of fondue. Open until 3 a.m.

SHOPPING

The phrase "shopping in Quebec" conjures up visions of wood carvings, ceramic jewelry, pottery, leatherwork, and Eskimo artifacts from James and Ungava bays. It is certainly true that these items are enormously popular, but Quebec City has many more things you may wish to look at—clothes, for instance. Quebec is rivaled only by Montreal in having the most fashion-wise women in Canada, and a look through any of the boutiques will show you how they got their reputation.

Also, antiques—although prices are high everywhere—
are much less expensive in Quebec than, say, New York
State or Ontario.

From a shopping point of view, Quebec City can be
divided into three main parts. The first is Upper Town,
where the busiest venue is Rue St-Jean, a narrow thoroughfare crammed with excellent boutiques. You'll
find a great deal of French ready-to-wear, and plenty of
bargains. Also worth a look is Place Québec, high
fashion and high prices. For browsing and window-
shopping, try Rue Ste-Anne and Rue St-Louis.

The second area is Lower Town. Here is where you
will find the arts-and-crafts stores—dozens of them,
around Place Royale and along Sous-le-Fort. Don't miss
the **St-Roch Mall**, a seven-block-long enclosed shopping
mall on Blvd. Charest between the bus terminal and
railway station. The most promising antique hunting
is to be had a block or so closer to the river, along
St-Paul: chiefly pine furniture, stained glass, and artifacts from old Quebec churches. But the best place of
all for antique lovers is not in the city itself, but a
few miles out of town, along Highway 20. Leave the
highway at the exit marked "Bernieres" and proceed
through the village along Highway 5 until you come
to **Dollard Trottier's**—five broken-down barns with a
hard-to-read sign. If Mr. Trottier is not there, he is
five miles away at his other establishment, roughly
in the opposite direction. Phone 832-8129 if you get
lost. Trottier's prices are about half those of everyone
else, and his name is renowned.

The city's third big shopping area is **Place Laurier** in
Ste-Foy. You can reach it by either bus or taxi. Here
are hundreds of shops and boutiques in what is described as "Canada's biggest shopping center." And sup-
plementing Place Laurier's attractions are the stores

and shops of Place Ste-Foy, much smaller in scope and number, yet well worth a visit in their own right. For more information, call 653-9318.

A BRIEF WORD ON A PHENOMENON

What began in 1954 as a modest attempt to cheer up an otherwise long and gloomy winter is nowadays considered one of Quebec City's major "industries." It is, of course, the Quebec Winter Carnival. For eleven blustery cold February days the town goes ga-ga, and out-of-towners (about half of them Montrealers) manage to unload some $3-million a day having the time of their lives. There's the annual boat race across the ice-clogged St. Lawrence, parades in both Upper and Lower Town (the one in Upper Town being the single most popular carnival attraction), car racing on an ice-covered course on the Plains of Abraham, pee-wee hockey, and ice sculpture contests. Try to imagine 400,000 revelers lurching through the slushy streets tooting plastic horns and, to keep warm, nipping away at a local brew known as "caribou"—a near-lethal mixture of red wine and distilled alcohol, usually carried in 15-ounce plastic canes with removable tops. No wonder the Quebec Liquor Corporation makes allowance for sales to be $1-million above normal in February, or that the local breweries can count on selling an additional 25,000 24-bottle cases.

The official symbol is "Bonhomme Carnaval," a seven-foot-high talking snowman, dressed in a patriotic *tuque* and wearing a *ceinture fléchée*. The grand finale is always the Upper Town parade: a three-hour procession of floats, marching bands, and vast numbers of shivering spectators. Everyone has a good time, and if you decide to go, so will you.

Sports

Whether you're an Olympic swimmer or a Sunday golfer, Montreal can amply accommodate you and your fellow sports buffs. You can play tennis when the thermometer hovers around zero, swim indoors or outdoors any time of the year, go skiing in the center of the city, rent a bike, play *pétanque, bocce,* or the latter's sedate English cousin, lawn bowls. The first cold snap reminds hockey fans it's time to crowd into the Forum to root for that fabulous home team, **Les Canadiens.** And what's a summer's day without a beer, a bag of *patates frites,* and a *chien chaud* while watching the **Expos** at Jarry Park. There is harness and flat racing respectively, at two outstanding tracks, **Blue Bonnets** and **Richelieu.** And when the air crackles, chills, and turns golden, it's time to head for the Autostade and cheer for the championship football played by the **Alouettes.** For current information: the list of sports events every day in the *Gazette, Star, Le Devoir, La Presse,* or *Le Jour;* or from either your hotel desk or the Montreal Visitors Bureau—85 Notre-Dame Street East, phone 872-3561—you can obtain a free copy of the *Montreal Calendar of Events.* In the summer months you can also get the calendar at the "log cabin" tourist office in Dominion Square.

For the serious amateur athlete, the best way to get a briefing on what's available is to pay a visit to or telephone **La Confédération des Sports du Québec,** a province-sponsored organization that supervises every kind of amateur sport in Quebec. Their office is at 881 Maisonneuve Boulevard East, phone 527-9311, and they are open seven days a week, 9 a.m. to 11 p.m. Another useful organization is the Sports and Leisure Service, City of Montreal, phone 872-2556. The YMCA-

YWCA is incredibly well organized in Montreal. Almost every sport and sporting activity from Alpine skiing to wrestling is part of the Y's roster of activities. Whether you need a place to jog, work out, take a swim, or meet a group that enjoys your kind of sport, give them a call at their headquarters, 1441 Drummond, or phone 849-5331.

SPORTS STADIUMS

MONTREAL OLYMPIC STADIUM ·
Maisonneuve Park
Métro: Pie IX.

Located in Montreal's East End, an eight-minute Métro ride from downtown, the 70,000-seat stadium complex is actually a combination of three structures. The giant "mast" contains eighteen floors of training facilities, plus a top-floor restaurant offering panoramic views of the city. At the mast's base is a 50-meter competition pool and a diving pool with room for 9,000 spectators. Finally, the stadium itself, an enormous flying saucer with a folding roof that shelters a football field surrounded by a 400-meter Tartan track. It's the biggest spectator sports complex in Canada.

JARRY PARK · *285 Faillon St. West*
Métro: No. 2 Line, Jarry.

Home of the Montreal Expos, the park offers big-league baseball in a small-town atmosphere. The regular season spans 162 games, half of them played on home turf. Tickets are available at Ticket Reservation Service outlets throughout the city. Phone 878-3811 for nearest location.

AUTOSTADE · *Man and His World, Cité du Havre*

Bus No. 12 at Union and St. Catherine.

Some of the best football in Canada seen here at the home of the Montreal **Alouettes**. It's an open-air arena, so check the weather before going. Tickets cost from $4 to $9 and are available at T.R.S. outlets. The regular season begins in late July and ends around the last week of October. Phone 878-3811 for information.

PAUL SAUVE ARENA · *4000 Beaubien St. East*

Métro: No. 2 Line, Beaubien.

Located in the heart of Montreal's working-class North End, the arena is best known for its weekly wrestling card, boxing matches, and roller derbies.

FORUM · *St. Catherine Street and Atwater*

Métro: Atwater.

The city's major commercial sports arena. Air-conditioned in summer, heated in winter, this indoor stadium can seat 16,000 comfortably. Boxing, wrestling, roller derbies, lacrosse, track meets, and, of course, home ice for **Les Canadiens** from October to April. For information, call 932-6131.

CENTRE CLAUDE ROBILLARD ·
Émile Journeault St., near intersection of Crémazie and Christophe Colomb

Métro: No. 2 Line, Crémazie.

The $40-million Centre Claude Robillard, named for Montreal's first parks director, was built specifically for the Olympic Games and is the most modern and complete sports installation in Canada. Artificial-turf football field, rubberized track, a 50-meter pool, and a 4,500-seat gymnasium are contained in this center.

INDIVIDUAL SPORTS
Auto Racing

After having been closed for several years, the big **Mont Tremblant** track reopened in 1975 on a "let's see" basis. "Le Circuit" (as it is popularly known) is widely regarded among drivers as one of the finest race courses in the world. It is carved out of the wooded Mont Tremblant area about 90 miles north of Montreal. Spectators who go up for the weekend schedule of racing events may find it a great opportunity for picnicking and camping as well.

There is also **Sanair**, in St-Pie-de-Bagot, which is not, however, really up to international formula class races. It is open from May to September, with mixed road racing and drag races. The biggest event of the year in Quebec City is the **Trois Rivières** race which usually takes place around the beginning of September. This race through city streets attracts world-class drivers.

There is also drag racing at **Napierville**, about 25 miles southeast of Montreal, and a few "crash and bang" courses around the city itself. Check local sports pages, schedules are erratic; or call Fédération Canadienne du Sport at 527-9311.

Baseball

See page 281.

Bicycling

Historically speaking, Montreal loves bicycle races, both track and long-distance, but hates leisure cyclists. Quite apart from the hills (a 10-speed bike is recommended),

there is the traffic. Best really to avoid the city altogether, pack your bikes in the car, and head for Île
Bizard, a quiet island just to the west of Montreal. Go
by way of Pierrefronds, and follow Route 37 north to
the Île Bizard Bridge.

To get expert and friendly advice, visit the **Peel
Cycle Centre** at 1398 Sherbrooke West (see also page
164). For the racing cyclist, either professional or amateur, no better shop exists than **Baggio Cycle and Sport**
(see page 164) at 6975 St-Laurent Boulevard. The
Canadian Youth Hostel Association (842-9048) is also
recommended. Each summer weekend, the CYHA
organizes two-day cycling tours through the Eastern
Townships and northern Vermont.

Boating and Sailing

Row boats, at 50 cents an hour, are available in Lafontaine Park, and you can board a paddlewheeler there
for a cruise around the lagoon. Boats are also for hire
at the La Ronde Amusement Park on St. Helen's Island
(see page 82).

Sailing: All summer long, Montreal Island is as completely surrounded by weekend sailors as by water. Some of the best sailing is to be found off the southwestern shore of Montreal Island, on an island-hemmed part of the St. Lawrence known as Lake St. Louis. If you are a sailor, you should contact the **Quebec Sailing Federation**, 881 Maisonneuve Blvd East (527-9311), a provincially sponsored organization that coordinates sailing activities at all levels of participation.

Bowling

Five-pin and ten-pin bowling available in about thirty locations around the city. One of the city's biggest and best is **Laurentian Lanes**, 66 automatic ten-pin lanes, open to midnight, 222 Montée-de-Liesse, near Côte-de-Liesse (341-4525). Another well-equipped bowling center is **Boulevard Lanes**, 72 automatic lanes, open round the clock, at 4400 Jean-Talon East (729-2829).

Bridge

If you want to learn to finesse with the finest, there are two excellent bridge clubs in Montreal: the **Brittany Bridge Club**, 3400 Jean-Talon West (733-8808), and the **Rosemont Bridge Club**, 2500 Rosemont Blvd (279-0739). Phone them for rates and hours.

Canoeing

Quebec is ideal for canoeists and kayakers: every possible variety of condition, from white water to tranquil streams. For information and advice, call the **Quebec Canoeing Federation**, 881 Maisonneuve East (527-9311).

Clay Pigeon Shooting

Not within city limits. Contact the **Montreal Anglers Sport Centre, L'Acadie** (348-5121) or **Coronet Guns** (878-2556).

Chess

Try **The Chess Nut**, 5500 Queen Mary Road (484-0681), one of the very few shops in Canada that specializes in chess sets. They not only sell everything needed for the game, but they're thoroughly wired into the local chess scene.

Curling

If curling is your game, Montreal has half a dozen clubs that warmly welcome out-of-towners. Among those closest to the city center are: **Montreal Caledonia Curling Club**, 11 Hillside (934-0897), **Greystone Curling Club**, 5055 Pare (738-4272), and the **Montreal West Bowling and Curling Club**, 17 Ainslie (486-5831).

Fishing

Quebec, according to its Tourist Office, is 600,000 square miles of the best fishing in the world. Geographers have estimated (although no one has ever counted) that the province has as many as a million lakes, rivers, and streams, with more fish than anywhere else on earth. The provincial Department of Tourism, Fish and Game operates parks and reserves double the size of Portugal, and everyone is welcome.

The keen angler can do no better than to pick up two indispensable free publications—*Sportfishing in Quebec* and the annual *List of Outfitters*—from the Government of Tourist Information Division, 2 Place Ville-Marie. You'll need a license of course. Residents of Quebec pay $3.25, senior citizens 50 cents, and this entitles the entire family to fish. Nonresidents pay $10.50 each for a season license that covers all fish with the important exception of Atlantic salmon. For salmon, a three-day license costs $10.50, and the season license $22.50. Licenses are sold at most resorts and by tourist outfitters, as well as sporting goods stores.

Flying

If you have the urge to fly in your own sky, the oldest established flying school is that operated by the **Aero Club de Montréal** (861-5878). **Won-Del Aviation** (861-8403) is another government-approved Class A school. Both are located at Montreal's principal airport for pleasure and business aircraft, St-Hubert.

Golf

There is one excellent golf course—Nun's Island Golf Club—within an easy 20-minute drive of the city center, half a dozen more within commuting distance, and half a hundred if you draw a circle 100 miles in radius around the city; all are quickly reached by one or another autoroute. For more information, obtain a free copy of *Golf in Quebec* from the Tourist Information Divison, 2 Place Ville-Marie.

Île des Soeurs (Nun's Island): Executive 18-hole course, 5600 yards, par 61. Considered an easy course. Electric carts, practice range, putting green, and restaurant. Clubs can be rented. Green fees $4 weekdays, $6 on weekends. Routes 20, 15, 10. Take the first exit before the Champlain Bridge toll booth (626-3992).

Hockey

Les Canadiens, of the National Hockey League, are the kind of home team that everyone wants. Since their founding in 1910, the "Habs" (short for their nickname, "Habitants") have rarely missed a playoff, and have captured the Stanley Cup eighteen times. Tickets are hard to get for home games; when available, they cost from $4.50 to $9.50. The season starts in early October and runs till April. Wednesdays and Saturdays at 8 p.m. at the Forum, St. Catherine Street and Atwater (Métro: Atwater).

After a game, you might want to savor the food and atmosphere in **Toe Blake's Tavern** (men only), Guy and St. Catherine, or at **Henri Richard's Brasserie,** at 3461 Park Avenue.

Horseback Riding

Here is a short but choice list of recommended riding academies and stables in or near Montreal. *The* saddle shop is **Blueberry Saddle and Harness,** at 2170 Crescent, just below Sherbrooke (844-2879). They're also very helpful with advice.

South Shore Stables (English Saddle): A riding academy and stables for boarding horses. You can take group lessons for $8 per hour, or 10 lessons for $70. Private lessons run $18 per hour. The Riding Academy is open 6 to 9 p.m. weekdays and 1 to 4 p.m. on weekends. The stables are open from 7 a.m. to 5 p.m. Winter lessons take place in a large, heated indoor arena.

To get there, cross the Champlain Bridge, take the Brossard exit, follow the service road (Lapinière Boulevard) for about three miles, and South Shore Stables is on your left (676-7757).

Mount Bruno Riding (English Saddle): The Riding Academy operates year round, between the hours of 9 a.m. and 7 p.m. The rates are $8 per hour, or 15 lessons for $100. If you are an experienced rider, you can rent a horse for $4 an hour and roam the miles of trails. Mount Bruno is located on Route 1 between St-Hubert and Chambly (676-0917).

Kirkland Ranch (Western Saddle): The rental is $3 an hour during the week, $4 an hour on weekends. The trail lasts about an hour. They also have draft horses, and give haywain rides. It costs about $30 for the ride, but up to 30 people can be accommodated atop the hay. To reach the ranch, take the Trans-Canada Highway to Exit 30, and follow the service road (St. Mary's Road) (695-4509).

Domaine Chez Hervé (Western Saddle): Forest, field and country roads abound. You can ride for an hour or all day. Rates are $4 an hour during the week, $5 an hour on weekends. Hours are 9 a.m. to 5:30 p.m. in winter, 9 a.m. to sundown during the summer months. Take Pie IX Bridge (pronounced pee-neuf), follow Route 25 to first traffic light, make a right onto Route 18, and follow road for about a mile. The stables will be on your left (474-2288).

Horse Racing

Big-time bettors and small-time punters from miles around know Montreal's **Blue Bonnets Raceway** as a cheerful spot to place a wager and watch the horses, particularly on a balmy summer's evening—though the season never stops, except around Christmas. It's the place to go to see some of North America's best harness racing. After many years of thoroughbred racing, the track is now completely given over to the trotters and the pacers.

Blue Bonnets is a 15-minute taxi ride from downtown, an easy drive (take the Décarie Expressway to the Jean-Talon exit), and all summer long there are special buses that will take you there for free (phone 739-2741). It's perfectly O.K. to bring along the entire family, and there's an outstanding dining room that overlooks the track. You can place your bet from your dining table. Admission is $1.75 to the grandstand, $2.75 to the club-house. Post-time is 7:45 p.m. nightly, Sunday at 2 p.m. The track is usually closed Tuesdays. Every Thursday is bargain day for women: 25 cents admission.

Blue Bonnets is the home of the Prix d'Été for 3-year-old pacers. The Prix d'Été ("Summer Prize") guarantees the winner a purse of at least $150,000, the richest prize in harness racing. For information, call 739-2741, or watch the local sports pages.

Richelieu is only open during the summer months.

Ice Skating

From October to the end of March, Montrealers use **Beaver Lake** in Mount Royal Park as their principal natural ice rink. But the lake is only one of more than a hundred outdoor ice rinks, natural and artificial, operated by the City Parks Department (hockey permitted on those rinks with boarded sides). For more information, call 873-2969. On a really beautiful winter weekend, nothing beats the short train ride to Ottawa for a day's skating along the Rideau Canal.

Orienteering

Orienteering—the art of getting from here to there using a map, a compass, and your own two feet—is one of the city's fastest-growing outdoor sports. Check with the **Quebec Orienteering Association**, at 527-9311, extension 287, for dates of its free clinics where beginners can get acquainted with the basics of the sport.

Parachuting

The old drop zones had to be moved because of the new Mirabel Airport. The new ones are near St-Antoine-sur-Richelieu, 24 miles southeast of the city, near Mont St-Hilaire. Of the four parachute clubs in Montreal, three are collegiate: McGill (392-8901), Concordia (879-8408), and Loyola (325-6267). The noncollegiate club is **Les Hommes Volontés**, c/o Pierre Milto, 575 Inverness Avenue, Montreal 305. Despite the name, it's open to both men and women. There is a fixed fee of $60 for training and equipment during first year of training, and a jump fee of $6. Experienced jumpers, $3 or $4.50 per occasion, according to height of jump.

Skiing
Cross-country

The fastest-growing sport in Quebec, and no wonder. Even if you are only in Montreal for a weekend, as long as there is snow on the ground you may wish to try out cross-country, or Nordic, skiing. It's cheap— total price for a good outfit is less than $100, and you can rent—and safe, because you proceed along trails rather than downhill. Here's how and where.

Most sporting goods stores sell cross-country equipment, and many advertise "bargain" packages. The three most reliable and best known are **The Mountain Hut**, 1324A Sherbrooke West, operated by the Canadian Youth Hostel Association; **Peel Cycle Centre**, 1398 Sherbrooke West; and, for people in the West End, the **Siren Ski Shop**, 6131 Sherbrooke West, which is owned by a tremendously helpful Finnish couple who really know their business. You'll get expert advice, friendly service, at all these shops. Mrs. Siren, however, doesn't rent equipment. At The Mountain Hut and Peel Cycle, you can rent boots, poles, and bindings together for about $4 weekdays and $10 for a weekend. If you have children, though, you'd better come prepared, or be willing to buy, since no one seems to have small-size gear for rent.

Now, as to where to go:

Montreal Parks: Maisonneuve and **Mount Royal** are two good places to start out with. There is plenty of room to maneuver. The City of Montreal gives lessons in Mount Royal and **St. Helen's** parks: $10 for adults, $5 for children. For these modest sums you get six 2-hour lessons. Call Mr. Millette at 872-4870 for more information. There are trails in Mount Royal and St. Helen's.

Morgan Arboretum: Miles of wooded trails. No lessons or rental facilities. The Arboretum is about 20 minutes from downtown. You pay $2 for parking. At Exit 26 off Route 40 West.

Provincial Parks: Oka is the nearest (and the most crowded), **Mont Tremblant** is the farthest (and the most attractive). **Mont Orford** is rather a long way, especially when the weather is bad, but has excellent trails.

Oka Park: 30 miles from Montreal. It has eight trails ranging from 2 to 6 miles in length. The 2-mile trail is perfect for the absolute beginner, although at times it reminds one of a department-store escalator, so crowded is it with skiers. No fees, no lessons or rentals. The park is located near the Laurentian Autoroute, between routes 640 and 29 West.

Downhill

The two main skiing areas near Montreal are the Laurentians and the Eastern Townships. The Laurentians are much more accessible—it's possible to be on a chairlift within an hour's drive of the city; whereas even in good weather it will take 2–4 hours to reach the slopes in the Eastern Townships. On the other hand, there is more snow in the Townships, and they are generally considered to offer better skiing: the crowds are thinner, the ski runs longer, and (in some keen skiers' view) the countryside is more beautiful. The two great peaks are Mount Orford (2,730 feet) in the Townships and Mont Tremblant (3,150 feet) in the Laurentians. Both offer intermediate-to-difficult slopes.

Voyageur buses leave the Montreal terminal, at Berri and Maisonneuve, on a regular schedule for the major slopes. For more information, call 842-2281.

The most useful guide to Quebec's 200-plus commercial and province-operated ski slopes is *Ski Quebec*. Obtain a copy at the Tourist Information Division, 2 Place Ville-Marie (873-2015). In New York, call (212) 581-1852. Professionals and amateurs interested in competition skiing should contact the Canadian Ski Association, Quebec Division, 881 Maisonneuve (527-9311).

Daily ski reports are published by most of the major newspapers; CJAD radio provides helicopter snow bulletins every Saturday morning, CBM's "Daybreak" program carries Guy Thibedau's ski report on a daily basis, while CBMT's "City at Six" has a television report twice weekly, on Wednesday and Friday.

Swimming

The St. Lawrence is not clean enough to swim in, and the majority of the city's thirty-six beaches are polluted and considered dangerous. For the visitor, the best bet is **St. Helen's Island** (Métro: St. Helen's), where there are three pools, one a 50-meter diving pool. The City of Montreal Parks Department (872-2556) operates both indoor and outdoor pools; the outdoor ones usually open on June 24 and stay open until Labor Day.

Tennis

Public courts are run by the City of Montreal Parks Department and anyone can play. Phone 872-2556 for more information. There is year-round tennis at the **Nun's Island Tennis Club**, on sixteen indoor courts. Anyone can play, and the rates are, in the summer, Monday to Thursday, $6 per hour before 5 p.m., $8 per hour after 5. In winter it is $9 per hour before 5 p.m. and $11 per hour after 5. On weekends the rates are reversed. Phone 769-5163 for more information.

Appendix

BASIC MENU FRENCH

A–B–C

agneau	lamb
aiglefin	haddock
ail	garlic
aïoli	garlic-flavored mayonnaise
à la carte	each item chosen separately
à la mode	in the manner of
amandine	garnished with almonds
ananas	pineapple
aperitif	before-dinner drink
artichaut	artichoke
asperge	asparagus
aubergine	eggplant
au choix	of your choice
au gratin	garnished with grated cheese and browned under broiler
au jus	served with pan juices
avocat	avocado
banane	banana
bar	bass
beigne	doughnut
beignet	fritter
beurre	butter
biftek	beefsteak
blanquette	veal, lamb, or chicken served in cream sauce
blé d'Inde	corn
boeuf	beef
bombe	ice cream, pudding

bordelaise	red wine sauce
boulettes	meatballs
bouquetière	a mixture of vegetables
bourguignon	thick red wine sauce with mushrooms and shallots
brioche	sweet bun; *en brioche*, surrounded by brioche pastry
brochet	pike
brochette	skewer; *en brochette*, on a skewer
brouillé	scrambled
canard	duck
caneton	duckling
carotte	carrot
céleri	celery
cèpes	wild mushrooms
cervelles	brains
champignon	mushroom
châteaubriand	porterhouse steak
chou	cabbage
choucroute	sauerkraut
chou de Bruxelles	Brussels sprouts
choufleur	cauliflower
coeur	heart
confiture	jam
coquille	served on a shell, as in *coquille St. Jacques*—a shell filled with scallops, creamy sauce, and gratinéed
côte, côtelette	cutlet or chop
courge	zucchini, squash
crêpes	thin pancakes
crevette	shrimp
croissant	crescent-shaped breakfast roll
croûte	crust; *en croûte*, baked in pastry
cuisses de grenouille	frog's legs

D–E–F

daube	meat or poultry in a covered casserole

dinde	turkey
dîner	dinner
doré	pickerel
eau	water
écrevisse	crayfish
émincé	ground or finely sliced
entrecôte	rib steak
épinards	spinach
érable	maple, maple sugar
escargot	snail
estragon	tarragon
faisan	pheasant
farci	stuffed
fève	haricot bean
flambé	flamed (usually with brandy or liqueur)
flétan	halibut
foie	liver
fondue	Swiss dish where each diner dips the given food into a hot mixture (usually cheese) set in front of him
fraise	strawberry
framboise	raspberry
frit	fried
fromage	cheese
fruits de mer	seafood
fumé	smoked

G–H

garni	garnished
gâteau	cake
gigot d'agneau	leg of lamb
glace	ice (as in ice cubes) or ice cream
grenouille	frog
haché	ground, chopped
homard	lobster
huître	oyster
huile	oil

J–L–M

jambon	ham
julienne	cut into small strips
lait	milk
laitue	lettuce
langue	tongue
langouste or langoustin	spiny rock lobster
lapin	rabbit
légumes	vegetables
marron	chestnut
marinière	steamed in a wine broth
mets	meals (sign on inexpensive diners)
meunière	lightly floured and sautéed in butter
morue	cod
moules	mussels
moutarde	mustard

N–O–P

navarin	lamb stew and vegetables
navet	turnip
noix, noisette	nuts
nouilles	noodles
oeufs	eggs
oie	goose
oignon	onion
pain	bread
pamplemousse	grapefruit
pâté	well-seasoned mixture of meats and/ or game and poultry, sometimes of fish and seafood, baked and then served cold as an hors d'oeuvre
pâtisserie	pastries
poché	poached
poire	pear
poisson	fish
pomme	apple

pomme de terre	potato
porc	pork
potage	thin soup

Q–R–S

quenelle	delicate dumpling made of fish forcemeat
quiche	open-faced pie made with egg mixture and a variety of ingredients
ragoût	stew
rillettes	a pork pâté
ris de veau	veal sweetbreads
riz	rice
rognon	kidney
rôti	roast
saucisse	sausage
saumon	salmon
sauté	fried, usually in butter, over moderate heat
sauvage	wild
sel	salt
sucre	sugar

T–V–X

table d'hôte	complete meal, including soup, entree, dessert, and often coffee
tarte	pie
tomate	tomato
tournedos	steak cut from the eye of the fillet
tourtière	meat pie
tranche	slice
truite	trout
veau	veal
viande	meat
vin	wine
vinaigrette	dressing of vinegar and oil
volaille	poultry
xérès	sherry

EMERGENCY

POLICE   Dial 872-1313
FIRE   Dial 872-1212
FIRST AID, AMBULANCE   Dial Police number

If You Fall Ill

Should you need medical attention in a hurry, there are several major hospitals within a five-minute drive from downtown. Among them: the **Montreal General Hospital**, 1650 Cedar Avenue (937-6011), **Royal Victoria Hospital**, 687 Pine Avenue West (842-1251), **Saint-Luc Hospital**, 1058 St-Denis (861-7321), and, for children, the **Montreal Children's Hospital**, 2300 Tupper, near Atwater (937-8511). In case of possible food poisoning, call the **Poison Control Centre** at the Montreal Children's Hospital to find out what to do. Emergency dental care is provided by McGill University at the Montreal General Hospital.

Visits to Emergency Rooms are charged for at a flat rate of $13 for a minor injury. Expenses for hospital treatment must be paid for in cash, except that Blue Cross or Medicare will be accepted for U.S. visitors.

All Montreal hotels have access to a doctor, and the rates for a room visit vary from $15 to $25.

Index

accommodations, 22–41; *see also* guest lodges; hostels; hotels; motels; tourist rooms
aircraft: flying school, 287; seaplane rides, 131
airport, 50–1
Alexis Nihon Plaza, 142–3, 156
Amherst, Gen. Jeffrey, 12
antiques, 144–8
Aquarium, 82, 125–6
Archambault, Louis, 84
Arnold, Benedict, 104, 265, 269, 274
art galleries, commercial, 173–6
Astor, John Jacob, 7, 12, 107
auctions, 149–50
automobiles, 52–4; parking, 53; racing, 283; rental, 53–4
Autostade, 282

baby-sitting, 124, 165–6
Bach, Frédéric, 48
Bank of Commerce Building, 70–2, 91, 129
Bank of Montreal, 14, 111; museum, 130
banks, 20–1
Banque de Logement, 40
bars, 196–9
baseball, 281
Battlefields Park, 268–9, 272
Beaver Lake, 129, 290
Bell, Alexander Graham, 131
bicycles, 164–5, 283–4
Bishop Street, 85–6, 174

Blue Bonnets Raceway, 289–90
boating, 284–5
Boîte à Chanson, 43, 107, 235
books, binding and repairs, 153
bookstores, 102, 150–3
Botanical Gardens, 8, 79, 127
bowling, 285
brasseries, 194–5
Bride's Church (St. Francis of the Birds), 63
bridge-playing, 285
Burns, Robert, 99
buses, 45, 48–50; out-of-town, 51

Cadillac, Antoine de la Mothe, 11
calèches, 44, 73
Callières, Louis-Hector, Chevalier de, 108
cameras, 180–2
camping, 41
Canadian Guild of Crafts, 163
Canadian Youth Hostel Association, 40–1
canoeing, 285
carpets, 154–5
cars, *see* automobiles
Cartier, Jacques, 10, 108, 261–2
catering services, 155
Cathedral of Mary Queen of the World, 60, 76, 100
Catholic services, 60
Caughnawaga Indian Reserve, 132

Centrale d'Artisanat du Quebec, 163
Centre Claude Robillard, 282
Centre d'Artisanat International, 164
Champlain, Samuel de, 108, 262
Charest, Joseph, 263, 267
Château de Ramezay, 75–6, 104
Château Frontenac, 269
chess, 286
Chevalier, Jean-Baptiste, 263, 267
children: baby-sitting services, 124, 165–6; day care centers, 166; entertainment, 124–34; theatres, 132–3; toys, 188
china, 156
Chinatown, 88–9
Chinese restaurants, 89, 228, 229, 234
Christ Church Cathedral, 61, 77, 101
church services, see religious services
cigarettes, 21; see also tobacco shops
cinema, 250–2
Citadel (Quebec City), 268
City Hall (Hôtel de Ville), 81, 105
clay pigeon shooting, 286
climate, 18–20
clothes: antique and recycled, 158; boutiques, 158–60, 162; and climate, 19; for men, 161–2; for women, 156–61
coffeehouses, 239
coins and medals, 163
concerts, 248–50; children's 132
Concordia Hall, 120

Concordia University: films, 252; student lodgings, 40
costumes, theatrical, 154
crafts, 163–4
credit cards, 20, 23
Crescent Street, 85–6, 174–5
Crescent Strip, 102
Cross of Christ, 71, 73
cuisine, 191–3; see also restaurants
curling, 286
Custom House, 108
customs regulations, 21

Davis, Dorothy, 133
day care centers, 166
delicatessens, 217
Demers, Pierre, 206
department stores, 137–41; The Bay, 101, 139, 161, 168; Dupuis Frères, 140–1, 161; Eaton's, 101, 137, 155, 161, 168; Holt Renfrew, 140, 161, 188; Ogilvy's, 102, 124, 140, 161, 188; Simpson's, 44, 102, 137, 138, 161
Dickens, Charles, 106, 256, 258
dining, see cuisine; restaurants
discotheques, 236–9
do-it-yourself hardware, 165
domestic help, 165–6
Dominion Square, 98–100
Drapeau, Jean, 15
driving, see automobiles
driving tour, 91–7
Du Calvet House, 106
Duceppe, Jean, 243
Du Luth, Daniel Greysolon, Sieur, 11

ear-piercing, 166–7
Église du Gesù, 60

electric current, 21
emergencies, 300
Eskimo art, 84, 128, 143, 163
Expo '67, 15, 126
eyeglasses, 176

fabrics, 167
films, 250–2
firearms, 22
fishing, 286–7
flower shops, 167
food, *see* cuisine; restaurants
food shops and groceries, 117,
    167–70; *see also* markets,
    street
football, 282
Forum, 247, 282
Franklin, Benjamin, 7, 12, 76,
    104, 108
French language, 6, 65–9;
    basic menu French, 295–9
Fuller, Buckminster, 83

galleries, art, 173–6
Garden of Wonders, 124–5
Gentlemen of St. Sulpice,
    10–11
George III, 272
glassware, 156
golf, 287–8
Greek restaurants, 89, 218–19,
    240
Greeks, 89, 116
Grey Nuns, 108, 109
guest lodges, 38–40
guns and ammunition, 22

hairdressers; 176, 177
handicrafts, 163–4
hardware, 165
health food stores, 172–3
Hébert, Philippe, 270

history: of Montreal, 10–15; of
    Quebec, 261–6
hobby shops, 177
Hochelaga, 10, 13, 78
hockey, 288
holidays, 63
horseback riding, 288–9
horse racing, 58, 289–90
hospitals, 300
hostels, 40–1
hotels, 22–38; airport row,
    36–8; city center east, 29–
    33; city center west, 34–6;
    midtown, 24–8
individual locations:
Argoat Tourist Lodge, 31;
Auberge Richelieu, 31;
Berkeley, 27; Bishop Guest
House, 36; Bonaventure, 26;
120, nightclub, 231, 233;
Château Champlain, 24–5,
121, nightclubs, 198, 231,
232–3; Château Versailles,
35; Colonnade, 36;
Constellation, 27, nightclubs,
233, 236, restaurant, 216;
Hôtel de Province, 35;
Iroquois, 32, 105, 197;
Jacques Viger, 31; Jardin
Saint-Denis, 31; La Salle,
28; Montreal Aeroport
Hilton, 36–7; Nelson,
31–2, 105, 197; Quality
Inn, 28; Queen Elizabeth,
27, 100, nightclub, 231, 232,
restaurant, 207; Queen's, 28,
discotheque, 237–8; Ritz-
Carlton, 24, restaurants,
197–8, 206; Royal
Roussillon, 30; Seaway
Capri, 38; Seville, 37; Sheraton-Mount Royal, 26–7;
Skyline, 37; Windsor, 28,
nightclub, 234; *see also*

hotels (*continued*)
    guest lodges; hostels; motels;
    tourist rooms
housekeeping services, 165
Hudson's Bay Company, 139

Indian art, 128, 143, 163
Indian Reserve, 132
indoor city, 44, 101, 118–22;
    shopping, 141–3
Info-Lodge, 40
information sources, 17–18
Irish immigrants, 12–13
Italian restaurants, 88, 133
    220–3
Italians, 87–8

Jacques-Cartier Bridge, 72
Jardin St-Denis, 44
Jarry Park, 281
Jesus People Hostel, 41
Jeunet, Serge, 208
jewelers, 101, 177–8
Jews, 13; synagogues, 62–3

kitchen equipment, 178

Lachine Canal, 12
Lafontaine Park, 124–5
LaPalme, Robert, 84
La Salle, Chevalier de, 11
Latulippe, Gilles, 248
Lauda, Georges, 49
Leacock, Stephen, 14
Lebrun, Jean, 204
Le Moyne brothers, 11
liquor: buying, 57–8; customs
    regulations, 21; pubs and
    bars, 196–9; taverns and
    brasseries, 194–5
Little Italy, 87–8, 172
locksmiths, 178–9
Lookout (Westmount), 44,
    73, 74, 94

Lotbinière, Marquis de,
    109–10
lotteries, 58

Macdonald, Sir John A., 99
Mackay Street, 85
Main, The (St. Lawrence
    Boulevard), 13, 87, 112,
    114–17, 136
Maisonneuve, Paul de
    Chomedey, Sieur de, 10, 73,
    77; monument, 111
Maisonneuve Park, 292
Maison Radio-Canada, 80
Man and His World, 72, 83–4,
    126
map stores, 179
markets, street, 117, 170–2;
    Atwater, 81, 167, 170–1;
    Bonsecours, 106, 108; Jean-
    Talon, 88, 167, 171–2;
    Marché-Central, 172; St.
    Lawrence, 172
Marks and Spencer, 141
Mary Queen of the World,
    Cathedral of, 60, 76, 100
McGill University, 14; book-
    store, 151; lodgings, 40; Red-
    path Hall, 249; Redpath
    Museum, 130
medical services, 300
Merchandise Mart and Inter-
    national Trade Center, 120
Mesplet, Fleury de, 108
Métro, 45, 48–9
Mirra, Angelo, 220
models, construction, 177
money, 20–1
Montcalm, Louis Joseph,
    Marquis de, 109–10, 264,
    268, 269, 271
Montgomery, Gen. Richard,
    76, 265, 274
Mont Tremblant, 293

Moore, Henry, 97
Morgan Arboretum, 293
motels: Fleur de Lys, 38; Holiday Inns, 26, 30, 37; Jacques-Cartier, 32; Lucerne, 32; Marquis, 32; Ramada Inns, 33, 35; Ruby Foo's, 38, restaurant, 234; Seaway Motor Inn, 36; Versailles, 33
Mountain Street, 85
Mount Orford, 293
Mount Royal, 7, 8, 13, 14, 70, 71, 73-4
Mount Royal Park, 14, 44, 95, 292
Murray Park, 93-4
museums: Bank of Montreal, 130; McCord, 128; Military & Marine, 126; Montreal Museum of Fine Arts, 85, 92; Musée Historique Canadien (Wax), 127; Railway, 130-1; Redpath, 130; Telephone, 131
music: folk and ethnic, 223-4, 226, 235, 236, 239; jazz and rock, 233-4, 235, 236, 237; *see also* concerts; night life
music stores, 179
Muslim services, 62

nature walks, 131
Nelson Monument, 75, 97, 104
news dealers, 179-80
newspapers, 55-7
night life, 231-40; dining and dancing, 232-4, 239-40; discotheques, 236-9; mostly music, 234-6
Notre Dame, Congregation of, 92
Notre-Dame Church, 7, 60, 76, 96, 111

Notre-Dame-de-Bonsecours, 60, 77, 97

O'Donnell, James, 76, 111
Oka cheese, 193
Oka Park, 293
Old Firehouse, 108
Old Fort, 82, 124, 126-7; Le Festin du Gouverneur, 214-15
Old Montreal, 7, 74-5, 96-7, 103-11; antiques, 147-8
Olmsted, Frederick Law, 14
Olympic Games, 8, 15, 72
Olympic Stadium, 281
opticians, 176
orienteering, 291
Outremont, 13

Palais de Justice, 105
Papineau House, 105
parachuting, 291
Parc Safari Africain, 132
party supplies, 154
passports, 18
Paul Sauve Arena, 282
Peterson, Arleigh, 246
photography, 180-2
Place Bonaventure, 120, 142
Place d'Armes: Montreal, 96, 111; Quebec City, 269
Place des Arts, 15, 84-5, 247, 248-9
Place-Desjardins, 142
Place du Canada, 121, 142
Place Jacques-Cartier, 43, 74-5, 97, 103-5
Place Royale: Montreal, 107-8; Quebec City, 267
Place Vauquelin, 105
Place Ville-Marie, 44, 78-9, 100, 119, 121-2, 141-2
Place Youville, 108
Planetarium, Dow, 128
Pointe à Callières, 108

Poison Control Centre, 300
police, emergency calls, 300
postal service, 54–5
Prince Arthur Street, 114–15, 136–7
Protestant services, 61–3
pubs, 196–9, 239–40

Quebec City, 256–78; Artillery Park, 273; Battlefields Park, 268–9, 272; Breakneck Stairs, 270; Cathedral of the Holy Trinity, 272; Château Frontenac, 269; Citadel, 268; history, 261–6; hotels, 258–9; Jardin des Gouverneurs, 269; Laval University, 273; Musée du Fort, 273; night life, 275–6; Notre-Dame Basilica, 271; Notre-Dame-des Victoires, 271–2; Parliament building, 270; Place d'Armes, 269; Place Royale, 267; Quebec Museum, 272–3; Quebec Seminary, 273; restaurants, 274–5; Rue du Trésor, 272; shopping, 276–8; Ursuline Convent, 270; Winter Carnival, 278

race track, 289–90
radio, 254
railroads, 51; museum, 130–1; stations, 14, 51, 121
Rainbow Bar & Grill, 40, 197
Ramezay, Claude de, 75
Rasco's Hotel, 106
religious services, 59–63; Catholic, 60; Christian Science, 62; Jewish, 62–3; Muslim, 62; Pentecostal-Gospel, 61; Protestant, 61–3;
Spiritualist, 61–2; Unitarian, 62
restaurants, 190–4, 200–29; for families and children, 133–4; Quebec City, 274–5; sidewalk cafés, 43, 231–2; vegetarian and health food, 134, 225
expensive, 200–7: Chez Bardet, 200–1; Chez la Mère Michel, 202; Le Fadeau, 202–3; Gibby's, 205; Guinguette les Trois, 205; Les Halles, 204; Hélène de Champlain, 82, 203; La Marée, 105, 191, Le Mas des Oliviers, 206; in Queen Elizabeth, 207; in Ritz Carlton, 206; St-Amable, 105, 199, 201; Le Vert Galant, 203–4
inexpensive, 102, 227–9
moderate to expensive, 208–15: Auberge St. Tropez, 210; La Bergerie, 208; Le Chalutier, 210; Chez Delmo, 209; Chez Fanny, 214; Chez Pauzé, 208–9; Chez Pierre, 191, 211; Club des Moustaches, 213; Colibri, 209; Dupont and Smith, 212; Le Festin du Gouverneur, 214–15; Les Filles du Roy, 192, 215; Le Paris, 213; Le Pavillon de l'Atlantique, 212; La Picholette, 211
national: American, 102, 134, 216–17; Argentine, 223; Chinese, 89, 228, 229, 234; Greek, 89, 218–19, 240; Hungarian, 227; Indian, 224; Irish, 197, 223–4, 240; Italian, 88, 133, 220–3;

restaurants (*continued*)
Japanese, 224; Polish, 227;
Portuguese, 226; Russian,
225; Swiss, 226; Vietnamese,
225, 228–9
Richler, Mordecai, 117
riding, 288–9
Ronde, La, 82–3, 124
Roux, Jean-Louis, 243
rugs, 154–5

sailing, 285
St. Andrew and St. Paul,
Church of, 61
St. Ansgar's Church, 61
St. Catherine Street, 14–15,
101–2, 136, 156
St-Denis Street, 44, 86–7,
136–7, 146
St. George's Centennial
Church, 100
St. Helen's Island, 81–2, 294
St. Helen's Park, 292
St. James United Church, 61
St. Joseph's Oratory, 60, 77–8,
127; concerts, 250
St-Lambert Lock, 80–1, 128–9
St. Lawrence Boulevard, *see*
Main, The
St. Lawrence River cruise, 129
St. Lawrence Seaway, 80–1,
128–9
St-Louis Square, 87, 112–14
St. Patrick's Church, 60
St-Paul Street, 43–4, 104
St-Sulpice, Order of, 92, 263
St-Sulpice Seminary, 7, 110–11
Salvation Army, 41, 62
saunas, 182
seaplane rides, 131
Sherbrooke Street, 33, 43, 45,
92, 136, 144, 146–7, 156
shoes, 183–4
silversmiths, 177–8

Siskind, Jacob, 248
skating, ice, 290
skiing, 292–4; equipment, 185,
292
Spence, Sir Basil, 83
sports, 280–94; equipment,
184–5, 292; stadiums, 281–2
steam baths, 182
Stock Exchange: modern, 72;
old, 110
student lodgings, 40
Sun-Life Building, 100
swimming, 294

tattooing, 186
Tavan, Louis, 213, 214
taverns, 194–5, 288
taxis, 50
telegrams, 55
telephone answering service,
186
Telephone Progress, Panorama
of, 131
telephones, 55; emergency calls,
300
television, 252–4; rentals, 186
temperature, 19, 20
tennis, 294
Terrasses, Les, 101
theatres, 242–8; Centaur, 110,
245; children's, 132–3;
Douglass Burns Clarke, 246;
French, 243–4, 247–8;
marionettes, 132–3; National
Theatre School, 244; La
Poudriére, 82, 246, 250;
Revue, 246; Saidye
Bronfman Centre, 245;
variety, 247–8; Youtheatre,
133
tipping, 58–9
tobacco shops, 102, 138, 186–8
tourist rooms, 38–41
toys, 188

traffic rules and signs, 52–3
travel information, 17–18
Tremblay, Michel, 244
Trudeau, Pierre Elliott, 8, 80
Turkish baths, 182

underground city, *see* indoor
  city
Université de Montreal, 40
Université du Québec à
  Montreal, 40

vaccination certificates, 18
Vauquelin, Jean, 105
Victoria Bridge, 12, 72
Victoria Hall, 93
Ville-Marie, 11

walking tours, 97–122
Washington, George, 265

Waters, Violet, 133
weather, 18–20
Westmount, 13, 93–4; Look-
  out, 44, 73, 74, 94
Westmount Baptist Church,
  61
Westmount Park, 93
Westmount Square, 143, 156
Wheelwright, Esther, 271
wines, 58
Wolfe, Gen. James, 110, 264,
  268, 269, 271

YMCA and YWCA, 39, 40
Youville, Marie Marguerite d',
  108
Youville Stables, 108–9

Zeckendorf, William, 79
zoos, 125, 132

A Note About the Author

Desmond Smith is a British-born journalist who spent fifteen years in the United States working as a writer-producer for ABC, NBC, and CBS News. He moved to Canada in 1972 and is presently the director of television in Montreal for the Canadian Broadcasting Corporation. He has contributed to *The Nation, The New York Times Magazine,* and *Harper's.* He lives in Montreal with his wife and two children.

A Note on the Type

The text of this book is set in Electra, a typeface designed by W. A. Dwiggins for the Mergenthaler Linotype Company and first made available in 1935. Electra cannot be classified as either "modern" or "old style." It is not based on any historical model, and hence does not echo any particular period or style of type design. It avoids the extreme contrast between "thick" and "thin" elements that marks most modern faces, and is without eccentricities which catch the eye and interfere with reading. In general, Electra is a simple, readable typeface which attempts to give a feeling of fluidity, power, and speed.

Printed and Bound in Canada